The Cartographic St

Why is today's world map filled with uniform states separated by linear boundaries? The answer to this question is central to our understanding of international politics, but the question is at the same time much more complex – and more revealing – than we might first think. This book examines the important but overlooked role played by cartography itself in the development of modern states. Drawing upon evidence from the history of cartography, peace treaties, and political practices, the book reveals that early modern mapping dramatically altered key ideas and practices among both rulers and subjects, leading to the implementation of linear boundaries between states and centralized territorial rule within them. In his analysis of early modern innovations in the creation, distribution, and use of maps, Branch explains how the relationship between mapping and the development of modern territories shapes our understanding of international politics today.

JORDAN BRANCH is an Assistant Professor in the Department of Political Science at Brown University.

Cambridge Studies in International Relations: 127

The Cartographic State

Cambridge Studies in International Relations is a joint initiative of Cambridge University Press and the British International Studies Association (BISA). The series will include a wide range of material, from undergraduate textbooks and surveys to research-based monographs and collaborative volumes. The aim of the series is to publish the best new scholarship in International Studies from Europe, North America and the rest of the world.

Cambridge Studies in International Relations

Series list continues after index

The Cartographic State

Maps, Territory, and the Origins of Sovereignty

JORDAN BRANCH
Brown University

CAMBRIDGE
UNIVERSITY PRESS

CAMBRIDGE
UNIVERSITY PRESS

University Printing House, Cambridge CB2 8BS, United Kingdom

Cambridge University Press is part of the University of Cambridge.

It furthers the University's mission by disseminating knowledge in the pursuit of education, learning and research at the highest international levels of excellence.

www.cambridge.org
Information on this title: www.cambridge.org/9781107499720

First published 2014
First paperback edition 2015

A catalogue record for this publication is available from the British Library

Library of Congress Cataloguing in Publication data
Branch, Jordan, 1976–
The cartographic state : Maps, territory and the origins of sovereignty / Jordan Branch.
  pages cm. – (Cambridge studies in international relations ; 127)
Includes bibliographical references and index.
ISBN 978-1-107-04096-0 (hardback)
1. Cartography–History.   2. Sovereignty.   3. International relations.   4. Territory,
National.   5. Boundaries.   6. World politics.   I. Title.
GA201.B69 2013
320.1'5–dc23
2013020832

ISBN 978-1-107-04096-0 Hardback
ISBN 978-1-107-49972-0 Paperback

For my parents, Eren and Watson Branch

Contents

Figures

Acknowledgments

Although this project has involved a lot of time working alone, with stacks of books, there is no way I could have completed it without the help of many people.

This book began as a dissertation at the University of California, Berkeley, so my first debt of gratitude is to my dissertation committee: Steve Weber, Chris Ansell, Ron Hassner, and Kate O'Neill. Nick Ziegler also served as a member of my prospectus committee, helping to get the project off the ground. Chris Ansell was instrumental, from the very beginning of this project, in helping me negotiate the back-and-forth between extreme breadth and complexity and making a coherent and defensible argument. Ron Hassner's enthusiasm and help have been amazing – who else, after all, combines such a depth of knowledge about our field, a limitless willingness to help, and an impressive collection of antique maps? Kate O'Neill provided extremely useful feedback in spite of facing the monumental task of reading an entire dissertation in one go, rather than in a more civilized piecemeal fashion. Finally, I could not have asked for a better dissertation chair than Steve Weber. From the very beginning, Steve provided me with exactly the type of guidance that I needed, allowing me the freedom to pursue whatever wild ideas came up, but keeping my historical study grounded in the key issues of International Relations. Steve was the kind of advisor I could – and did – call to ask about how to phrase specific parts of a response letter for an article revision. His support has been priceless.

My fellow graduate students at Berkeley have also earned my thanks – for transforming classes, exam preparations, and everything else that could make graduate school a burden into positive experiences. Jessica Rich and Naomi Choi deserve special mention as close friends who have always put up with me and as colleagues who have given me honest and supportive feedback on my work. In addition, the broader International Relations community at Berkeley, including the numerous students and faculty affiliated with the Institute for International Studies, provided a stimulating environment for exchanging ideas and papers – even for someone like me, whose work has sometimes been at the periphery of our field. (The Institute for International Studies also funded part of the research for this book.)

In 2011, I was extremely fortunate to receive the Hayward R. Alker Postdoctoral Fellowship at the Center for International Studies at the University of Southern California. The year I spent there allowed me the time, resources, and support needed to convert a somewhat unwieldy dissertation into a focused and vastly improved book. Particularly valuable were the support and feedback I received from Patrick James, the director of the Center, and from many of the faculty in USC's School of International Relations (including, in particular, Mai'a Cross, Robert English, Brian Rathbun, and Ann Tickner). In addition, while at USC, I was fortunate to be able to meet with Nicholas Onuf, who provided invaluable comments on this project, as well as sage advice that was particularly helpful to a new Ph.D.

In 2012 I joined the political science department at Brown University, where I finished the revisions on this book. My colleagues at Brown immediately welcomed me and made me feel like a valued member of the department; they have helped make the transition to being a faculty member completely painless. The students in my fall 2012 "Maps and Politics" class were also helpful in their questioning of the arguments in this book. I am extremely pleased to have finished this project – and to begin new ones – in this friendly and rich academic environment.

Additionally, this project benefited from the extensive pushing, prodding, and questioning that I have faced at a number of venues outside Berkeley, USC, and Brown when speaking at conferences and at other universities, including the political science departments at George Washington University, Northwestern University, the University of Chicago, and the University of Toronto. When you start talking about maps, people become interested, and I have always benefited from the incisive comments, questions, and suggestions that I have received. Others who provided valuable advice include Daniel Nexon, Hein Goemans, Christian Reus-Smit, and Jeppe Strandsbjerg. Also helpful was the extensive feedback from reviewers and editors at *International Organization* and the *European Journal of International Relations*, where some of this book's arguments have previously appeared (reprinted with permission from: "Mapping the Sovereign State: Technology, Authority, and Systemic Change," *International Organization* 65(1), Winter 2011; "'Colonial Reflection' and Territoriality: The Peripheral Origins of Sovereign Statehood," *European Journal of International Relations* 18(2), June 2012). The questions and suggestions of the two anonymous readers of the book manuscript also improved the final product immensely. John Haslam at Cambridge University Press has guided the book through the publication process flawlessly, and, from our very first meeting, his enthusiasm for this project has been invaluable.

Finally, I have to thank the people who have made it possible for me to bring this project to fruition. Helen Lee, whom I had the unbelievable good fortune to meet in a graduate seminar on research methods (of all places!), gives me the kind of support and encouragement that one can only dream of. My brother, Adam Branch, has played an instrumental role in my whole academic career as well as in this project. Leading by example, Adam first showed me that graduate studies in political science could be fun. Then, before I began at Berkeley, he gave me a copy of Hendrik Spruyt's *The Sovereign State and Its Competitors* – guiding me toward the questions that eventually led to this book. My parents, of course, deserve more gratitude than I can offer. Their support – of every imaginable kind – has always been beyond measure. Their example and love continue to keep me going, every day. This book is dedicated to them.

1 | Introduction

In the 1680s, King Louis XIV of France was presented with a new map of his realm, the product of decades of work using the most advanced scientific mapping techniques of the early modern period. Funded largely by government resources and based on the combination of trigonometric surveying and exacting measurements of latitude, the map showed the correct coastal outline of France, in contrast to where that coastline had previously been pictured as lying. (See Figure 1.1.) The updated image revealed that earlier maps had significantly over-estimated the total area of France – with a difference of about 54,000 square miles – and Louis is reported to have expressed his dismay at this "loss" of territory, greater in size than any of his successful military conquests to date.[1]

The map, of course, revealed that Louis had never ruled a territory that was as large as he had imagined it to be. The map itself changed nothing, other than the ruler's idea of his realm – but the *idea* of what is ruled is central to how political actors pursue their interests. Since the early modern period, maps have continued to shape how rulers and subjects understand politics, defining everything from divisions between states to internal jurisdictions and rights. At the global level, the mapped image of the world dominates ideas of political organization: states are understood as territorial claims extending to a mapped linear boundary. Although this may appear perfectly natural to observers today, how we got here is anything but straightforward.

In other words, why is today's world map filled with territorial states separated by linear boundaries? Answering this question is central to understanding the foundations of international politics. In today's international system, all political units are sovereign territorial states,

---

[1] While the exact words of Louis' reaction are unknown, when the map was presented to the Royal Academy of Sciences and members of the court, its implications were clear. See Konvitz 1987: 7–8; Petto 2007: 7.

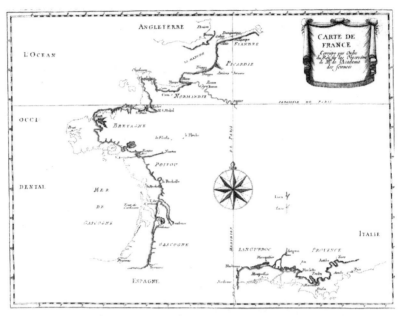

Figure 1.1 Map of the coastline of France, 1693

Note: This image is of a 1693 printed copy of the map, but an original manuscript version had probably been prepared in 1683. The coastline describing a larger expanse (drawn in a lighter outline) represented the earlier estimation from the mid 1600s, while the coastline depicting a smaller area (drawn in a heavier outline) was based on the new measurements (Konvitz 1987: 7–8; Petto 2007: 7).

defined by linear boundaries and with theoretically exclusive claims to authority within those lines. This provides the basis for international law and practice – the foundational terms for how states bargain with one another. Although the ideal may not describe reality in some parts of the world, it nonetheless shapes the goals toward which almost all political actors aspire. Yet this system is actually unique to our modern world and emerged out of a complex set of processes inside and outside early modern Europe – processes that we need to understand in order to grasp both the origins and the future trajectory of the sovereign state.

Asking why our maps look the way they do is more complicated – and more revealing – than we might think. The role of maps in the emergence of sovereign states was not merely to depict the political world as it existed. Maps were fundamentally involved in producing this outcome as well. Maps have shaped, and continue to shape, how people understand the world and their place within it. Early modern Europe saw a revolution both in mapmaking technologies and in the ideas and practices of political rule. That was no coincidence: how rulers conceived of their realms was altered as they, and others, increasingly used maps that depicted the world in a new way. The origins of our international system of sovereign territorial states can be found at the intersection of cartographic depictions, political ideas and institutions, and the actions of rulers and subjects. That intersection is the subject of this book.

Evidence from the history of cartography, peace treaties, and political practices reveals how new mapping technologies changed the fundamental framework of politics in early modern Europe. Key characteristics of modern statehood – such as linear boundaries between homogeneous territories – appeared first in the representational space of maps and only subsequently in political practices on the ground. Authority structures not depicted on maps were ignored or actively renounced in favor of those that could be shown, leading to the implementation of linear boundaries between states and centralized territorial rule within them. For their part, mapmakers never intended to change politics. Instead, they were concerned with making money, creating art, and advancing the science of cartography. Furthermore, the European encounter with the Americas and subsequent competition therein required new means for making political claims – new means that were provided by mapping. These intertwined dynamics reshaped political organization and interaction, leading to the system of exclusively territorial states that has continued to structure international politics to this day.

Mapping and the emergence of the sovereign state

The territorial state is familiar to observers today, but the fundamental novelty of this form of political organization is often missed. The drastic nature of the early modern transformation of political rule is revealed when we look at changes in how political authority was conceptualized from the Middle Ages to the nineteenth century. For example, in 1086 a contemporary observer wrote as follows concerning the creation of the Domesday Book, the inventory of William the Conqueror's rule in England:

Then sent he [King William] his men over all England into each shire; commissioning them to find out "How many hundreds of hides were in the shire, what land the king himself had, and what stock upon the land; or, what dues he ought to have by the year from the shire." ... So very narrowly, indeed, did he commission them to trace it out, that there was not one single hide, nor a yard of land, nay, moreover (it is shameful to tell, though he thought it no shame to do it), not even an ox, nor a cow, nor a swine was there left, that was not set down in his writ. And all the recorded particulars were afterwards brought to him.[2]

The passage illustrates the medieval tradition of claiming political authority over a collection of diverse persons and places, recorded in this case in an exhaustive written survey. Rule, in other words, was not about how extensive a territory was on a map, but instead concerned what and who exactly was under a ruler's authority.

After the introduction of new mapping techniques and their widespread adoption beginning in the sixteenth century, however, rule began to be understood differently. The change is evident in a passage from Christopher Marlowe's play *Tamburlaine the Great* (*c.* 1588), spoken by Tamburlaine on his deathbed:

Give me a map; then let me see how much
Is left for me to conquer all the world[.][3]

A novel shift has occurred toward using maps to picture territorial authority as a spatial expanse – in the case of the fictionalized Tamburlaine, to lament all that remained unconquered at his death. He has no interest in seeing a list of his enemies' vassals, holdings, and manors.

Several centuries later, map-based political claims were no longer aspirational, but instead defined actual political claims on the ground.

---

[2] *The Anglo-Saxon Chronicle* (1912), entry for AD 1085.

[3] *Tamburlaine the Great*, Christopher Marlowe, *c.* 1588. Available online at Project Gutenberg: www.gutenberg.org/etext/1589. This sixteenth-century play is a fictionalized account of the life of Tamerlane, or Timur, the fourteenth-century Central Asian conqueror.

For example, Article II of the 1815 General Treaty of the Congress of Vienna reads:

That part of the Duchy of Warsaw which His Majesty the King of Prussia shall possess in full sovereignty and property ... shall be comprised within the following line ...[4]

This post-Napoleonic treaty represents the culmination of centuries of change, as political rule is assigned as exclusive and complete sovereignty over a space defined by cartographic lines. Yet the careful delineation of boundaries in 1815 was revolutionary: only a century earlier, most negotiated settlements – as well as actual divisions – between European polities more closely resembled medieval lists of places and rights than they did modern linear boundaries.

This progression not only illustrates the epochal transformation of politics in early modern Europe – a shift from the complex authorities of the Middle Ages to the territorial exclusivity of the modern state – but also suggests the importance of mapping to this process. In early modern Europe, the rediscovery of key classical texts and contemporary technological innovations led to a revolution in the creation, distribution, and use of maps. Thanks to their wide dissemination, maps provided new tools for rulers to gather and organize information about their realms, but they also had far greater effects. New maps restructured the very nature of what it meant to "rule," leading eventually to modern territorial states as we know them today. The impact of mapping on political ideas, practices, and structures is the focus of this book.

In short, maps were a necessary – though not sufficient – condition for the emergence of the sovereign-state system. The dynamics examined in this book, in other words, were one essential component in the centuries-long shift to exclusive territorial claims represented by the sovereign state, although they were not the only process at work. Numerous other social, political, and economic changes also drove the centralization of rule and the creation of states. Yet mapping and its effects were necessary for a key characteristic of the sovereign state as it emerged by the early nineteenth century: namely, the purely territorial and boundary-focused character of the authority claims made by

---

[4] Article II; in Israel 1967: 520.

states. As the rest of this book argues, without maps of the type that appeared and were widely adopted in the early modern period, the expansionary and centralizing efforts of rulers could have taken on a fundamentally different form.

Near the end of the fifteenth century, the techniques of map creation, production, and distribution changed dramatically, resulting in the wide use of maps throughout Europe. Ptolemy's *Geography* was reintroduced to Western Europe and translated into Latin in the early fifteenth century, exposing humanist scholars to a set of mapmaking techniques unknown during the Middle Ages. Specifically, Ptolemy described how to use the celestial coordinate grid of latitude and longitude to define terrestrial locations geometrically and then to map such locations using mathematical projection methods. The geometric approach to the depiction of space, which diverged significantly from medieval techniques, has remained the foundation of cartography to this day. Fifteenth- and sixteenth-century innovations in printing and the expansion of a commercial market for books created an explosion in map production and use, spreading the new geometric means of depicting the world throughout European societies.

These new representational tools subsequently changed how rulers made political claims and thereby redefined the character of states and the international system. During the seventeenth and eighteenth centuries, rule was reconceptualized in exclusively spatial terms, with cartographic linear boundaries separating exhaustive claims to territorial rule. The shift was in large part the result of the increasing use of maps by political actors, particularly as a tool of negotiation and treaty-making. These cartographic tools enabled increased precision in boundary demarcation, but they also did much more. The way in which the world was depicted in maps reshaped actors' fundamental ideas about political rule, driving a change in how states were defined, internally and externally. In short, forms of authority not depicted in maps were undermined and eventually eliminated, while map-based authority claims became hegemonic. As rulers continued to centralize internally and compete externally, the changing ideas about how authority and rule should be defined gave a particular shape to political claims. International negotiations and treaties reveal this shift, as what was contested, traded, and seized changed from a listing of places and non-territorial jurisdictions to a careful delineation of spaces separated by discrete boundaries.

By the nineteenth century, rulers had put these new ideas into practice, projecting linear divisions on to the material landscape and reshaping their interactions to embody the new focus on exclusively territorial rule and sovereign equality among states. The transformation extended to the deep grammar of political rule, rather than merely affecting the surface level of particular political claims or boundaries. Traditional political goals, such as territorial expansion or defense, were redefined to fit with the cartographic ideal of rule as a linearly defined space rather than as a collection of places and jurisdictions. Conflicts over territory took on their modern form of conquering – and defending – spatial areas defined by discrete boundaries. The exclusive use of linear territoriality to define political rule is a unique feature of the modern state system, which was only fully consolidated in the post-Napoleonic reconstruction of European politics – not, as is often asserted, at Westphalia in 1648. (Settlements throughout the seventeenth century, in fact, continued to reveal persistently medieval notions of place-focused territoriality and feudal rule.)

The transformation, however, was not entirely internal to Europe: the early modern period witnessed a global expansion of economic exchange and military conquest, resulting in a new degree of interchange across regions. One of the most important dynamics of this period was colonial expansion, with similar processes occurring globally, including rapid growth of European maritime empires and territorial expansion and consolidation by the Qing emperors in China. Especially important for the territorialization of authority were the efforts of European rulers to assert political claims in the previously unknown spaces of the "New World" of the Americas, which made possible the application of novel ideas and practices of rule. Colonial expansion offered the first opportunities and incentives to implement cartographically defined territorial authority. Although contemporary practices within Europe still reflected medieval forms of rule, expansion to spaces previously unknown to Europeans demanded the use of new techniques and ideas. Spanish–Portuguese agreements of the 1490s, seventeenth-century North American charters, and eighteenth-century disputes among colonial powers were all structured by linear definitions of space. Claims were made from afar, with little or no actual information on the relevant places – the geometric division of space required only that the lines themselves be agreed upon. This use had repercussions within Europe, as the implementation of authority claims in the colonial world based exclusively on territorial demarcation later reshaped intra-European practices along the same lines. In other words, expansion to the New World created a demand for new practices, a demand that was essential to driving – rather than just enabling – the shift to cartographically defined authority and modern territorial statehood.

Mapping, in short, was more than a tool enabling rulers to pursue their existing interests. While technological changes had direct effects on actors' capabilities – such as the ability to claim territory from afar or to delimit boundaries with increasing precision – there was more to this process. More fundamentally, mapping technology changed rulers' foundational norms and ideas about how politics *should* and *could* be organized, altering the conditions of possibility for political rule and interaction. The change in ideas also created new demands for the further development of those cartographic technologies that would later enable the implementation of an exclusively territorial form of rule. Out of the subsequent restructuring of political practices emerged a new international system composed exclusively of territorial states. Cartographic technology both enabled new capabilities and practices and simultaneously constituted new goals as legitimate.

This book thus reframes how we understand international systems in general and how we delineate the character, origins, and future trajectory of today's system of sovereign states.[5] Territorial states have been seen as recurring patterns throughout history, as inventions of the late Middle Ages, or as constructs emerging only in the more recent past.[6] A focus on the connection between representational technologies and the authoritative basis of political structures provides new traction on this problem. Considering how political authority is represented, understood, and operationalized, reveals the historical novelty and unique character of our sovereign-state system – in particular, the exclusive reliance on territorial authority and discrete boundaries

[5] For a variety of theorizations of international systems, see Bull 1977; Buzan and Little 2000; Reus-Smit 1999; Ruggie 1993; Spruyt 1998; Waltz 1979; Wendt 1999; Wight 1977.

[6] For the realist view that international structures are relatively static, see Fischer 1992; Gilpin 1981; Waltz 1979. For arguments that many key elements of territorial statehood emerged during the Middle Ages, see Krasner 1993; Spruyt 1994; Wight 1977. Finally, for the contention that states only emerged in the more recent past (a view also supported by this book), see Hall 1999; Hall and Kratochwil 1993; Osiander 2007.

to define the highest level of political organization. By establishing the historically unique character of statehood, we can more effectively consider the possibility of future change in the international system, an issue examined in this book's concluding chapter.

Changes in the fundamental character of political organization and interaction involve more than shifts in material resources or capabilities. Constructivist scholars in International Relations (IR) argue that ideas, beliefs, and practices are integral to political structures. Ideas and norms provide meaning to material facts and thus structure political behaviors and outcomes.[7] Examining the ideational effects of material cartographic technology offers a useful means of studying technological drivers of change while acknowledging that the effects of such material factors are constructed by, and operate through, the ideas that give them meaning. This also illustrates the complexity of the relationship between agents and structures, in which actors promulgate structural conditions and simultaneously are constrained and driven by them.[8] Furthermore, the importance of practices and habits as structural conditions is reflected in the particular ways in which maps – and the ideas both implicit and explicit in them – restructured political outcomes in early modern Europe.[9] A mutually constitutive relationship exists among three relevant factors: representations of political space, the ideas held by actors about the organization of political authority, and actors' authoritative political practices manifesting those ideas. Exogenous sources of change act through this relationship: the cartographic revolution in early modern Europe created new representations that, first, led to changes in ideas of authority and, subsequently, drove a transformation in the structures and practices of rule.

Building on these foundations, this book examines the effect of cartography on the transformation in political authority – both in ideas and practices – that constituted the shift from complex medieval forms of rule to modern territorially exclusive statehood. A useful general framework relating mapping to social and political change is provided

[7] See, among many others in this tradition, Kratochwil 1989; Onuf 1989; Reus-Smit 1999; Ruggie 1983, 1993; Wendt 1999.
[8] Doty 1997; Giddens 1984; Wendt 1987; Wight 1999.
[9] This builds on recent efforts to apply Pierre Bourdieu's "logic of practice" (Bourdieu 1990) to International Relations. See, in particular, Adler and Pouliot 2011; Hopf 2010; Jackson 2008.

by spatial and cartographic theory, and a few existing studies have begun to draw a connection between mapping and state formation.[10] Building on these allows for a new, comprehensive analysis of the impact of cartographic technology on early modern political change. Mapping, in short, undermined medieval structures of rule while simultaneously suggesting new possibilities for political authority, shaping the emergence of sovereign territorial statehood as we know it today. The ideational effect of cartography explains why, in a period with a number of possible political structures, the particular model of the sovereign territorial state eventually came to be implemented as the *only* legitimate form of rule. Functional efficiency alone does not explain this outcome, unique to the modern international system.[11]

Existing studies of early modern political change have focused on a wide range of causal factors and processes involved in the emergence of territorial statehood.[12] In spite of their variety, however, nearly all explanations have omitted the role played by cartography in the development of modern territorial statehood. In general, studies either emphasize material driving forces, such as military technology, organizational competition, property relations, and economic systems, or they rely on changes in ideas, including shifts in religious norms, new representational epistemes, and developments in political theory.[13] All of these factors were undoubtedly involved in the complex process whereby the modern state was created.

[10] The notion of the "social construction of space" builds on Lefebvre 1991. Broadly theoretical works on the ideational effects of mapping include, most prominently, Harley 2001; Pickles 2004; and Wood 1992, 2010. For other approaches to the directly political effects of mapping, see Biggs 1999; Neocleous 2003; Steinberg 2005; Strandsbjerg 2008. Bartelson 2009 also explicitly examines changes in cartographic and cosmological ideas and the effects of those changes on political ideas but focuses specifically on the notion of "world community" rather than territorial statehood.

[11] This contests the argument that territorial rule can be explained primarily as a practical, logic-of-consequences choice by rulers from a repertoire of acceptable principles (e.g. Krasner 1993). The way in which that repertoire was *reduced* over time to include only cartographic territorial claims – rarely with any direct connection to efficiency or practicality – is fundamental to the process examined in this book.

[12] For useful recent reviews of this literature, see Spruyt 2002 and Vu 2010.

[13] For example, Anderson 1974; Downing 1992; Ertman 1997; Gorski 2003; McNeill 1982; Philpott 2001; Rosenberg 1994; Ruggie 1993; Skinner 1978; Spruyt 1994; Teschke 2003; Tilly 1992; Wallerstein 1974.

The state, after all, can be effectively understood as an "assem- *def.*
blage" of authorities, institutions, and ideas, which all originated and
combined in complex ways.[14] However, without the specific changes
driven by mapping, other pressures toward the expansion and centralization of political organization would not have yielded our particular system of exclusively territorial states. The effect of mapping
technology, in fact, connects some of the key material and ideational
shifts of the early modern transformation: mapping technology is
a set of material tools and practices, but it is also closely tied to a
mapmaker's or map user's repertoire of ideas about how the world is
organized. This argument also links changes at the broadest level of
entire societies (ideas about how authority should be asserted) with
shifts in individual behaviors (such as treaty-making practices or map
use by rulers).[15]

Other explanations thus account for certain aspects of the modern
state system but are more effective when combined with the impact of
cartography. For example, the competitive advantages, both military
and economic, enjoyed by territorial states help to explain why, in
early modern Europe, large centralized political units became dominant. Yet these advantages fail to account for the particular form
that states assumed by the early nineteenth century: exclusively territorial entities separated by discrete boundaries. Organization based
on authority and control over a collection of places, rather than linearly divided space, could also have satisfied the need for efficient
extraction. A similar point can be made with regard to other driving
forces behind early modern political change, such as the Protestant
Reformation or economic transformations. These factors explain only
part of the outcome we are interested in, and they fail to address the
origins of the particularly territorial and boundary-focused character
of the modern state system. What is not included in these analyses is
the essential role played by mapping in shaping territorial statehood
as we know it today. In fact, outside the military sphere, technological
changes and their potential impact on political transformations have
predominantly been understood to play only a secondary role, as a

---

[14] Sassen 2006.
[15] See Spruyt 2002 on the divergence between macro and micro levels of
explanation for the origins of states.

small part of larger economic or social changes.[16] Yet the relationship between material technologies like mapping, ideas about political
authority and organization, and the material practices of rule is central
to the origins of the modern state.

The extra-European aspects of this book's argument also build on
other approaches to the origins of our state system that have advocated broadening our scope beyond a single continent. Recent work
has emphasized that, in order to understand international systems in
general, and the modern state system in particular, we need to expand
our inquiry to encompass political arrangements from all regions and
historical periods.[17] Other scholars have explicitly pointed out the
interaction between European and global developments and the potentially extra-European origins of key ideas, technologies, and practices
underlying European political modernity.[18] The global expansion of
early modern political interactions was a key impetus for the earliest
implementation of cartographically defined territorial claims and the
eventual worldwide consolidation of the sovereign state.

This book's argument holds that changes in mapping techniques
and uses – while clearly tied to other major early modern transformations – played a significant and independent role in the emergence
of political modernity. By weaving these threads together, this book
provides a new explanation for the particularly territorial character of
sovereign statehood.

Method and plan of the book

The impact of map use on political organization and interaction did
not involve the sudden transformation of any individual actor's point
of view; instead it constituted a long-term change in society-wide
normative structures and mentalities. The change occurred through
generational turnover and socialization, as political advisors and decision-makers were educated in an increasingly map-filled environment
and as they began to use maps in their everyday activities. The resulting

---

[16] In large part, this may be due to the way in which the relevant academic
disciplines (in particular, historical sociology and International Relations) train
scholars to focus on these possible driving forces and not others.

[17] For example, Buzan and Little 2000; Ferguson and Mansbach 1996;
Watson 1992.

[18] Hobson 2004, 2009; Keene 2002.

changes in cognitive frameworks were slow and unintended and may have had effects far beyond what actors themselves were aware of. The character of this impact has implications for how we study its political effects. Technological changes are observable, as are transformations of material political practices. Yet ideas about political authority and organization are not directly observable, particularly when changes are intergenerational, as individual actors might not even note in journals or letters that their thinking has changed. In other words, what actors consider normal or even imaginable can be restructured without their conscious recognition of the changes.

The best means of documenting changes in these ideational frameworks is to study their observable implications or effects. To this end, this book examines changes in practices, both cartographic and political, theorizes an explanation that accounts for those changes, and then traces the causal pathway between the two.[19] Thus this book relies on the methods of narrative analysis and process-tracing, which make it possible to specify the links between technological drivers of change, the ideational structures those changes work through, and the material political outcomes that result. Both primary and secondary historical material help to establish the connection between mapping and political change in early modern Europe.[20]

Each chapter of the book provides support for this connection, beginning with a close specification of the particular outcome being explained. Chapter 2 thus proposes a new approach to describing international systems and systemic change and then uses that framework to delineate the character and timing of the early modern transformation of European political structures. In particular, fundamental ideas about political authority – who has the right to rule over what kind of domain – structure the identity and organization of political actors, shaping outcomes such as the nature and causes of conflict. Authority structures defined by territory can be distinguished from forms of rule defined by non-spatial principles, such as authority over persons. In the European Middle Ages, political structures were defined by a variety of authority types, both territorial and non-territorial (such as

[19] For a similar approach, see Thomson 1994: 5. See also Wendt 1987.
[20] On narrative analysis and process-tracing, see George and Bennett 2005; Mahoney 1999. For a useful discussion of historical evidence in IR, see Trachtenberg 2006.

personal feudal bonds). Territories, moreover, were not always delimited by boundaries between homogeneous spaces but rather were
defined more often by centers of strong control that faded at the peripheries. The result was a political structure with overlapping claims
to authority, hierarchy among actors, and unclear divisions between
internal and external relations. It was only in the early nineteenth century that medieval heteronomy was fully displaced by political rule
defined exclusively in terms of territory delimited by discrete boundaries. Focusing on political authority undermines the conventional
Westphalian narrative (which sees states appearing earlier) and thus
allows for a more accurate understanding of when and how sovereign
states emerged.

Chapter 3 then examines the development of new cartographic
tools in Europe from the fifteenth century onward and highlights the
socially embedded – and influential – character of this technology.
Maps in the European Middle Ages were rare and were drawn without the geometric definition of accuracy implicit in modern mapping.
Medieval cartographic images manifested an understanding of the
world that emphasized the uniqueness of individual places rather than
the homogeneity of spatial expanses. In the fifteenth century, however, the rediscovery of key classical texts and innovations in printing
led to fundamental transformations in the character, prevalence, and
use of European cartography. Maps came to resemble today's images,
reflecting and reinforcing a new view of space as a geometric expanse.
The world could now be envisioned – and acted upon – from afar
using abstract ideas and divisions. In short, early modern Europeans'
understandings of the world were restructured by the visual language
of maps.

Chapter 4 draws the connection between the broad technological and
societal transformations discussed in Chapter 3 and the directly political effect of cartography on authority structures. As rulers increasingly
used and created maps, cartography both shaped the transformation
in how territorial rule was understood and helped to undermine non-
territorial bases for authority. Territorial authority went from being
defined by claims over particular places, often presented in a textual
list, to being asserted over homogeneous spatial expanses, defined by
cartographic ideas and inscribed upon maps. Non-territorial authority structures such as personal feudal bonds did not appear on maps
and therefore no longer formed part of the conversation among actors

who increasingly defined their identities and interests in cartographic terms. After centuries of map use, rule had been redefined, both in ideas and in practices, as a claim over a territory circumscribed by a discrete boundary.

Expanding the scope beyond Europe, Chapter 5 highlights the process of colonial reflection, whereby the new ideas and practices of exclusively territorial rule were first used in the Americas and then later applied to intra-European interactions. European expansion to the New World demanded a new set of ideas and tools for asserting rule from afar. The newly developed techniques of mapping and cartographically inspired ideas formed a key part of this new repertoire, as early modern mapping allowed rulers to make and contest political claims without any actual knowledge of the territory being claimed or what lay within it. Thus, cartographic tools of government – and the exclusively territorial form of rule that they made possible – were first put to work in sixteenth- and seventeenth-century colonial expansion, providing a foundation for their application later within and between European states.

In order to provide further empirical support for the role of mapping in this political transformation, Chapter 6 examines major early modern European peace settlements. The negotiation goals and practices of political actors and the texts of the resulting peace treaties reveal the manner and timing in which the complex authorities of the medieval political system were replaced by the homogeneity of territorial claims defined exclusively by linear boundaries. From the eighteenth century onward, mapping and cartographically structured ideas displaced earlier, more complex forms of authority. This textual and behavioral evidence provides an analytical link between changes at the level of ideas and their implementation in political practices on the ground.

Chapter 7 narrows the focus to one illustrative case: France. The territorialization of rule in France followed a representative, though often misinterpreted, trajectory from a complex agglomeration of medieval authority claims to the boundary-defined, exclusively territorial, post-Revolutionary state. Maps were fundamental to this transformation, both as material objects that reshaped political ideas and as tools that enabled new assertions of authority and control. The new commercial depictions of France in the sixteenth and early seventeenth centuries created new conditions of possibility for how

French rulers thought about their realm, lending new strength to the notion of discrete boundaries around a homogeneous spatial territory. Subsequently, rulers began to put this transformed idea into practice (both at frontiers and internally), including by commissioning extensive mapping projects to delineate French territory. Yet these projects built on the foundation provided by commercial mapping, making use of the latter's visual grammar and geometric structure. These maps then made it possible for French rulers to delineate their territorial boundaries with a degree of precision previously unavailable – but they did so only because earlier mapping had made hegemonic this particular way of defining and asserting authority. By overturning the conventional reading of pre-Revolutionary France as a modern territorial state, this chapter demonstrates the interplay between sixteenth- and seventeenth-century cartography and the late eighteenth-century implementation of territorial rule.

Finally, Chapter 8 applies the theoretical insights from the preceding historical analysis to particular questions about fundamental political change today. Using the generalizable implications of this historical case, this chapter focuses in particular on the implications of digital cartographic technologies for contemporary political ideas, practices, and outcomes. The application of information technology to mapping is now creating the most fundamental transformation in cartography since the early modern period, making this a particularly auspicious time to consider potential changes to the state. By focusing on the intersection between representational technologies and political authority, this book's theoretical lens reframes contemporary issues and provides a new means of examining the ways in which the sovereign state is simultaneously supported and challenged today.

2 | Authority, sovereignty, and international change

Over a period of several centuries, in a contested, uneven, and layered evolution, the structure of international politics in Europe underwent a fundamental transformation. The complexity of late medieval political organization was regularized and homogenized, yielding our familiar international system, constituted by territorially exclusive sovereign states. This system of states remains the foundation for political organization to this day. In spite of the momentousness of this change, important causal drivers and processes remain unexamined, and key aspects of statehood remain unexplained. This book considers the overlooked but significant role played by cartography in the emergence of modern territorial sovereignty out of the complexity of medieval political rule.

In order to understand just how important mapping was to the constitution of our state system, however, we need first to reconceptualize what we are explaining when we account for the origins of political modernity. What exactly do we mean by the formation of sovereign states? Which aspects of statehood have been explained, and which have been ignored? These questions are made more complicated by our propensity to read backwards into history from the political arrangements of today. In fact, our system of sovereign, territorial states is not a standard from which rare periods of complexity have diverged; instead, states today represent a unique configuration of political authority requiring close scrutiny and explanation.[1]

This chapter offers a historically directed approach to understanding our world of territorial states and its origins in early modern Europe. In particular, I highlight the importance of ideas and practices of political authority to the constitution of sovereignty, statehood, and the modern international system. With this focus, the character

---

[1] On the tendency to read backwards, particularly in IR theory, see, among many others, Osiander 2001a; Smith 1999; Walker 1993.

and timing of the shift from medieval to modern political structures becomes clear.

Conceptualizing political change: authority and the international system

In order to identify and explain transformations of international political structures – historical and contemporary – we need a means for describing any particular set of organizations and institutions in terms that are both historically appropriate and, at the same time, comparable across periods and cultures.[2] Neorealist International Relations theory contends that the relevant features of any international system are captured by three characteristics – two of which are assumed to be unchanging – and thus represents the extreme in terms of developing abstract categories comparable across periods. Unfortunately, this approach fails to capture the possibility of change or the existence of systems with characteristics different from those of modern states.[3] The other end of the spectrum is represented by theories that recognize the particularity of the modern state system and the contingency of its origins. Yet most of these theories tend to describe modern statehood in terms of a set of unique characteristics, removing the possibility of developing categories for effective historical comparison.[4]

Instead, we should describe political institutions in a way that is clearly defined, applies to a wide range of contexts, and avoids assuming that all eras have shared the basic characteristics of the modern state system. This can be accomplished by narrowing our focus to the dominant ideas of political authority and their instantiation in political

[2] Avoiding anachronistic terms such as *international* or *interstate* to describe political structures that existed before either modern nations or states would clearly be ideal. However, due to the overwhelming use in the International Relations literature of such terms, I will refer throughout to *international* politics, structures, and systems (as do many other historically minded IR authors). It should be noted, however, that this analysis is applicable to any system composed of interacting polities (with or without the particular characteristics of modern states or nations).

[3] Waltz 1979. Much subsequent neorealist theory has built on Waltz's basic formula; see, for example, Gilpin 1981. For critiques of neorealism relevant to this discussion, see in particular Ruggie 1983, 1993; Spruyt 1998.

[4] The English School is the most prominent example of this approach, as key works have usefully highlighted the particularity and historical contingency of modern states. See Bull 1977; Wight 1977.

practices. Authority – defined as the right and ability to demand obedi-   def
ence – is integral to politics in all eras and circumstances.[5] Ideas and
practices of political authority are thus central both to the structure
of the international system and to the constraints and incentives presented to actors within that system.[6] In International Relations, for
example, *internal sovereignty* (effective control over a territory) is
distinguished from *external sovereignty* (recognition of that authority by other states). Both, however, are defined by the character of the
authority that a political actor holds, both internally vis-à-vis subject
persons, jurisdictions, or territory and externally in terms of the divisions between political entities.[7]

The state sovereignty of today's international system is, therefore,
defined by a particular collection of ideas and practices of political
authority: specifically, territorial demarcation and mutual exclusion.
These fundamental features of state sovereignty are unique to the
modern state system, rather than immutable properties of all human
political organization.[8] The authoritative ideas and practices that
undergird modern state sovereignty should therefore be directly inter-
rogated in order to understand both how they emerged from a very
different set of arrangements in the late Middle Ages and how they
may be changing today.[9]

[5] This point has been made most famously by Max Weber's description of three
   ideal-types of authority and their application.
[6] This conceptualization builds on a number of works that have noted the basis
   of sovereignty and international structure in political authority. See, among
   others, Ferguson and Mansbach 1996; Lake 2003, 2009; Milner 1991; and
   Thomson 1994. See also Wendt 1999.
[7] This is a similar point to that made by Thomson (1994: 14–15) differentiating
   the constitutive dimension of sovereignty from the functional dimension. The
   former concerns the principle by which authority is claimed, while the latter
   addresses the narrower question of the activities that an authority holder
   controls. Related distinctions are made by Holsti (2004) on foundational versus
   procedural institutions of the international system and by Buzan (2004) on
   primary versus secondary institutions.
[8] As Agnew (1994) points out, too much International Relations scholarship has
   fallen into the "territorial trap" of assuming the permanence and inevitability of
   our uniquely territorial form of political organization. See also Elden 2010.
[9] Most IR authors approach sovereignty as a collection of predefined ideas and
   practices rather than examining variation in authority, including those theorists
   who treat sovereignty as contested and problematic. For example, Krasner
   (1999) breaks down sovereignty into two external and two internal types, and
   then asks when and how these principles have been violated. This is a useful
   approach for examining the modern period (as he does). Yet if we wish

Ideas and practices of political authority can be investigated by focusing on rule: who rules? Who has rule over what domain? How is that domain defined? How are the rules of different authority-holders separated? Answering these questions allows us to compare foundational political ideas and practices across historical periods.[10] The following paragraphs pursue this approach, presenting a typology of authority types. This is by no means exhaustive of the possible variations in authority, but it nonetheless captures the key differences between medieval political structures, the modern state system, and many other possible arrangements.[11] Furthermore, it reveals the specific features of modern statehood that are explained by mapping and its effects, allowing us to distinguish these territorial elements of the sovereign state from other features – such as centralization or bureaucratization – that have been explained by other theories. Two forms of variation in authority are fundamental: the conceptual basis for authority (territorial versus non-territorial, with variation also existing within each category) and the exclusivity of authority (exclusive versus overlapping).

All authority claims have some conceptual basis: ideas defining who or what is subject to the authority in question and how the limits of that authority are understood. The primary distinction is between authorities defined in territorial or spatial terms (in various forms) and authorities defined without reference to space or place.[12]

Territorial authority is familiar to us today, although modern territoriality is merely one of many possible spatial forms of authority.[13] Territorial claims can be made based on authority radiating outward from a center of control, or they can be made over spaces defined

---

to account for the transition from the medieval to the modern system – or to consider the possibility of a transformation in the international system today – it is not a question of particular fixed principles being violated or honored, but rather a change in what those principles are.

[10] Focusing on the issue of *rule* builds on Kratochwil 1989 and Onuf 1989, among others.

[11] Agnew 2009 provides a similar analysis, also revealing that the modern nation-state is merely one territorial political form among many possibilities.

[12] This is similar to a narrower distinction made by Sahlins (1989: 28) between territorial sovereignty and jurisdictional sovereignty.

[13] This point has been noted often by constructivist IR theorists. See, for example, Kratochwil 1986; Ruggie 1983, 1993. On territoriality in general, see Sack 1986 and Gottman 1973.

by clear boundaries. Rulers in many pre-modern polities defined their realms as a center of strong control that faded toward the peripheries.[14] This was the case even in polities with ostensibly linear boundaries such as the Roman *limes* (including Hadrian's Wall) and the Great Wall of China: rather than linear bounds, these fortifications were seen as temporary stopping places on the way to world conquest and were used for internal control as much as for external defense.[15] Political actors did not conceptualize their rule in terms of exhaustive claims defined by discrete and absolute divisions. Territorial authority defined by boundaries, however, is fundamental to the modern state system, as states are defined, in theory if not always in practice, by fixed and discrete boundaries. These boundaries neatly delineate the complete authority of one state from the similarly complete authority of its neighboring states.

Another source of variation in territoriality is the degree of distinction among diverse parts of the spatial claim. Differentiated conceptions of territory posit space as a succession of unique places, each with particular (and perhaps incomparable) characteristics. Homogeneous territoriality sees an undifferentiated space, without qualitative differences between different areas.[16] When considered together, these two forms of variation (center-focus versus boundary-focus, differentiated versus homogeneous) reveal the possibility of fundamentally divergent forms of territorial authority: on the one hand, many historical eras' notion of rule over collections of *places* and, on the other, the modern notion of boundary-defined political *spaces*. The dominant position enjoyed by the latter understanding is unique to the modern world.

Non-territorial authority, in contrast, encompasses claims to political rule that are defined in ways that do not incorporate spatial terms.[17] This category includes a wide range of authority claims, including most prominently those made over individual persons or collections of persons, without regard to their spatial location or distribution.

---

[14] Holsti 2004: 73.
[15] Kratochwil 1986: 36; Whittaker 2004. Also, see a similar point concerning precolonial authority in Africa made by Herbst (2000: 45).
[16] Agnew 2009: 35–39; Harley 2001: ch. 3.
[17] While there is an inherent danger of reading backwards when using a residual category such as this, it is nonetheless useful for analyzing early modern political change in terms of a distinction between, first, changing forms of territoriality and, second, the disappearance of non-territorial authorities.

Authorities claimed on a universal level over particular issue areas or types of transactions are also effectively non-territorial: with no boundaries to those claims, they are not operationalized in spatial terms. Although non-territorial claims are the exception in today's state system, they have constituted a common form of authority in other historical settings.

Independently of its conceptual basis, authority can also vary between the complete exclusivity held by a single authority figure and the overlapping or sharing of authority among multiple holders. If it is exclusive, authority is by definition final; that is, there is only one locus of authority over the particular persons, territories, or issue jurisdictions in question. Overlapping or non-exclusive authority, by contrast, exists when the same subject or target of authority has more than one ruler. Historically, non-exclusive authority has existed in many forms, including multiple homage in feudalism or nomadic claims to territory only as a periodic route of migration rather than as permanent and exclusive claims.[18] The modern state system is defined by exclusive authority, at least in theory; overlaps and shared rule are treated as exceptional.

These ideas about political authority – how it is defined, how it is exercised, and who holds it over what or whom – do more than define abstract notions of sovereignty or political rule. These ideas shape the fundamental structure of political organization and interaction, by determining the identities of actors and their internal and external organization.[19] Internally, how is authority defined? Rule could be defined as territorial control over diverse places or over delimited spaces, or as a claim over collections of persons. Externally, how are the divisions between different rulers' domains conceptualized and effected? Modern states are understood to have discrete and precise boundaries, but other polities have had very different forms of divisions. The identity of a political actor is defined by these ideas, and thus an actor's interests are shaped by them as well. What is meant by

---

[18] Note that authority can be decentralized without being overlapping, and vice versa. On nomadic territoriality, see Ruggie 1993.

[19] This is not to say that these ideas are the only thing that gives shape to international political structures, but rather to point out that particular elements of structure – recognized as such by most prominent IR theories – are strongly influenced by these ideas. See Wendt 1999 on the interaction between ideational and material factors in system structure.

security or conquest, for example, changes depending on the domain that is being defended or expanded.[20]

The organization of the actors within an international system is also shaped by those same ideas and practices of political authority. Ideas concerning how actors are related to one another – that is, if any has authority over another – provide the underlying structure to how the system is organized. Contrary to the assumption by neorealist theory that anarchy is permanent and immutable, an examination of authority reveals that every international system has hierarchical elements. International systems historically have varied widely in their degree of hierarchy, and even today's sovereign-state system – though built on the principle of formal equality – contains hierarchical authority relations.[21]

These ideas, about who are the recognized actors and how they are organized, fundamentally structure behaviors and outcomes in international politics. Actors' interests are informed by their identities, and the degree of recognition of the legitimacy of other actors' claims shapes interaction. By exploring the particular character and timing of the shift from medieval to modern political authority structures, the following pages highlight key elements of this transformation that require explanation. The medieval period was characterized by diverse authority types – territorial and non-territorial, overlapping and complex – which, by the early nineteenth century, were reshaped into the modern uniformity of mutually exclusive territorial statehood.

Political authority in the late Middle Ages

In late medieval Europe, ideas and practices of political authority were complex, mixing a range of territorial and non-territorial bases for rule and thus constituting international structures very different from those of the modern state system.[22]

---

[20] Bukovansky 2002.
[21] See, among others, Lake 2003, 2009; Milner 1991; Watson 1992.
[22] Setting clear historical or geographical boundaries to the "late Middle Ages" is difficult, but there are enough commonalities among political ideas and practices within what we label as Western and Central Europe, during the thirteenth through mid fifteenth centuries, that this can be treated as an analytical category.

Some political authorities were understood and operationalized in territorial terms, though in a way that was distinct from modern territorial statehood. Most territories were defined by a center of control rather than being delineated by discrete boundaries. Contiguous political entities were most often separated by loosely controlled frontier zones rather than by clear linear demarcations, and the peripheries of larger polities were more loosely controlled than the centers. For example, authority in independent city-states was understood to radiate outward from an urban center into a rural hinterland. Although there were some linear divisions – such as waterways used to delimit authority – these were the exception rather than the rule.

Another aspect of medieval territorial authority that differs from modern concepts of authority is the high degree of differentiation among diverse places in the territory. For example, French kings held some parts of France as personal possessions and other parts through feudal vassals. Also, in the Italian city-states, the central city was ruled very differently from the outlying subject towns, let alone the rural space in between. In short, territorial authority was center-focused and constructed on a diverse collection of ideas.[23]

In addition to these territorial claims, political authority in medieval Europe was also based on non-spatial forms of rule. In fact, contrary to how we might read backwards from today, the non-territorial forms of authority were often more important to the structure of rule than were territorial claims. The primary form that non-territorial authority took was the system of feudal ties between lords and vassals. Medieval polities were built around networks of homage and vassalage running from kings down to low-level knights. Although feudalism involved the granting of fiefs in land, the superior's authority was based on a personal bond, not on territory.[24] In addition to direct feudal bonds, which were, in theory if not always in practice, based on face-to-face interactions, political rule on a larger scale was also understood as rule over persons rather than over territory. Medieval kingship was founded on the notion of a connection between the king and "the people," and subjects expressed their side of this bond through symbolic oaths of

[23] Fischer 1992; Ganshof 1970; Martines 1979.
[24] Bloch 1961; Mitteis 1975; Poggi 1978. Although Spruyt (1994) argues that feudalism had waned as a significant political principle by 1300, evidence exists supporting the persistence of feudal structures *alongside* other forms of rule, both territorial and non-territorial, well into the fifteenth century.

loyalty. Law, similarly, was applied to peoples rather than to states or territories.[25]

Non-territorial authorities also included claims over particular offices or issue jurisdictions, which were made without clear spatial definitions. For example, the Treaty of Verdun (AD 843) divided Charlemagne's empire into three parts. Although in retrospect this looks like a simple territorial partition, in fact the division was framed in terms of jurisdictions and revenues, not territory per se. The shares were meant to be "equivalent in regard to revenues and equivalent in regard to the amount of lucrative offices (*honores*) and benefices that could be distributed among the aristocracy."[26] Both the ends and the means of this division were conceived of in jurisdictional, rather than territorial, terms.

Overall, rule in the late Middle Ages included various territorial and non-territorial authorities. These forms of authority coexisted not just throughout the region, but also often within a single political entity. A king could claim different parts of his realm based on different principles, territorial or non-territorial.[27]

These authorities, moreover, were not exclusive, as the vague jurisdictional frontiers and complex feudal networks made overlapping claims normal. Feudal relations created situations of overlapping control, as vassals could owe fealty – and military service – to more than one lord.[28] These complexities made resolutions among actors at the highest level far from simple. For example, during the Hundred Years War, the obscure origins of the rights of lords to rule their fiefs sometimes left the French and English negotiators unable to settle claims – even when the two parties agreed on who should get what – because the local lords refused to recognize the right of *either* side to assign control.[29] These complexities and overlaps blurred the modern distinction between internal and external affairs, both in terms of diplomacy (as actors at many levels within one kingdom would send embassies) and in terms of taxation (where internal and external tariffs and duties were identical).[30]

Thus, while it has been argued that state sovereignty appeared in the late Middle Ages – at least in a nascent form – this runs against

---

[25] Dunbabin 1988; King 1988; Procopé 1988; Sahlins 1989.
[26] Ganshof 1970: 48.   [27] Sahlins 1989.   [28] Bloch 1961; Duby 1968.
[29] Fowler 1971: 192.   [30] Dickinson 1955; Ganshof 1970: 53.

the evidence concerning how political authority was conceived and operationalized.[31] Although authority claims were made based on territorial designations, these by no means reflected the underlying principles of sovereign statehood. Notably absent was the modern idea of authority being *solely* defined by discrete territorial boundaries and being theoretically exclusive within those lines. Instead, both in theory and in practice, authority was constituted by diverse territorial and non-territorial claims, often overlapping and with vague divisions between them. In other words, although there had been some movement toward a more territorial form of rule by the end of the Middle Ages (including, in one well-known example, the shift in title from the "King of the Franks" to the "King of France"), this did not represent a transition to modern territorial statehood or sovereignty.[32]

This range of authority types constituted an international system composed of a diverse collection of polities, organized with a complex mix of hierarchical and anarchical relationships. Medieval political theory reflected this diversity, as discussions of political organization incorporated a wide range of terminologies and doctrines.[33] Political conflict and cooperation involved kingdoms such as France or England, the Holy Roman Empire, the papacy, city-states in Italy and elsewhere, independent city-leagues, and non-territorial corporate groups. None of these polities resembled small-scale versions of the exclusively territorial states of the modern world, nor could they be considered the direct precursors to modern states. In kingdoms, for example, rulers held only incomplete authority over their realms, founded as much on feudal ties and rule over the *gens* (or people) as on territorial claims.

[31] For an influential example of the former view, see Joseph Strayer's *On the Medieval Origins of the Modern State* (1970). Strayer sees elements of statehood in the late Middle Ages because he defines the state simply as a strong form of political organization, not because polities in this period exhibited the particular characteristics of sovereign territorial states. It is not that Strayer's analysis is incorrect, per se, but that it only traces the earliest origins of a small piece of what makes up sovereign statehood, and ignores the particularly territorial character of modern politics. The impact of this short volume on discussion in IR of the origins of political modernity has been significant; see, for example, Gilpin 1981: 116ff.; Krasner 1993: 252ff.; Ruggie 1993: 150; Spruyt 1994: 79; and Thomson 1994: 21.

[32] Kantorowicz 1957.

[33] For example, a multitude of terms – including *res publica, regnum, civitas, commune, dominium,* and others – were often used interchangeably to refer to political entities. See Black 1992; Dunbabin 1988.

The latter, in any case, were asserted over places, not over delimited spatial expanses.[34] The Holy Roman Empire was even more divergent from our norm of modern statehood, as the emperor was simultaneously a German king, the arbiter among a loose federation of small principalities, and a largely symbolic authority figure over all of Christendom.[35] City-leagues, such as the Hansa, performed many functions we now associate with states but remained non-hierarchical and only loosely confederated, with limited control over hinterlands. City-states were also common in the late Middle Ages but were not the miniature territorial states they are often declared to be: cities did not have complete or exclusive authority over subject towns or the countryside, and boundaries between city-states were rarely discrete territorial demarcations.[36]

This complex collection of political actors, founded on numerous overlapping authorities, created an international system organized around a mix of anarchical and hierarchical relationships.[37] Concerning the latter, medieval political theory often advocated for the unity of all of Christendom under a single authority – of the Church or the emperor. While such arguments by no means determined the actual relationships between political actors, they did create the possibility for authority relations to exist, if not throughout the system then at least in parts of it. Similarly, although feudalism may have been in decline by the fourteenth century relative to the preceding period, feudal bonds still constrained the interactions of key actors. For example, the lord–vassal relationship between the French and English kings was part of what instigated the Hundred Years War in the mid 1300s and continued to frame the interactions between the two rulers throughout the conflict.[38] The status of the Holy Roman Empire similarly reflected the continuing influence of hierarchical elements into the late Middle Ages. While polities outside Germany rarely acknowledged any de facto authority of the emperor, the principalities within the boundaries of the empire continued to be subject to limited imperial authority and interacted through imperial institutions.[39]

---

[34] Bloch 1961; Finer 1997; Reynolds 1997.   [35] Osiander 2001a.
[36] Covini 2000; Guarini 2003; Martines 1979; Spruyt 1994.
[37] Or, as Ruggie (1993) labels the system, "heteronomous."
[38] Curry 1993; Reynolds 1997.
[39] Ganshof 1970; Leyser 1975; Muldoon 1999: ch. 4; Ullman 1949.

This mixture of hierarchical and non-hierarchical organization among medieval actors shaped political interactions, as was particularly evident in late medieval diplomacy. Envoys, ambassadors, and other representatives were sent between various actors, rather than today's practice where only recognized, sovereign states treat with one another.[40] For example, the Congress of Arras (1435) is seen now as a three-way summit between England, France, and Burgundy, but it actually involved a much larger number of actors. The French contingent included not only representatives of the crown, but also those of the nobles and the towns, with an unclear relationship to the royal embassy. Towns ostensibly under the authority of England, France, or Burgundy had semi-independent policies. Paris itself had three groups representing it, one each from the clergy, the city burghers, and the university. Finally, the English embassy was actually a "double embassy" – England proper and Lancastrian-controlled France had separate representatives. Even this apparently simple diplomatic meeting demonstrates the variety of political units active within what is now France.[41]

These actors, moreover, saw themselves as members of a single society of Christendom with a shared set of goals for diplomatic interaction. In theory, this society was hierarchical, with the pope held as the highest authority. Although historians have rightly noted that popes rarely if ever achieved this position in practice, the papacy often served as a key mediator in diplomatic interactions, and thereby shaped outcomes indirectly.[42] For example, papal mediators were essential in negotiating many truces – so much so that during the Great Schism (1378–1417), warring parties found it much harder to settle their differences because they often backed different papal claimants and refused to recognize mediators from rival factions.[43] After the end of the Schism, papal representatives once again took a central role in negotiations, such as at the Congress of Arras, where the French–English negotiations were held entirely through papal mediators, without any face-to-face meetings.[44]

Treaty-making practices also reflected the complexity of medieval political authority, as treaties were signed between various actors and were seen as personal obligations rather than as legal agreements

[40] Holzgrefe 1989.   [41] Dickinson 1955.
[42] Black 1992; Curry 1993; Mattingly 1955.
[43] Allmand 1988; Fowler 1971.   [44] Dickinson 1955.

between institutionalized states.[45] Medieval laws of war also differ from their modern equivalents, largely due to the concept that all of Christendom was a single hierarchical society. The type of law applied to war, *jus gentium* (law of peoples), was seen as common to all Christian peoples, and simultaneously governed what we would consider internal and external military conduct. Ostensibly public crimes such as treason were treated as personal offenses against the ruler, based on the nature of the lord–vassal bond.[46]

In short, late medieval political rule, organization, and interaction were built on a complex collection of territorial and non-territorial authorities, with hierarchical ties connecting rulers throughout the region. This was fundamentally transformed during the early modern period as a system of exclusively territorial states emerged.

Modern political authority and sovereign statehood

Today's international system rests on an authoritative foundation of rule entirely different from what has just been outlined. We now have exclusively territorial states, separated by discrete boundaries and claiming absolute authority within those lines. This set of political structures, though appearing fundamental to us, was only fully consolidated in the post-Napoleonic reconstruction of European politics. Traditionally, the beginning of the modern state system has been placed at the Treaties of Westphalia (1648), which ended the Thirty Years War in central Europe.[47] Even those scholars who do not attribute the modern state system directly to the treaty tend to see this period generally as marking the consolidation of sovereign statehood after its initial appearance in the sixteenth century, or earlier.[48] These approaches, recognizing some common features between the modern and medieval periods, ascribe too much continuity to two eras that are essentially different.

---

[45] Ganshof 1970; Holzgrefe 1989.
[46] Dessau 1968; Keen 1968.
[47] This view, usually traced to a 1948 article by Leo Gross, is effectively debunked by Osiander 2001b. For extensive lists of IR works that attribute great importance to 1648, see Krasner 1993: 239 and Osiander 2001b: 260–61. This attribution also appears in scholarship on international law; see, for elaboration, Beaulac 2004.
[48] Wight 1977, for example.

Political organization in the first century and a half after Westphalia, though exhibiting forms of rule transformed from those of the late Middle Ages, was by no means identical to the system of exclusively territorial and anarchically organized states of the nineteenth and twentieth centuries. The "Westphalian myth" has been criticized by many authors, including Andreas Osiander, who convincingly argues that the idea that a system of states was created in 1648 is a fallacy, "a product of the nineteenth- and twentieth-century fixation on the concept of sovereignty" and based on seventeenth-century anti-Hapsburg propaganda.[49] The shift to modern uniformly territorial states was not complete until more than a century after 1648.

In terms of how political rule was conceptualized and put into practice, the seventeenth and early eighteenth centuries witnessed the persistence of medieval ways of defining, and separating, political realms.[50] For one, political boundaries between actors were not the modern linear frontiers of our state system. The Treaty of the Pyrenees (1659), which placed the boundary between Spain and France on the Pyrenees mountains, was merely the first phase in creating this modern idea of a territorial border: it recognized the legitimacy of the geographic idea of a natural boundary. Other clauses of the same treaty delineated jurisdictional divisions that actually contradicted the geographic boundary. Discrete territorial divisions along the entire length of this frontier were made clear on the ground only in the 1860s.[51] Furthermore, the description of seventeenth- and early eighteenth-century rule as "absolutist" reflected rulers' aspirations better than their actual abilities, as these purportedly absolutist states are better understood as "conglomerate" or "composite" polities – agglomerations of complex and decentralized contractual relationships – rather than as unified entities.[52]

These kingdoms and republics, therefore, differed fundamentally from the territorial states of the nineteenth and twentieth centuries, in terms of both their internal organization and their external relations. Composite states such as France or Spain coexisted with a broad range

[49] Osiander 2001b: 251.
[50] See Chapter 6 for evidence of this timing from peace treaties.
[51] Sahlins 1989.
[52] Bergin 2001; Black 1999; Gustafsson 1998; Munck 1990; Nexon 2009; Te Brake 1998: 198.

of other political forms, such as those that persisted within the Holy Roman Empire, including electorates, free cities, and secular and ecclesiastical principalities. Contrary to the conventional modern view, relations among these German polities were not completely transformed by the events of 1648, as imperial judicial institutions continued to function and the principalities were understood to be "autonomous" rather than "sovereign."[53] International politics, in short, remained anything but an anarchical order among formally equal, sovereign states.

The sixteenth and seventeenth centuries did witness a key institutional innovation that has been declared to represent the birth of modern statehood: the system of extraterritorial jurisdiction for embassies. This system – resting on the idea that part of one state's territory is actually subject to another ruler's authority – is held to be a key milestone in the emergence of sovereign statehood.[54] Yet the early modern ideas and practices relating to extraterritoriality demonstrate that, rather than *creating* modern territorial authority, the form of extraterritoriality in use in the sixteenth and seventeenth centuries instead *reflected* the contemporary form of territorial authority: that is, it focused on places rather than spaces and was defined by centers rather than boundaries. Unlike today's explicit delineation of the property of an embassy (which is then considered the sovereign territory of the embassy's state), the immunity of early modern embassies was not demarcated cleanly. Instead, early modern extraterritoriality offered a gradually diminishing sense of immunity as one moved away from the embassy.[55] Thus, the form of extraterritoriality that developed was fundamentally derived from the existing form of territoriality, based on the era's ideas about authority in general. Extraterritoriality is variable, just as territoriality is, and is not a cause of change but a sign of it – a particular implementation of territoriality in the practices of rulers and states.

Instead, the early nineteenth century is the period in which the transition from medieval complexity to modern sovereign statehood was

---

[53] Black 1987; Munck 1990; Osiander 1994; Sturdy 2002.
[54] Mattingly 1955: 236–44; Ruggie 1993: 165.
[55] For example, some embassy-filled areas of cities exhibited a "notorious *franchise du quartier* which made each embassy *and its adjacent area* a privileged sanctuary for debtors, smugglers, and all sorts of notorious criminals" (Mattingly 1955: 242, emphasis added).

consolidated. Unlike the 150-year period following Westphalia, after the Congress of Vienna (1814–15) all actors were defined in terms of exclusive territorial authority, and both system-wide and subsystem hierarchies and heteronomies (such as the Holy Roman Empire) were replaced by a great-power-managed anarchical system. In key ideas and practices of rule, the early nineteenth century was not a reactionary "restoration" of pre-Revolutionary absolutism but instead represented the implementation of a collection of ideas and techniques of rule that had developed slowly during the early modern period and that were consolidated during the French Revolution and its aftermath.[56]

By the middle of the nineteenth century, rule had taken on an exclusively territorial form, rather than the earlier mix of territorial and jurisdictional authority claims. In political theory, for example, after the mid eighteenth century, authors such as Emerich de Vattel or Christian Wolff came to define states as sovereign and formally equal and noted the importance for such states to demarcate their boundaries carefully.[57] This theoretical backing for exclusively territorial authority found expression in the French Revolutionary regime's doctrine of the state as "an exclusive sovereign authority exercised by a single government over a clearly defined territory."[58] Many of the jurisdictional complexities represented by foreign or independent enclaves within the boundaries of states were eliminated by the Revolutionary and Napoleonic conquests, and they were not restored at Vienna. Territorial rule was reconceptualized as a space defined inward from the boundaries rather than outward from a center (or from multiple centers).

This period also saw the final termination of the complex overlapping and shared authorities that had existed in many parts of the continent in the late Middle Ages and in the Holy Roman Empire through the eighteenth century. The Revolution's concept of sovereignty as having a single locus of authority was among the new tools of power that the ostensibly reactionary post-1815 regimes were happy to keep. This reflected the culmination of a long-term effort by all governments, conservative or revolutionary, to end the sharing of authority over particular domains with other actors. The process was accelerated and completed in particular by Napoleon's conquests and the

[56] Lyons 2006; Osiander 2007; Schroeder 1994, 2000.
[57] Onuf and Onuf 1993: 15; Sahlins 1989: 93.
[58] Schroeder 1994: 72.

resultant vacuum in authority in many realms after his defeat.[59] This process was supported by many of the preceding centuries' political writings, such as those of Bodin or Hobbes, which offered useful theoretical backing to the practical imposition of the conception of exclusive sovereignty.

The early nineteenth century, therefore, witnessed the consolidation of the territorial state throughout the European system. Although actors differed greatly in terms of size and power, their constitutive characteristics were, for the first time, almost completely homogeneous. This was the result of two trends progressing since the fifteenth century: the elimination of non-state actors such as the Empire or the city-leagues, and the shift toward exclusive territorial sovereignty as the basis for state rule. The Holy Roman Empire, for example, was formally dissolved in 1806, and city-leagues such as the Hansa had ceased to be important organizations by the eighteenth century. The states that emerged in the post-Napoleonic period were transformed from their composite and weakly centralized precursors: rulers now wiped clean the remaining medieval complexities and overlapping claims in favor of exclusive territorial rule over clearly delineated states.

The possibility of a single hierarchical order extending across Europe was also fully eliminated by 1815, as neither the emperor nor the pope had even a remote possibility of being recognized as a legitimate authority over European rulers.[60] Instead, the system as a whole was subject to a form of "collective hegemony" under the tutelage of the self-described great powers.[61] Though the terminology has changed, the management of the international system by the most powerful actors has remained a constant feature of the state system since 1815.

The homogeneously territorial definition of the modern state has not been without exceptions, but those exceptions remain defined by the framework provided by the territorially exclusive ideal of statehood. (Today's challenges to the territorial state are discussed in Chapter 8.) Similarly, features of nineteenth-century political organization that are sometimes considered violations of statehood actually reflect the same exclusively territorial ideal. For example, uniform territoriality extended into European overseas expansion: although the

---

[59] Osiander 1994; Schroeder 1994; Tombs 2000.
[60] Parker 2001; Skinner 1978.
[61] Watson 1992: ch. 21. See also Elrod 1976; Schroeder 1986.

hierarchical *internal* organization of colonial empires diverged from
the anarchical relations among European states, many colonial possessions were nonetheless defined *externally* in similarly territorial
terms, as homogeneous spatial entities separated by linear boundaries.[62] In fact, Europeans made political claims based on cartographic
territoriality earlier in the Americas than within Europe (a process
that is detailed in Chapter 5). The contrast between hierarchy within
empires and anarchy among sovereign states does not contradict the
homogeneously territorial character of the nineteenth-century international system; instead, the difference represented a variation within
the framework of exclusive territoriality. This framework remains the
baseline against which states are compared, and to which many state-
less peoples aspire.

Conceptualizing authority, explaining the territorial state

Medieval authority had various conceptual bases, ranging from territorial to jurisdictional and personal. Complementing this diversity was
the prevalence of overlapping and shared rule. In the shift to the modern international system, two major changes to authority occurred.
First, the jurisdictional and overlapping forms of authority were eliminated. Second, territorial authority became the sole basis for sovereignty in the modern system. It also underwent a significant change:
medieval territorial authority, based on a center-out concept of control
of places, was transformed into the modern form of territorial authority, in which control is conceived of as flowing in from firm boundaries
that delineate a homogeneous territorial space.

Understanding the particular character and timing of this transformation is a necessary foundation for any explanation of the emergence
of modern states. The present chapter's conceptualization – focusing
on the definition and operationalization of political authority – allows
us next to examine particular elements of modern statehood that have
not been explained sufficiently. The exclusively territorial nature of
rule – and the exclusive definition of territories as spaces with discrete boundaries – is fundamental to modern statehood, but it is

---

[62] Bassett 1994; Brotton 1997; Edgerton 1975; Pickles 2004; Sack 1986. This
does not apply to the more complex forms of jurisdictional concessions and
agreements in places such as nineteenth-century China (Kayaoglu 2007).

poorly explained by existing approaches to the emergence of the state. Territorial exclusivity is in fact closely linked to the processes examined in this book: the interaction between mapping technologies and political organization. The next chapter thus examines the early modern revolution in cartographic techniques and uses, providing context essential for explaining the origins of the state.

3 | *The cartographic revolution*

How did it come to be that whereas in 1400 few people in Europe used maps, except for the Mediterranean navigators with their portolan charts, by 1600 maps were essential to a wide variety of professions?[1]

In effect, every map is a theory.[2]

Two related phenomena emerge from the history of European mapping in the early modern period. The first is the explosion in the production of maps and their transformed usage. At the beginning of the fifteenth century, European cartography was extremely limited, comprising a very small number of coastal maps for navigation, schematic land itineraries, and symbolic representations of religious time and space. By the end of the sixteenth century, however, the situation was entirely different: there had been a radical transformation both qualitatively in terms of the character and uses of maps and quantitatively in an exponential increase in their production. All kinds of actors were now using the new maps to pursue their economic, social, and political goals.

Yet this admittedly monumental shift in material objects and in practices is only half of the story. Maps also serve to embody, shape, and reshape map users' ideas about the world in which they live, even to the point of altering the goals they are pursuing with the help of these cartographic tools. As the second epigraph above suggests, maps, like theories, shape our understanding of the world by highlighting – and obscuring – particular spatial or social features. Mapping is thus closely linked to societal norms and ideas: how mapmakers depict the world shapes map users' view of the world. In early modern Europe, the new, immensely popular forms of cartography had an enormous impact on Europeans' spatial ideas. In short, the sixteenth

---

[1] Buisseret 1992a: 1.   [2] Ziman 2000: 126.

and seventeenth centuries laid the foundation for our map-filled – and map-shaped – world.

This argument does not require a teleological assumption of progress in technological development.[3] Reading early modern changes in cartography as a story of increasing accuracy and scientific precision is anachronistic and reflects our post-Enlightenment assumptions.[4] Leaving aside the narrative of progress, however, changes in mapping inarguably occurred, which led to and shaped important social and political outcomes. Moreover, how we define *maps* and *cartography* should not be based on the practices of our particular historical period. Instead, as the editors of the monumental *History of Cartography* project suggest, maps can be defined more broadly as "graphical representations that facilitate a spatial understanding of things, concepts, conditions, processes, or events in the human world."[5] This allows us to approach early modern cartography from the point of view of those who lived during that period, enabling us to understand the social and political effects in a non-teleological manner. *def.*

Before we investigate the early modern cartographic revolution – the technological changes in mapmaking and the ideational impact of these new ways of depicting and understanding the world – we need a theoretical framework for analyzing the history and social effects of mapmaking, a framework which is provided in the next section. With this as a basis, the following sections will, first, outline medieval mapping and spatial ideas; second, describe the technological and ideational effects of the early modern cartographic revolution; and, third, briefly summarize the varied map traditions of ancient and non-Western civilizations.

---

[3] I am defining *technology* here in its most general sense as the practical application of knowledge, most often of a particular area. This means that new cartographic technology includes all the new applications of knowledge to depicting the world visually – an admittedly broad designation, but one that is useful for its inclusion of developments in map production and distribution as well as map drawing.

[4] A point made by Edney 1993 and others.

[5] Harley and Woodward 1987a: xvi. See Wood 2010 for an opposing view, that maps should be defined more narrowly. I follow the former definition because spatial representations from a variety of historical and cultural settings (whether we want to call them maps or not) can be linked to political and spatial practices.

Theorizing mapping and space

Maps not only provide the means for gathering and displaying information about the world; maps also shape how actors understand the
world they inhabit. Because maps are fundamentally connected to spatial ideas, the study of mapping involves more than simply examining
artifacts and material objects. This broader approach, which builds on
recent studies of cartographic history, provides the foundation for a
theoretically informed examination of the technological revolution in
early modern cartography.

The past several decades have seen a move away from the traditional
approach to the history of cartography, which emphasized scientific
progress and increasing accuracy in modern mapmaking. Historians
have shifted their focus to the authorship, power relations, and worldviews inherent in maps and map technologies. Maps have come to be
seen as more than mere representations of reality, "mirrors to nature,"
or "communication devices," and instead are being studied in terms
of their embodiment of, and influence on, how map users view their
world.[6]

Concepts central to the traditional narrative of progress in mapmaking – such as the notion of geometric accuracy – are thus reframed
as inventions of a particular era, of questionable applicability to other
periods or cultures.[7] Recognizing the contextual nature of cartographic
accuracy allows us to interrogate conventional notions, such as the modern idea of a clear distinction between accurate scientific maps (seen as
good) and propaganda maps (seen as bad). Although some examples
of propagandistic maps are obvious in their distortions of reality, *all*
maps elide certain features and construct a particular representation
of space; no map offers a truly "undistorted representation" of the

[6] This transition in approach is represented in essays and books by authors
explicitly studying the societal embeddedness and impact of maps (e.g.
Brotton 1997; Cosgrove 2001; Crampton 2001; Harley 2001; King 1996;
Klinghoffer 2006; Pickles 2004; Wood 1992, 2010), in recent work on maps
from particular cultures and historical periods (such as, for example, medieval
Europe: Edson 1997; Woodward 1985), and in the ongoing multi-volume
History of Cartography project (Harley and Woodward 1987a, 1992, 1994;
Woodward 2007b; Woodward and Lewis 1998), which has explicitly "moved
away from the positivist model toward the constructivist one" (Woodward
2000: 33).

[7] Harley 1987: 3; Wood 1992: 41.

world. We need to look at each map in terms of what it includes and excludes, whose interests are served or rejected, and what social context shapes and is shaped by the map and its use.[8]

By examining the actors, interests, and belief systems involved in mapping we can understand better the power that maps both represent and operationalize. First, maps directly embody power relations between those who produce and those who use them, and they also exhibit the conscious goals and interests that led to their production and use. Second, implicit norms and unquestioned practices of mapmaking also shape depictions and thereby can create or reinforce ideas about how human space is structured, including its social and political aspects. These two forms of power can be classified as *external* and *internal* to the map: the former referring to the ability of patrons or powerful individuals to make maps for their own purposes, and the latter denoting the way in which maps – with or without the conscious intent of their creators – influence how actors view their world.[9]

The external, conscious expression of power in maps has often received attention from scholars, because it is exemplified by maps that are clearly propagandistic and fits with the assumption that scientific maps can be unproblematic representations of the world. Nonetheless, although maps are used by political actors in the pursuit of their own interests, sometimes those very interests have been constituted by the indirect, or internal, power of maps. This capability of maps to construct, reflect, and reify particular worldviews shapes social and political interaction to a degree unrecognized by – and unrecognizable to – the traditional narrative of cartographic history. Yet this dynamic operates both historically and in the present.

---

[8] King 1996: 18; Pickles 2004: 45; Wood 1992, 2010. The possibility of constructing an "accurate" map at a one-to-one scale has long been ridiculed by imaginative authors, illustrating how useable maps are *always* schematic representations of the world and include only certain features. Borges' ironic discussion of the construction and later abandonment of the "Map of the Empire which had the size of the Empire itself and coincided with it point by point" is probably the most famous, but the possibility – and absurdity – of creating a map so accurate that it is at a scale of 1:1 is also discussed by Umberto Eco, among others (Borges 1990; Eco 1994). In fact, of course, even a 1:1-scale map would have difficulty including the three-dimensional, overlapping, or social features of space.

[9] Harley 2001.

permanent v. temporary features.

Consider what a map depicts or leaves out. While we tend to see modern maps as accurate – though incomplete – representations of the objective world, we also tend to ignore what implicit decisions may have been made about what is "mappable." For example, in most of today's maps, the features to be included are those defined as permanent: topography, settlements, roads, and so on. Yet the distinction between what is seen as permanent and temporary is an arbitrary one, and reflects an implicit norm that values settled and built human space over temporary or migratory forms of activity.[10] The relationship between what is judged to be important and what is mapped goes both ways: as maps that include particular features or phenomena are widely used, the normative importance of those spaces or features depicted is further reinforced.[11] As Brian Harley argues, although a map is created by us, "through its internal power or logic the map also controls us. We are prisoners in its spatial matrix."[12]

The particular "spatial matrix" created by today's mapping is just one of many possible ways of understanding space. Henri Lefebvre was one of the first to point out that "(social) space is a (social) product"; and that "every society ... produces a space, its own space."[13] In other words, space as we understand it is not an objective, natural, or pre-existing entity, but rather is constructed by cultural and material practices – practices that can differ across societies and eras, constituting diverse understandings of space and hence different ways of seeing the world. The way in which space is viewed in a particular society is structured in part by the character of that society's cartography. In early modern Europe, therefore, cartographic developments constituted not only a technological change but also a "cognitive transformation" in which maps served to both "*record* and *structure* human experience about space."[14]

This is not to argue for a technologically deterministic point of view – these effects of mapping on social ideas and relations are

[10] Pickles 2004: 63.
[11] For example, Akerman 2002 examines this mutual reinforcement dynamic in the relationship between early twentieth-century road maps in America and the perceptions people have of the importance of highways versus other features of the landscape.
[12] Harley 1989: 85.
[13] Lefebvre 1991: 26, 31. For a recent discussion of Lefebvre, see Brenner and Elden 2009.
[14] Harley and Woodward 1987b, emphasis added. See also Pickles 2004: 5.

mirrored by the influence of ideas, practices, and social structures on the ways in which cartographic technologies are developed and used.[15] As Manuel Castells has argued, "technology *is* society, and society cannot be understood or represented without its technological tools."[16] Cartography is particularly integral to this dynamic. Mapmakers create maps that instantiate their ideas about how the world is organized – both consciously in terms of geographic knowledge and unconsciously in terms of how to structure the depiction of space. Map users' ideas about the world, then, are shaped by these depictions, in ways that the users may or may not be aware of. This can be a stable relationship, where shared ideas about space simultaneously shape and are shaped by the maps being produced and used. Yet when an exogenous change is introduced – such as the early modern technological revolution in mapping discussed below – this can lead to a transformation in this relationship. The character, uses, and contents of maps change, leading to changes in spatial ideas and related social and political practices. This transformation, however, operates through the mutually embedded nature of cartographic technology and ideas about space – actors create and alter technological, social, and political structures, while simultaneously being constrained by them.[17] A particular understanding of space can be produced at a historical juncture, but it is also continuously *reproduced* by ongoing spatial depictions and practices.[18]

Mapping, in other words, shapes the conditions of possibility of how actors conceive of space, territory, and political authority. New technologies and their uses can enable new ways of thinking about space – and undermine other understandings – thereby shaping both

---

[15] This mutual, reciprocal relationship cuts a middle ground between purely deterministic interpretations of technology and the opposite misunderstanding, that technological developments are entirely dependent on the social context. See Bijker *et al.* 1989; Fritsch 2011; Latour 1987.

[16] Castells 1996: 5. See also Burch 2000; Herrera 2006; and Sassen 2002.

[17] This relationship between actors, their ideas, and their representational technologies builds on structuration theory (Giddens 1984). This approach has pointed out the way in which a mutually constitutive relationship can lead to recursive transformations in both agents and structures. Actors create structures that simultaneously constrain and incentivize their action, leading over time to change, rather than stasis (Carlsnaes 1992; Sewell 1992). On the agent–structure problem, see also Adler 2005; Dessler 1989; Doty 1997; Wendt 1987; Wight 1999.

[18] Brenner and Elden 2009.

social practices and political institutions.[19] This involves a change in the "depth knowledge" of how actors understand their world, rather than merely the "surface knowledge" of geographic information.[20] The effects of mapping technologies offer a particularly complex example of this dynamic: maps are used instrumentally by actors, and, at the same time, maps influence those same actors, although they may not be conscious of the influence. Not only do maps enable certain actions – thanks to their ability to gather and present particular information cartographically – but the power internal to mapping also constructs the very usefulness of maps as a political or social tool.

Thus material and ideational factors interact, both in mapping and its effects and in the broader context of institutions and practices of international politics.[21] This interaction is apparent both in the transformative role played by maps in early modern Europe, discussed at length later in this chapter, and in the character and use of maps in the Middle Ages, considered next.

Medieval European cartography and space

Because the modern world is permeated by maps built upon techniques developed in the European Renaissance, it is important to recall that, in other cultures and at other times, this type of mapping was rare or nonexistent – as was the modern, geometric view of space. Medieval Europe offers a particularly striking illustration of the absence of mapping (as do many other eras and civilizations, discussed briefly at the end of this chapter). Contrary to the anachronistic assumption that medieval actors shared our cartographic tools and understandings about how human space is structured, medieval European mapping and spatial ideas differed greatly from their modern counterparts. In fact, maps saw only limited use in the Middle Ages, as written texts performed many of the functions we now ascribe to mapping. Maps were used only sporadically for claiming property, delimiting political

---

[19] This approach builds on one of the methods pioneered by Michel Foucault (1970), and put to particularly effective use by Ian Hacking's studies of the emergence – and impact – of modern ideas of probability and statistics. See Hacking 1975, 1990.

[20] See Hacking 1995, 2002 for the distinction between changes in depth and surface knowledge.

[21] Wendt 1999.

authority, or even navigating on land or sea. The maps that did exist were extremely rare, reflected several disparate traditions, and served a variety of purposes. Nonetheless, medieval mapping did serve to construct – and was constructed by – a particular understanding of space.[22] Discussed below are several key traditions reflecting this understanding: schematic and religious world maps, maritime navigational charts, and regional, local, and itinerary maps.[23]

Mapping in medieval Europe

One tradition of mapmaking in the Middle Ages depicted the three continents of Asia, Europe, and Africa, encompassing the entire world known to Europeans. Large maps along these lines were often hung on the walls of cathedrals and were known as *mappaemundi*. (See Figure 3.1.) Instead of purely geographic information, *mappaemundi* typically illustrated biblical and classical history, and they placed Jerusalem at the center of the image. Although they may not be accurate according to modern geographic standards, they served the purpose for which they were intended: religious instruction. What they did not do – and were not intended to do – was represent contemporary political entities. Instead, these images mapped spiritual knowledge onto a schematic representation of the known world.[24]

Portolan charts, on the other hand, were explicitly practical, intended as shipboard navigational maps. (See Figure 3.2.) They had been preceded by written sailing directions, which, by the thirteenth century, were supplemented with visual depictions of coastlines with an overlay of compass directions, or rhumb-lines, for finding the shortest route between two coastal points. Although these maps may appear geometrically sophisticated because of the rhumb-lines, they actually make no use of the latitude–longitude grid and present distances in travel time,

[22] Later in this chapter I address the mapping traditions of a variety of non-Western cultures, illustrating the same connection between diverse cartographic depictions and understandings of space, as well as the unique character of post-Renaissance Western mapping.

[23] To contemporaries, however, these categories were distinct: "scholars in the Middle Ages would not have recognized the products of these varying traditions, these groups and subgroups, as constituting a single class of object" (Harvey 1987b: 283). It is only in our retrospective categorization that all these images are seen as maps. See also Edson 1997; Woodward 1985.

[24] Woodward 1987.

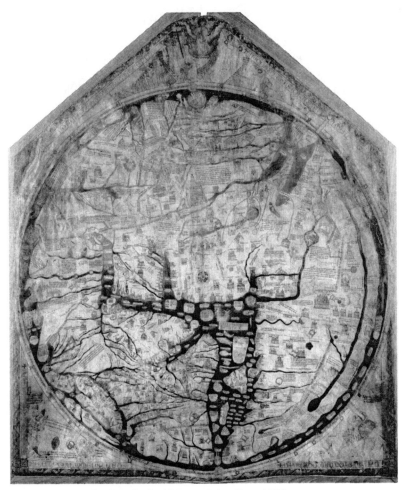

Figure 3.1 Hereford Cathedral Mappa Mundi, *c.* 1290
Note: As with many *mappaemundi*, this map depicts Europe, Asia, and Africa, with east at the top and Jerusalem in the center. Britain, for example, is in the lower left corner.

not linear measurements. Yet these maps fit the practical requirements of shipboard navigation in the Mediterranean: they gave the most direct routes between coastal points, labeled and exaggerated pertinent coastal features, and were based on the firsthand knowledge of the sailors who used them. As will be discussed in detail below, although these maps appear to us as surprisingly "accurate" visual depictions of space during a period whose other mapping traditions seem archaic

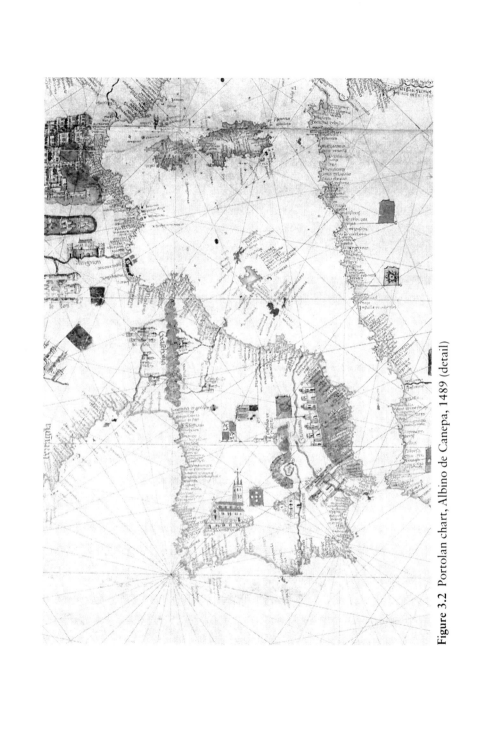

Figure 3.2 Portolan chart, Albino de Canepa, 1489 (detail)

and primitive, their "shipboard perspective" and the absence of a latitude–longitude grid reveal that these maps lacked the defining characteristics of later mapping techniques.[25]

Portolan charts depicted land only inasmuch as they delineated coastlines and labeled coastal points with a dense series of names. Medieval
regional and local maps that were primarily intended to portray land
geographically were much less common and varied widely in character and technical features. Many medieval regional maps are itinerary
maps, schematically depicting routes such as those taken by pilgrims,
without any intention of conveying accurate geographic representation in terms of scale or orientation. (See Figure 3.3.) These maps were
not geometric, two-dimensional projections of the surface of the earth,
but were rather graphical representations of a single, linear dimension
of travel.[26] Their apparent "inaccuracy" again reflects our expectation
that medieval maps were intended to represent the world according to
our own standards, rather than as a means of providing the information required for activities such as land travel.[27]

The dearth of maps in medieval times was in part due to the privileging of textual description over visual depiction, a dominance which
survived at least into the early Renaissance.[28] This applied particularly
to geographical information: "In the Middle Ages, the normal way of
setting out and recording topographical relationships was in writing,
so in place of maps we have written descriptions: itineraries, urban
surveys, field terriers, and so on."[29] Rulers used textual description
for their realms, relying on "geographical explanations that were an
extremely codified literary form inspired by ancient models."[30] These

---

[25] Campbell 1987; Cosgrove 2001: 85; Randles 2000 [1988]: 1–2.
[26] Padrón 2004: 54. See also Harvey 1987a.
[27] In fact, well into the twentieth century, personal navigation while traveling
    on land continued to be easiest by following written itineraries or schematic
    diagrams rather than by using accurately scaled maps. In the early automobile
    age in the United States, due to the absence of reliable sign-posting on
    highways, massive written itineraries were still more reliable than small-scale
    highway maps. Only once routes were effectively marked in the field was
    map-based navigation made possible, quickly followed by an explosion in the
    production of the familiar road maps we still use today (Akerman 2002).
[28] Grafton 1992.
[29] Harvey 1987a: 464. See also Kain and Baigent 1992.
[30] Revel 1991: 147.

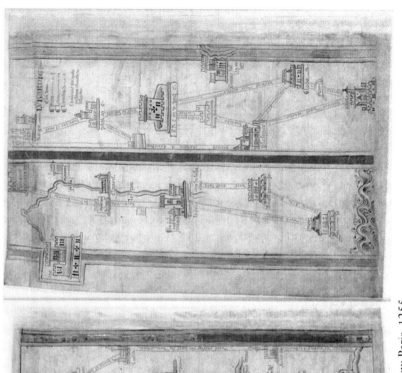

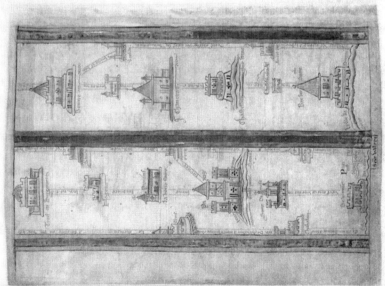

Figure 3.3 Medieval itinerary map, Matthew Paris, 1255

Note: These are two pages from an itinerary of the route from London to Jerusalem. On the left is southern England and northern France, on the right is northern Italy.

descriptions were based on official observation, often made during the monarch's personal travels around his realm.

In short, although maps existed in the European Middle Ages, they were limited in number, extraordinarily diverse, and used for few of the purposes for which modern maps are created. These mapping and textual traditions, however, shared certain key characteristics that simultaneously reflected and constituted the way in which medieval actors understood spatial relationships.

Medieval spatial ideas

Two key features of the medieval view of space can be discerned: first, the world was understood as a series of unique places rather than as a geometric area or expanse; and, second, space was conceived in terms of time as much as distance.[31] Both features are closely related to the cartographic depictions – and textual descriptions – in use during this period.

Medieval Europeans perceived the world as a series of places, each with its own, possibly unique, characteristics. Ricardo Padrón sums this up well:

For the medieval imagination, places were charged with a positive sense of thickness, stability, and indivisibility. Space, by contrast, was nothing but the empty "in between," something that only came into existence as the distance separating two places, two significant points of reference.[32]

This view of the world as a series of locations is evident both in maps common at the time and in contemporary literary descriptions of space.

Medieval world maps both appear to us to distort geography and greatly emphasize the importance of places over the spaces between them. Locations seen as significant by the mapmakers are depicted

---

[31] Although one scholar has argued that "It has yet to be shown that there even was such a thing as a 'medieval way of describing and representing the world'" (Dalché 2007: 287), there is enough evidence of commonalities in how thinkers, political actors, and others in the Middle Ages understood their world to enable us to posit a dominant, if not completely homogeneous, medieval view of space.

[32] Padrón 2004: 58.

completely out of scale by modern standards – cities are often represented by huge images of walls, towers, and churches, rather than as point locations. Itinerary maps also schematized this idea of the world as a series of places by showing only the important stops along linear routes, with little effort to depict overall geographic relationships. The blank spaces on itinerary maps did not represent areas to be filled in through discovery but rather "portions of the space of representation that are not inscribed upon."[33] Even portolan charts – the medieval maps with the most modern appearance – represent an extension of the route-focused bias of itinerary maps. Through the use of rhumb-lines for navigation, the expanse of the ocean is depicted as a set of linear routes between places (coastal locations) rather than a geometric plane.[34] All of these map types embody the medieval view of the world; they also reinforce, for those using the maps, that particular way of understanding space. Readers would focus on the places included and the human-defined routes between them, rather than seeking to understand their geometric location or the spatial expanse upon which they are located.

Furthermore, the literary mode of knowledge, which dominated the visual in the high culture of the European Middle Ages, also highlights the medieval emphasis on places over space. While purposes such as religious education for the illiterate masses were often accomplished with purely visual means (including church paintings depicting biblical stories or lessons, as well as *mappaemundi*), the literate elite strongly favored the written word – a tendency only reinforced by the non-literate character of mass culture. Textual description easily fits with a view that understands the world as a series of places, since each location can be listed and carefully described in writing without the need to depict or understand the spaces in between.[35] The eleventh-century Domesday Book, for example, is an exhaustive inventory of England ordered by its recent Norman conquerors – but exhaustive only in terms of the medieval view of the world as a series of places. The fundamental unit is a single lord's manor, the entry for which lists resources, underlings, and tax assessments. Although the overall survey is organized geographically by county, the spaces within those

[33] Padrón 2004: 54.   [34] Padrón 2004: 62.
[35] Grafton 1992; Revel 1991.

counties are understood as sets of distinct places, without geographical referents or any information on overall spatial extent.

In addition to the world being understood as a series of places, the
medieval concept of space was built on time as much as distance. The
words used for "space" often meant an extension of time: for example,
it was not until the sixteenth century that the Spanish word *espacio*
came to mean "planar extension," and that was only among a small
group of elite cartographers and cosmographers.[36] This concept of
space as a measure of time related to the understanding of spatiality in medieval Christianity. For example, in many works from the
Middle Ages, "time is visualized as a linear space through which an
individual's life passes."[37] Even when the world was measured spatially, the measurements used in maps incorporated elements of time:
for example, distance was measured by the number of days of travel or
land area by the amount one man could plow in a day.[38] This combination of time and physical distance to define space is also evident in the
medieval *mappaemundi* discussed above. These world maps depicted
a religiously inspired view of the world that emphasized historical and
biblical events rather than contemporary places, thereby collapsing
historical and contemporary time into one image.[39]

Medieval mapping, in short, reflected and reinforced an understanding of the world as a collection of places, linked by religious belief or
the human scale of travel. Although these ideas and technologies had
been relatively stable during the Middle Ages, in the early modern
period they would be transformed fundamentally.

The cartographic revolution of the Renaissance

The fifteenth and sixteenth centuries saw a revolution in how maps were
created, distributed, and used.[40] This transformation of cartography,

---

[36] Padrón 2004: 51.   [37] Delano-Smith 2000: 181.
[38] Bauman 1998: 27; Kula 1986.
[39] Woodward 1985, 1987.
[40] See Woodward 2007a for a discussion of the question of whether the changes
    in cartography during this period represent a "revolution." Although some
    argue that this is an overstatement, when we take into account the massive
    increase in map production and use, the fundamental change in the character
    of maps, and the extensive social impact of cartography, calling this a
    revolution makes sense.

in turn, made possible and shaped equally drastic changes in how Europeans understood their world.

Early modern mapping

Renaissance cartography is conventionally seen to begin in the early fifteenth century with the Latin translation of Claudius Ptolemy's *Geography*, a Greek text of the second century AD. This book contained both a discussion of the methods of mapping according to the celestial coordinate grid and an extensive list of cities by coordinate location. The Greek original may have also contained maps based on Ptolemy's projection methods, but all copies that survived into the early modern period contained only maps produced later. While his other works on astronomy and astrology were well known in Christendom during the Middle Ages, the *Geography* was apparently neither read nor circulated. This changed, however, in the early 1400s when a Florentine scholar obtained a Greek manuscript copy of the *Geography* and translated it into Latin, probably as early as 1406.[41] This book circulated quickly and widely in humanist circles (as did many other recently rediscovered classical texts) and was in printed editions by the 1470s.

Yet the actual story is more complicated: for most of the fifteenth century, interest in the *Geography* was almost exclusively of a humanist, text-focused nature. What in retrospect ended up as the book's most important contribution – Ptolemy's instructions for map projections – was not emphasized by many fifteenth-century scholars, even those who saw the work as an unimpeachable source of geographical knowledge.[42] Instead, it was not until the early sixteenth century that interest expanded in the mathematical aspects of the *Geography*, particularly in map projections. At this point, new translations were made to replace those of the early fifteenth century, which had contained many errors in the more technical sections.[43] This shift in focus, however, was decisive. Ptolemaic techniques – particularly the foundational idea of using celestial coordinates and geometric map

---

[41] Randles 2000 [1994].

[42] For example, many mid-fifteenth-century German *mappaemundi* had references to Ptolemy, but only in textual terms. Meurer 2007: 1180.

[43] Dalché 2007.

projections – quickly came to dominate the new market for maps during the sixteenth century. Although sixteenth-century mapmakers improved upon Ptolemy's text in terms of accuracy, global coverage, and projection methods, the *Geography* had nonetheless transformed cartographic techniques and restructured the fundamental grammar of European cartography.[44]

Mapmakers soon began to draw maps according to Ptolemaic principles, using the grid of latitude and longitude. (See Figure 3.4.) Mapping came to focus on the depiction of land surfaces with the coordinate grid and mathematical projections, so that, by the middle of the sixteenth century, these techniques were central to the continuing development of mapmaking. Ptolemaic projection methods were refined and new ones were invented, all built upon the key contribution of the *Geography*: that the world can and should be depicted visually with reference to a coordinate-based grid system, thereby establishing geometric accuracy of scale, distance, and orientation as key cartographic goals. In the centuries following, these principles guided the continuing change in mapmaking technologies, with the development of surveying techniques, astronomical observation, and, eventually, chronometer-based position-finding.[45] Even today, while nearly every technology of mapmaking continues to evolve, the foundational structure provided by the coordinate grid remains the same.

The rapid growth of grid-based cartography, however, did not immediately eliminate the use of textual descriptions of space or non-geometric mapping traditions. Texts continued to be used for travel itineraries and descriptions of places, and maps were often presented in conjunction with textual forms. Non-grid-based maps also persisted and even increased in use. Depictions of cities, for example, were commonly in oblique, bird's-eye-view form. Local property mapping also expanded dramatically after the sixteenth century, adopting geometric surveying techniques after the early seventeenth century.[46] Nonetheless, because of its popularity and influence during the sixteenth, seventeenth, and

---

[44] See Wood 2010 for a skeptical view of the influence of Ptolemy's *Geography*. Although it is clear that the "heroic" role played by this one book has been overstated, there is no question that the breakthrough of commercial mapmaking was closely tied to – if not caused by – the adoption of Ptolemaic techniques.

[45] Thrower 1999.

[46] Kain and Baigent 1992; Pelletier 2007; Wood 2010; Woodward 2007a.

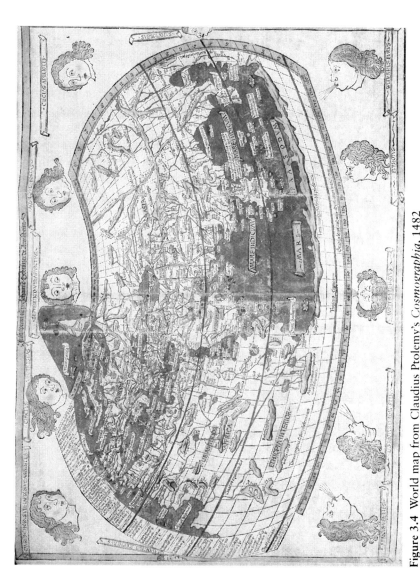

Figure 3.4 World map from Claudius Ptolemy's *Cosmographia*, 1482

eighteenth centuries, one particular early modern mapping tradition provides the focus for this book's analysis: namely, the small-scale mapping of regions, continents, and the world in printed atlases and maps. This form of mapping represented the fundamentally novel development of cartography during the early modern period: the growing popularity and use of maps as a means of "seeing from afar" – and seeing more than one person could otherwise observe.

Ptolemaic, grid-based mapping expanded rapidly in production and use, thanks particularly to the adoption of printing techniques after the late fifteenth century – part of the broader "communications revolution" initiated by the printing press.[47] The increase in map production accelerated even more dramatically in the sixteenth century: "Between 1400 and 1472, in the manuscript era, it has been estimated that there were a few thousand maps in circulation; between 1472 and 1500, about 56,000; and between 1500 and 1600, millions."[48] Although some early modern mapping was commissioned by rulers, the mass printing of maps was directed toward the literate public as a whole and was driven by commercial motives from the very beginning. For the first time, middle-class Europeans understood maps and their uses, thanks to the commercial map-printing houses of Italy and the Netherlands. This printing revolution increased the number of maps in circulation, and it also increased the possibility of standardizing the maps used and distributed across Europe, creating the conditions for a similar standardization in how Europeans depicted – and thus understood – their world.[49]

The consumer-based aspect of map printing is illustrated by the production of atlases, which began with the 1570 publication of Abraham Ortelius' *Theatrum Orbis Terrarum*. This atlas was a collection of disparate pre-existing maps, but it was unified by the ideal that cartography was useful "not simply as a tool for trade, but a means for approaching and appreciating the orderliness of the earth and patterns of human domination over it."[50] The immediate popularity of

---

[47] Eisenstein 2005.
[48] Woodward 2007a: 11. The implications of the scale of this growth is further illustrated by per capita estimates of maps in Europe: "In 1500, there was one map for every 1,400 persons; by 1600 there was one map for every 7.3 persons" (Karrow 2007: 621).
[49] Eisenstein 1979; McLuhan 1962; Mukerji 2006; Woodward 1996.
[50] Mukerji 2006: 661.

atlases is evinced by their rapid profusion and their variety: "The first modern world atlas was published in Antwerp in 1570. It was followed, not long after, by the first town atlas (1572), pocket atlas (1577), regional atlas (1579), nautical atlas (1584), and historical atlas (1595)."[51] Within decades atlases ranged from extraordinarily expensive works for rulers and the richest elite to smaller, cheaper volumes for the general public, often published in vernacular languages.[52] These works were not necessarily useful for rulers wishing to gather detailed information about their or others' territories, but they did serve to put cartographic images, accurate or not, in the hands of the general public. These images, moreover, consistently made use of the coordinate grid and mathematical projections, rather than the non-geometric techniques of medieval cartography. (See Figure 3.5.) This fundamental change in mapping began the process of reshaping how Europeans understood their world.

Modern spatial ideas

This cartographic transformation eventually yielded our modern view of space, which differs drastically from that of medieval Europeans (and from that of other cultures and historical periods, discussed later in this chapter). In short, the modern conception sees space – particularly land areas – as a surface that is homogeneous and geometrically divisible and on which different areas or places differ only quantitatively, not qualitatively. This stands in stark contrast to the medieval view of the world as a series of unique places, connected by routes of travel rather than by geometric relationships. The modern Euclidean understanding of space presents the world as an empty stage for human action, where space is homogeneous and all places can, in theory at least, be treated as qualitatively equivalent.[53]

In early modern Europe, this transition was closely connected to new developments in cartographic technology. New mapping techniques enabled the creation of new kinds of maps, which in turn reshaped the view of space held by Europeans, particularly as mass-printing technology and consumer demand led to a huge increase in map production and use. Maps rapidly became a tool used by the

---

[51] Koeman *et al.* 2007: 1318.   [52] Mukerji 2006.
[53] Harley 2001; Lefebvre 1991; Sack 1986.

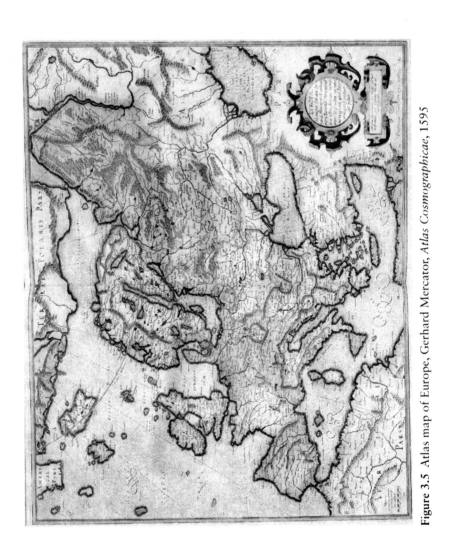

Figure 3.5 Atlas map of Europe, Gerhard Mercator, *Atlas Cosmographicae*, 1595

wider European public to understand the changing world that they inhabited. "Cartographic reason seems to have been so powerful a force in the sixteenth and seventeenth centuries that it came to signify the most important forms of reason. *To map was to think.*"[54] The new strength of the visual language of maps was boosted by their practical usefulness: maps in early modern Europe came to be used in a variety of settings, shaping how a wide range of actors understood their world and influencing their behavior in it.[55]

A key part of this technological driver of ideational change was Ptolemy's application of the celestial coordinate system to the earth's surface. This grid system, or graticule, represented a major shift from medieval mapping techniques, which, for all their variety, shared a common focus on particular human places and the travel routes or moral relationships among them. Denis Cosgrove sums up this transformation well:

The implications of representing earth space through an infinite array of fixed points are more than merely instrumental. The graticule flattens and equalizes as it universalizes space, privileging no specific point and allowing a frictionless extension of the spatial plot. At the same time it territorial- izes locations by fixing their relative positions across a uniformly scaled surface.[56]

Modern mapping's homogenization of space has two immediate effects: first, it reduces the tendency of mapping itself to privilege one location over another; and second, it makes the world a surface that can be divided geometrically, even from afar.

On the first point, mapping according to Ptolemy's graticule was a shift toward *homogeneity of scale*. The geometric grid means that "[e]ach point on the map is, in theory at least, accorded identical importance."[57] Although there have been arguments since the sixteenth century over map projections, orientations, and centering (including

[54] Pickles 2004: 77, emphasis in original.
[55] Brotton 1997; King 1996. While Padrón 2002 questions the penetration of the modern view of space before the seventeenth century, at the level of European elites (including rulers) maps were unquestionably used and new spatial ideas were evident.
[56] Cosgrove 2001: 105–6.
[57] Harley and Woodward 1987b: 505.

all space is equal, contradicts the previously established power of the map-maker

nineteenth-century disputes over the location of the prime meridian and the late twentieth-century battle between the Mercator and Peters projections), opposing sides in each dispute have framed their position within the same coordinate grid.[58] The Ptolemaic mapping techniques themselves have the potential both to be centered at any location on the globe and to fit with numerous social or political agendas.

Contrast, for example, medieval and early modern world maps. Medieval *mappaemundi* depicted the three Old World continents, often in a circular frame. This allowed them to center on Jerusalem, or at least near the Mediterranean. This centering was dictated by – and reified – the cultural and moral importance accorded to this region by European political and religious leaders of the Middle Ages as well as by the mapmakers themselves. Ptolemaic mapping, on the other hand, can be centered anywhere. The advantage of this feature is illustrated by the efforts of Jesuit missionary Matteo Ricci to introduce European mapping to China in the sixteenth century. After the first world maps he presented to the imperial court displeased the Chinese authorities because they were centered on Europe, he produced another Ptolemaic map of the world with one structural difference: the map was centered on China. The second map proved to be far more acceptable, the revolutionary character of its graticule hidden by the familiar position of China in the middle.[59]

Modern mapping enables a view of space that considers all points to be implicitly equal, whether the location is a place of great importance in terms of human activity or is simply a geometric point on the earth's surface. This equalization, however, also provides an effective platform for promoting unequal relationships: grid-based maps can always put the mapmaker at the center of the map and thereby undermine the political or cultural claims of other regions or peoples. Colonial and imperial cartography by Europeans, for example, supported social and political hierarchies through their Western-centered imagery. Space may be homogenized visually without being equalized politically.

The homogenization of space and its definition as a geometric surface measured by the graticule, which made possible a purely geometric division of space and territory, proved to be a useful tool for asserting control. Medieval space, understood as a sequence or collection

[58] Monmonier 1995.   [59] Day 1995; Mignolo 1995: 219.

of unique places (as in an itinerary, a *mappamundi*, or a written list), could be divided in non-geometric ways, as places were categorized or separated by particular symbolic or qualitative characteristics rather than simply by location on the grid. Ptolemy's graticule, on the other hand, was based on a "geometrical rather than symbolic principle."[60] In the broadest sense, this meant that the world could be divided by lines into homogeneous areas, replacing the notion that places should be distinguished and categorized by their qualitative characteristics. (The implications for political space and authority – discussed in the next chapter – have been particularly transformative.)

This geometric division of space also made it possible for as yet unknown places to be claimed, so long as they fell within the geometric division proposed by the map. Even if parties had different ideas about what lay in unexplored areas, they could agree on a geometric division of spaces in a way that would have been difficult or impossible with pre-Ptolemaic techniques. Without geometric cartography, in order to claim territory one had to describe it in terms of place-specific characteristics. If proved later to be inaccurate, this description could no longer support a claim to those places. With a geometric division of space, however, the accuracy of beliefs about what lay within unexplored areas was made irrelevant to the possibility of claiming them.[61] The importance of Ptolemaic mapping techniques to this ability to understand new discoveries is apparent in the practices of early modern navigators. As one scholar describes it, a navigator could use portolan charts for coastal regions, "but if he wanted to locate these coasts in relation to the known world and make their position understandable, he had to resort to 'the manner of Ptolemy,'" that is, to the grid-based view of space.[62] (Chapter 5 addresses this in relation to New World mapping and political claims.)

Modern mapping, based on the graticule, is significant in that space *can be* understood as homogeneous and geometrically divisible. Perhaps more important, though, modern mapping is effectively unable to depict space as anything other than homogeneous and geometric. The very nature of grid-based mapping dictates this: all modern mapping is founded on the ideal of the geometrically accurate depiction of the curved surface of the earth on a flat plane. These techniques both make certain types of map possible and make other kinds

[60] Brotton 1997: 32.   [61] King 1996.   [62] Dalché 2007: 330.

of maps impossible. The rapid disappearance of many medieval map formats – such as *mappaemundi* – in the face of Ptolemaic mapmaking reveals the tendency of some mapping technologies to destabilize and undermine others. Medieval ideas of cartographic accuracy – such as the practice of highlighting places of particular religious or cultural importance, or the goal of portolan charts to facilitate navigation by overemphasizing coastal landmarks – came to be seen as inferior because of the modern tendency to equate "scientific" mapmaking and geometric accuracy.[63]

The effect of Ptolemaic cartography on the European view of space was so strong and so pervasive that the ideal of the world as a measurable, geometrically divisible surface outran the actual techniques or even the capabilities of early modern cartography. The understanding of the world as a grid where every point has a coordinate location was instilled by the use of maps based on the graticule, long before accurate measurements could be completed. Through the early seventeenth century, for example, accurate latitude measurements or triangulation-based land surveys required more resources (in terms of both finances and training) than most public or private mapmakers were willing to expend, leading to the creation of maps based on inaccurate or estimated measures even after the technical ability to improve them existed.[64] Furthermore, cartographers lacked the capability to measure longitude at sea – with the exception of imprecise and exceptionally difficult celestial observations – until the invention of the marine chronometer in the 1760s. Thus, although cartographers were in practice unable to fix locations according to the norm of coordinate-based accuracy, the belief never wavered that this was essential, and it served to promote the further technological developments that finally made such accuracy possible in the late eighteenth century.

Figure 3.6 illustrates schematically the dynamics that followed the technological revolution in mapping. First, maps were created based on Ptolemy's system of latitude–longitude coordinates and projection techniques (1). This eventually shaped a view of space in which the world was seen to be geometrically calculable and divisible (2). This geometric view of space in turn both drove further mapping efforts with these techniques (3) *and* created demands for technological

---

[63] Crampton 2001.   [64] Konvitz 1987; Woodward 2000.

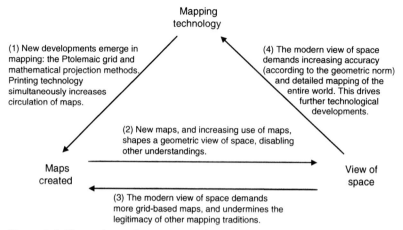

Figure 3.6 The early modern cartographic revolution

improvements that would make the exacting standards of scientific accuracy achievable (4).

The changes introduced by new mapmaking and printing techniques, therefore, initiated a series of interconnected processes culminating in the consolidation of a new complex of material technologies and spatial ideas. The modern view of space that came out of this process continues to be supported by the maps produced today, in spite of the continual transformation of the technology of map production. The technological developments in cartography from the Enlightenment onward have served to reinforce, rather than undermine, the Ptolemaic ideal of geometrically accurate mapmaking. None of the improvements in surveying, printing, or even aerial imaging has altered the fundamental understanding of our world as a geometric surface; instead, these developments have allowed maps to approximate that Ptolemaic ideal even more closely.[65]

Ancient and non-Western mapping traditions

The particularly modern understanding of space originated in a correspondingly particular region and historical period: Western Europe

[65] This may be changing today. Contemporary and future developments in mapping technologies and their potential social and political impact are discussed in Chapter 8.

in the sixteenth and seventeenth centuries. Many other cultures have created and used maps, but no other period has seen the same type of cartographic revolution. Non-Western mapping traditions, in spite of their complexity, lacked the key elements that drove the shift to the modern view of space: the Ptolemaic graticule and the quantitative expansion of printing. This meant that the maps created in other societies did not enable a geometric understanding of space in the way that early modern European mapping did. Without attempting an exhaustive review of mapping traditions worldwide, what follows summarizes key features of, first, ancient and classical cartography and, second, several non-Western mapping traditions.

Many ancient civilizations show evidence of mapping, although without anything near the level of map use in early modern Europe. The cultures of Mesopotamia and Egypt used some maps, including local maps for the purposes of demarcating property ownership.[66] Some of the key ideas of early modern cartography, particularly the use of celestial coordinates for terrestrial positioning, were inherited from classical Greece. Nonetheless, the number of maps in circulation and the level of map use was extremely low throughout the classical world: for example, Greek and Roman "travelers, tourists, pilots and military commanders probably never used maps."[67] This was particularly true in terms of the widespread, general-purpose mapping that would appear in the sixteenth century.

In the Roman empire, however, maps were used in specific circumstances, particularly for property allotment and as ownership records in newly colonized areas.[68] Although the basis of Roman land mapping in a grid system suggests a geometric conception of space, the Roman grid was very different from the Ptolemaic graticule. Roman maps divided land on the basis of square measures unconnected to a celestial coordinate system or to the globe as a whole.[69] Without this key link, the major ideational impact of modern mapping was absent: if all places are not fixed on to a predetermined grid of coordinate location, then space is not homogenized to the same degree, nor is it knowable or claimable without direct observation. Instead, land is divided only after being conquered, observed, and possibly cleared.

[66] Dilke 1987; Kain and Baigent 1992.
[67] Jacob 1996: 195.   [68] Kain and Baigent 1992.
[69] Edgerton 1987: 24.

When compared to modern European colonial divisions of territory – based on the Ptolemaic graticule and its geometric conception
of space – Roman divisions of land took much more account of local
human and geographic features. Modern divisions and claims, such as
the division of the American west by cartographers in the late 1700s,
were made on generally unknown territory in a way that took little
account of local conditions.[70] The tendency to make such claims and
divisions without any local knowledge was made possible only by a
cartographic system based on a global coordinate grid, which gives
every place – known and unknown – a fixed-point location.

Outside local property delimitation, moreover, Roman map use was
rare. Instead, Roman cartographic and literary traditions yielded a "linear" conception of space: space was understood in terms of lines of
travel, not planar expanses.[71] "Space itself was defined by itineraries,
since it was through itineraries that Romans actually experienced space;
that is, by lines and not by shapes."[72] The geometric approach of land
surveyors (*agrimensores*) did not extend beyond their narrow field and
did not define how Roman rulers or citizens imagined their world.

Similarly, classical Chinese cartography also differs from modern European mapmaking and its resultant view of space. Although
maps were used extensively by governmental officials and scholars
even in early imperial China, this cartographic tradition shared few
traits with early modern mapping.[73] Throughout the period of traditional Chinese cartography (i.e. predating the increasing exchange
of mapping techniques with Europeans that began in the sixteenth
century), map images contained "little quantitative information" and
were "not meant to be used alone but ... in conjunction with text."[74]
Furthermore, although some ancient Chinese maps involve a grid system, these appear to be the exception rather than the norm, even into
the period after contact with Western mapmakers.[75] Just as in many
Roman maps, the grid on traditional Chinese maps was not a graticule and was not linked to a global system of coordinates. Unlike the
Ptolemaic grid that links all points on the earth to one another and
geometricizes space, on Chinese maps "the square grid seems to have

[70] King 1996: 68–69. See also Chapter 5, below.
[71] Talbert and Unger 2008.   [72] Whittaker 2004: 76.
[73] Yee 1994a.   [74] Sivin and Ledyard 1994: 29; Yee 1994a.
[75] Yee 1994a.

been superimposed arbitrarily on a given area of interest." Thus, "map space was not treated analytically in China; points were located not by coordinates, but solely by distance and direction."[76] The key elements of Ptolemaic mapping were absent from this mapping tradition.

Traditional Islamic cartography also exhibited very little in the way of mathematically derived geographic mapping. This is particularly surprising, since Ptolemy's *Geography* was well known in the Islamic world long before its fifteenth-century "rediscovery" in the West. Ptolemy's work was widely read, and his list of cities by coordinate location was often noted by scholars. Yet, among Islamic scholars, "the link between Ptolemy's mathematics and actual map production seems never to have been made."[77] Arabic texts of the *Geography* appear not to have contained Ptolemy's key chapter on map projections.[78] In other words, although the mathematical basis for understanding the world as a homogeneous, geometric space was available, without the translation of this knowledge into a widely used visual form, the societal effect on how actors view space was limited. Only in early modern Europe did the cartographic revolution combine the mathematical understanding of places as located on a coordinate grid covering the entire globe with the visual depiction of that understanding in maps and the printing-driven explosion in map production, distribution, and use.

Instead, key features of Islamic mapping closely resemble those of medieval European cartography. Maps were almost exclusively in manuscript form, with little or no printed cartography – in spite of the knowledge of Chinese block-printing techniques.[79] In addition, there were few if any individuals or institutions engaged exclusively or specifically in cartography, making maps extremely rare.[80] Even in the Ottoman empire – more closely linked to early modern Europe – land ownership was recorded in written cadasters rather than on maps, property disputes were resolved in courts without visual aids, and the routes for the state's official courier network were recorded in verbal itineraries.[81] All of these practices reflect the greater authority attributed to textual rather than visual knowledge.

As global trade and travel expanded in the sixteenth century, the growing exchange of ideas and technological tools led to increasing

[76] Yee 1994b: 124.
[77] Tibbets 1992: 95. See also Karamustafa 1992a.
[78] Tibbets 1992: 101 n.51.   [79] Karamustafa 1992a.
[80] Harley and Woodward 1992.   [81] Karamustafa 1992b.

convergence on the use of maps by rulers throughout the world. Qing emperors in China, for example, faced some of the same incentives toward centralization of rule and pursued similar strategies of gathering information about their realm as did their European contemporaries. When Jesuit missionaries presented the court with new geometric techniques for measuring and mapping territory, the Chinese authorities quickly saw their utility and adopted similar mapping projects – sometimes even hiring the foreigners to conduct the surveys.[82]

Similarly, at the end of the sixteenth century, mapmaking by Japanese rulers and commercial printers accelerated rapidly, with maps being quickly adopted as tools of commerce, travel, and administration. Particularly in terms of the commercial production of maps, this period of Japanese cartography closely resembles contemporary European developments (including some exposure to Western atlases and maps among Japanese elites by the late sixteenth century). Yet a fundamental difference remained: during the seventeenth-century expansion of map production, Japanese maps rarely made use of the coordinate grid or any other means of establishing an abstract, geometric scale. This changed only with the reopening of Japan to foreign imports in 1720: subsequently, Japanese maps began to adopt the latitude–longitude grid and the related geometric depiction of space.[83] Until this point, Japanese mapmaking practices had completely lacked this essential feature of European cartography.

As European power and influence expanded over the subsequent centuries, cultures with different cartographic technologies and spatial understandings were increasingly confronted with an imperative to adopt Ptolemaic techniques. For example, in the second half of the nineteenth century, Western mapping was introduced to Siam (Thailand) from the top down, as a series of reforming kings used European mapping techniques and brought in European mapmakers (among other modernization efforts). This process exhibits some of the same dynamics as had occurred centuries earlier in Europe, and it illustrates the power of Ptolemaic mapping to change actors' conception of space.[84] Before the mid nineteenth century, Siamese

[82] Elman 2006; Hostetler 2001.   [83] Berry 2006; Yonemoto 2003.
[84] The following discussion relies on the excellent study of the intersection between Siamese modernization and mapping by Thongchai Winichakul (1994).

mapmaking contained several loosely connected traditions, varying from cosmological treatments of the Buddhist universe to itinerary-based depictions of terrestrial space. These visual depictions of the world reflected – and supported – various conceptions of space, all of which lacked the homogenizing character of the Ptolemaic grid. This changed quickly, however, as King Rama IV (r. 1851–68) became personally involved both in importing Western astronomy and cartography and in making astronomical observations and measurements himself. His efforts, although resisted by other Siamese elites, eventually led to the creation of official mapmaking institutions and the introduction of Western-style geography into education. The power of modern mapping lies in its ability to undermine and destabilize other forms of geographic knowledge: once the Ptolemaic grid has been imposed on the world, other understandings of space are made untenable, except for purely metaphorical uses. The previously dominant views of the world as a sacred space were replaced by the modern notion of the globe as a homogeneous expanse which can be divided up geometrically.

The case of Siam illustrates the clear direction of the relationship between mapping technology, the maps created, and the view of space: Western mapping technology was introduced from the top, leading first to the creation of new maps based on these techniques and then, only later, to the widespread adoption of a geometric understanding of space. Yet the Siamese case was more than an accelerated version of the process that had occurred in Europe centuries earlier. Modern mapping was backed not just by the reigning monarch but also by the outside pressures of European colonial powers. The British and French made extensive use of maps in their dealings in the region and arrived with a geometric view of space, which in turn structured their interaction with Siamese leaders, even when the latter had a different understanding of the world. The tendency of modern cartography to move the conception of space toward the abstract, the geometric, and the homogeneous was accelerated and reinforced by other political pressures.

Similarly rapid and transformative adoptions of Western cartography and conceptions of space occurred in many parts of the world, as European imperial powers reached their zenith in the late nineteenth century. Embracing Western mapping, however, did not necessarily represent an acquiescence in imperial or colonial domination – these (and other) technologies of modernization also came to form part of the toolkit of anti-colonial resistance. Yet the instrumental use of these tools, even for overtly anti-hegemonic purposes, simultaneously represented an acceptance of the deep, constitutive grammar of Western spatiality: the notion that the world is composed of a geometric, divisible surface, knowable and claimable from afar with sophisticated cartographic tools.

This understanding of the world was particularly influential on early modern European political ideas and practices, as rulers increasingly used and created maps. The resulting political transformation, driven and shaped by early modern mapping, is the subject of the next chapter.

4 | *Mapping the territorial state*

The territory no longer precedes the map, nor survives it. Henceforth, it is the map that precedes the territory.[1]

Jean Baudrillard describes the postmodern condition of simulation as a world in which the map predates the territory, rather than vice versa. Yet this ostensibly reversed order is not new; the same sequence also appeared in the cartographic foundation of early modern territorial ideas and claims. New forms of mapping in early modern Europe – originally produced by non-political actors and later adopted by rulers – reshàped ideas and practices of political authority, leading to a transformation in the nature of territoriality and the elimination of non-territorial authorities. This shift from medieval heteronomy to modern sovereignty laid the foundation for the territorial state. In short, maps have preceded territories from the very birth of the modern international system.[2]

First, the character of territorial authority was restructured by the map-driven transformation of the conception of space. Europeans' understanding of space shifted from seeing the world as a series of unique places to conceiving of the globe as a homogeneous geometric surface, which had direct implications for how political space – and hence territorial political authority – was understood. Medieval territorial authority over a series of locations, such as towns along a route of travel, was replaced by modern territorial authority over a uniform, linearly bounded space. Changes in mapping technologies both made possible the modern concept of territory and also undermined the authority of medieval spatial ideas.

Second, the elimination of non-territorial authorities resulted from this same explosion in the production and use of maps in early modern

---

[1] Baudrillard 1988: 166.
[2] This argument builds on a number of discussions of the relationship between mapping and political rule (Biggs 1999; Neocleous 2003; Steinberg 2005; Strandsbjerg 2008). See Chapter 1 for more discussion of existing theories.

Europe. Political interactions and structures during the medieval period involved both territoriality and forms of legitimate authority divorced from territory, including personal feudal bonds and jurisdictional rights and duties. With maps increasingly used at all levels of European society, these forms of political authority not amenable to cartographic depiction were undermined, resulting in the exclusively territorial authority of modern states and the international system. The combination of these two processes – transformation of territoriality and elimination of other authorities – made possible our world of sovereign territorial states.

Yet the relationship between the maps in circulation in early modern Europe and major actors' understanding of sovereignty was not unidirectional: beliefs, norms, and conceptualizations about authority also influenced which maps were produced and what characteristics they exhibited. Figure 4.1 illustrates these relationships, building on the analytical scheme from Chapter 3 (Figure 3.6). The view of space directly constituted the form that territorial authority took (1), the quantity of maps created and used determined whether non-territorial notions of authority would be undermined and eliminated (2), and changing ideas about what constituted legitimate sovereign authority subsequently drove the creation of more maps reflecting that view (3).

In this reciprocal process, mapping technology both enables certain practices and validates the legitimacy of those practices. Maps were not simply a tool adopted for the pursuit of pre-defined goals or interests; instead, the use of maps reshaped some of the fundamental goals of political actors, such as the control of territory. A mutually constitutive relationship exists between representations of political space, the ideas held by actors about the organization of political authority, and actors' authoritative political practices manifesting those ideas. Actors are constrained by the structural ideas and practices of the system and also create those constraints through their ongoing interactions. Exogenous sources of change act through this relationship: the cartographic revolution in early modern Europe created new representations that produced, first, changes in ideas of authority and, subsequently, a transformation in the structures and practices of rule.[3]

---

[3] This accords with theories of structural change that allow for the possibility of transformation in the agent–structure dynamic, such as theories of cognitive evolution and morphogenesis. See Adler 2005; Archer 1995; Carlsnaes 1992.

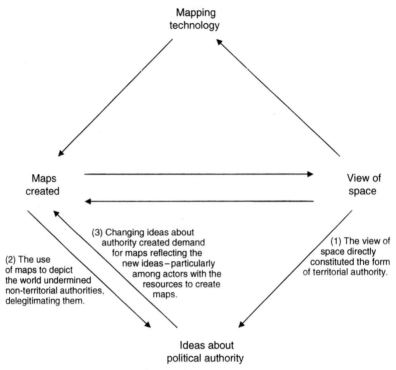

Figure 4.1 Maps, space, and sovereignty

As many constructivist International Relations theories have argued, the effect of material factors on political institutions and outcomes often works through changes in the ideas that give those material facts meaning.[4] Particularly important for the transformation of ideas and practices of rule was the increasing use of maps by those in positions of political power, detailed in the next section.

Map use by rulers in early modern Europe

Chapter 3 addressed the ways in which maps changed dramatically in form, content, and quantity in early modern Europe. The political implications of this revolution were sweeping. Although maps often were seen initially as simply decorative artifacts, they quickly came

[4] Wendt 1999.

to be used as tools of directly political interaction and rule. During the sixteenth and seventeenth centuries, the use of maps by rulers expanded dramatically: beginning in Italy in the late fifteenth century, and then spreading to Germany, France, England, and Spain in the sixteenth century, by the seventeenth century map use by governmental actors was common throughout Europe.[5] This extensive adoption of mapping created the conditions of possibility for a transformation of ideas and practices of rule.

The trajectory of government map use followed a pattern unfamiliar to observers today, accustomed as we are to states investing heavily in cartographic projects. For the first two centuries of early modern cartography, rulers made use of maps but rarely commissioned their own. Most of their cartographic tools were based on commercially produced maps and atlases that were in relatively wide circulation. This was particularly true for maps covering larger areas rather than local maps of specific fortifications, towns, or routes. During the sixteenth and seventeenth centuries, therefore, commercial mapping was more influential on rulers than rulers were on mapping, and maps thereby reshaped political ideas and practices.

This began to change in the seventeenth and eighteenth centuries with a progressive increase in attention and resources given to cartography that culminated in major mapping projects commissioned by rulers and in the dominance of official cartography in the nineteenth and twentieth centuries. Yet this state-sponsored mapping followed and built directly upon the foundations laid by commercial mapping in early modern Europe. By the time that rulers and governments became heavily involved in map production, the fundamental ideas of what should and should not be mapped – and how – had been consolidated by several centuries of map production and use. Official mapping projects did little to challenge the geometric understanding of space and political authority; instead they adopted the same ideational framework and cartographic tools to achieve rulers' political goals.

---

[5] Buisseret 2003: 69. It should be noted that it can be difficult to study map use directly, as the artifacts themselves have often been lost and actors rarely comment on their own use of maps once it becomes commonplace (Kokkonen 1998: 64). Nonetheless, historians have managed to put together a reasonably complete record of when maps began to be used, and in what ways. Particularly useful for this survey is vol. III of *The History of Cartography* project (Woodward 2007b).

Early government map use

Beginning in the second half of the fifteenth century and continuing into the sixteenth, rulers began to take a new interest in using maps for domestic administration and military planning. This trend, however, proceeded only gradually. Few examples of government map use exist from before 1450, and even into the sixteenth century, rulers rarely adopted cartography as the dominant means for gathering information about their realms.[6] In short, map use was sporadic and uneven through at least the late sixteenth century. Maps were used as supplements to traditional means of information-gathering, administration, and military planning, and most of the maps commissioned were of local areas and for single purposes.

At the end of the fifteenth century, rulers who used maps were still the exception. While the state-sponsored mapping of Venice's local land holdings in 1460 offers one of the first examples of a Renaissance government commissioning a modern topographical map of its territory, in other Italian city-states official map use was rare until at least the end of the sixteenth century.[7] In other fragmented regions such as Germany, map use was similarly sporadic and decentralized. For example, there was no "official" map of the entire Holy Roman Empire: "all general maps of Germania were products of the private initiatives of their authors," not of any political authority.[8] During the first half of the sixteenth century, many regions were mapped only by commercial cartographers – and by non-native cartographers at that. All early sixteenth-century maps of Denmark, for example, were produced by outsiders.[9]

In some centralizing polities, however, the sixteenth century saw a trend toward increased use of maps. For example, map use by the English governing class expanded rapidly during the reign of Henry VIII (r. 1509–47). After 1530, "maps begin to appear regularly with other, more traditional types of documents, as tools in the processes of government and administration."[10] Similarly Emperor Charles V (r. 1519–56; king of Spain 1516–56) "grew up with a full awareness of cartographic possibilities, and throughout his life he was in close

---

[6] Buisseret 1992a: 2.
[7] Casti 2007; Marino 1992; Quaini 2007; Rombai 2007; Valerio 2007.
[8] Meurer 2007: 1245.   [9] Strandsbjerg 2008.   [10] Barber 1992: 32.

contact with maps and mapmakers."[11] Although for much of his reign few accurate maps of peninsular Spain existed, Charles used maps when planning his foreign adventures.[12] Yet most of the maps used by rulers during this period served only narrow administrative or defense-related purposes, rather than being useful as a means of envisioning – and thus ruling – one's entire realm.

The timing of when rulers began to use cartographic governance tools is explained by several related factors. The first was the popularity of writings by Machiavelli and others advocating the use of maps. Thomas Elyot's 1531 *Boke named the Governour*, for example, argued that governments would benefit from using maps both as practical tools of administration and as propaganda devices to support claims of legitimacy.[13] Additionally, in the early sixteenth century many cartographically sophisticated Italian scholars visited courts throughout Europe, bringing with them knowledge about governmental map use in Italy. The most important factor, however, may have been generational turnover, as the advisors and ministers who came to the fore in the first half of the sixteenth century were educated when Ptolemy's *Geography* had already achieved its widespread translation and influence.[14] This created a critical mass of political elites open to the use of new cartographic depictions as tools of government.

Government-commissioned cartography: first phase

Rulers eventually began to move beyond the sporadic and limited use of maps and into the creation of their own general-purpose cartography. During the sixteenth century, small official cartographic institutions were established, suggesting rulers' growing desire to avoid relying on commercial map publishers for geographic information.[15] While the timing varies across different European polities, many rulers first commissioned maps covering all or most of what they ruled in the later sixteenth century. For example, Spanish king Philip II (r. 1556–98), influenced by his father's use of maps, demonstrated a "personal near-obsession with maps" for the administration of his kingdom.[16]

---

[11] Buisseret 2007b: 1081–82.   [12] Hale 2007.
[13] Barber 2007: 1598.   [14] Barber 2007: 1594–95.
[15] Kagan and Schmidt 2007: 666.   [16] Barber 1997: 102.

Other rulers made similar requests for cartographic tools. The duke of Bavaria commissioned cartographer Philipp Apian to map his realm in the 1550s, probably the first official cartographic project in the German Empire.[17] In England the first government-sponsored effort to map the entire realm was undertaken by Christopher Saxton in the 1570s. This attempt to create a unified series of maps of the entire country – based, as nearly all such projects were at the time, on the collation of existing source material rather than on firsthand surveys – was intended to fulfill all three of the common purposes of mapping in this era: improving national defense, aiding domestic administration, and supporting propagandistically the authority of the crown.[18] A number of other mapping projects were initiated but never came to fruition. For example, the Danish king requested maps in the 1550s, but few if any were ever completed.[19]

In spite of the expansion of mapping, therefore, many sixteenth-century cartographic projects were not particularly useful for governance by centralizing rulers. The maps that were completed were often for specific, local purposes, and lacked the standardization and comprehensiveness that could come with later projects. In addition, some rulers during this period never made any attempt to use the new cartographic tools: for example, neither Prussia nor the Austrian Hapsburg realm was officially mapped during the sixteenth century.[20]

Government-commissioned cartography: second phase

In the seventeenth century, rulers began to put more substantial resources toward cartographic projects, in an effort to produce maps that would actually be useful for administrative or military purposes. The unsatisfactory character of "armchair" cartography – as existing projects relied on gathering together sources of varying quality and thus suffered from a lack of precision in scale and detail – led to a desire by government actors to commission maps based on direct surveying. For example, King Gustavus II Adolphus of Sweden (r. 1611–32) brought in German engineers to draw large-scale town maps for the planning of defensive fortifications, and he commissioned court mathematician Andreas Bureus to provide maps of Sweden for

<hr>

[17] Meurer 2007.   [18] Barber 2007: 1629–30.
[19] Strandsbjerg 2008: 348.   [20] Scharfe 1998; Vann 1992.

administration, taxation improvement, and defense.[21] King Christian IV of Denmark (r. 1588–1648) likewise commissioned maps that, by the 1640s, served as useful cartographic tools for the court.[22]

Probably the most comprehensive and influential mapping project of the seventeenth century was the survey of France begun by Jean-Dominique Cassini in the late 1660s, at the request of the finance minister, Jean-Baptiste Colbert. This survey, which spanned decades and multiple generations of the Cassini family, involved the careful triangulation-based measurement of the entire French realm and the subsequent publication of maps. (See Chapter 7 for a detailed discussion.) This represented the first successful attempt by a government to map its entire territory using the latest surveying techniques – mathematical tools that had existed since the 1620s but that had, until Cassini, proved too expensive and technically difficult to be successfully used on such a scale.[23]

In the following century, the massive French project was emulated in other European government efforts, such as the initiation in the 1780s of a unified, survey-based collection of maps covering all of Great Britain in what became the Ordnance Survey.[24] Similar projects were soon undertaken throughout the continent when administrative motivations combined with the interests of military general staffs in demanding detailed maps.[25] Surveys initiated by the Bavarian government in 1759, for example, were directly modeled on the Cassini project, not just through emulation from afar, but also because French surveyors had actually crossed Bavaria in their efforts to establish long-distance measurements.[26] These new mapping projects paralleled an overall shift in what was seen as the most scientifically advanced mapmaking: atlas maps of broad geographical regions based on observations of latitude and longitude were being superseded by topographical maps built on direct surveying and measurement.[27]

Mapping, however, was never the sole preserve of centralizing rulers, nor was it an irresistible force for centralization. Regional authorities and local revolts both made use of cartographic tools, and

---

[21] Kain and Baigent 1992; Mead 2007: 1805.
[22] Strandsbjerg 2008: 351. [23] Konvitz 1987; Turnbull 1996.
[24] Thrower 1999: 114. [25] Hale 2007; Thrower 1999.
[26] Wolfart 2008: 4. [27] Edney 2009: 41.

surveying projects were often resisted by local populations and elites.[28]
For example, local rulers commissioned Guillaume Delisle to map
Burgundy without any involvement of the French crown.[29] Examples
of local resistance were numerous, including when the state cartographer working for the Prince-Bishopric of Augsburg was repeatedly
sued by local villages in the region he was commissioned to map.[30] Yet
this type of resistance proved to be futile, as even the rebellious parties
often ended up making use of the same mapping techniques – and thus
all sides ended up framing their interests in cartographic terms. The
narrow interests of one party were often contested by the other side,
but the deep grammar of cartographic territoriality became fundamental to all claimants to authority.

The national survey projects, such as the Cassini in France, were
made particularly powerful by their combination of two of the dominant cartographic traditions of the early modern period: small-scale atlas
maps of entire regions, continents, or the world and large-scale local
mapping of property in both private and official cadasters. Surveying
an entire realm using triangulation linked the growing importance of
clear demarcation and mapping of private property with the graticule-
based mapping of regions and continents – both of which had been
widely used separately since the late sixteenth century. The power of
local mapping as a tool of capitalist land ownership (well established
by the 1700s) combined with the power of atlas mapping as a way of
seeing the larger world – a link that was further cemented by the direct
involvement of centralizing states.

All these factors – the transformation of mapping technologies, their
widespread use by rulers, and the synthesis of diverse cartographic
traditions – created the conditions necessary for a fundamental transformation of political authority and the practices of rule, the result of
rulers' ideas being restructured by mapped images.

Maps and the territorialization of political authority

In early modern Europe, the medieval notion of the world as a set of
unique places, related by human experiences and ideas about them,
was transformed into the modern notion of space as a geometric,

[28] Barber 1997: 87; Kagan and Schmidt 2007: 674; Konvitz 1987: 14.
[29] Petrella 2009.   [30] Wolfart 2008.

homogeneous expanse. This shift had specific consequences for political territoriality, particularly since geography during this period was increasingly understood in political terms.[31] Although modern statehood is constituted by a bundled set of overlapping ideas and practices, three distinct aspects of the transformation from medieval authority structures can be distinguished: (1) the transformation of territorial authority from a differentiated collection of centers to a homogeneous space defined by discrete boundaries; (2) the elimination of non-territorial forms of authority; and (3) the implementation of exclusively territorial rule in the political practices of states. Together, these three processes constituted the shift to the exclusively territorial and boundary-focused character of modern states, an outcome for which new mapping techniques and their widespread use were a necessary condition.

The shift to bounded, homogeneous territorial authority

Between the fifteenth century and the eighteenth century, the medieval notion of political authority over a collection of differentiated places, with control radiating out from the center or from multiple centers, was replaced by an emphasis on boundaries between homogeneous political spaces. The result was the modern perception of spatial authority defined exclusively by discrete boundaries, and seen as homogeneous within those lines. Cartography was integral to this transformation, as rulers' ideas were first reshaped by using maps that drew clean boundaries between homogeneous entities, long before such divisions or political units existed on the ground. The process proceeded in several distinct – and historically sequential – steps: first, maps depicted political authority as a collection of discretely bounded spaces; second, political ideas shifted toward an acceptance of bounded territorial authority as preferable to authority over a collection of places; and, finally, new political practices (and hence international structures) were put in place on the ground.

The transformative character of Ptolemaic mapping becomes clear when it is contrasted with previous techniques. Within medieval European cartography, there were several mapping traditions that supported a notion of political authority as rule over a differentiated

---

[31] Mukerji 2006: 653.

collection of centers. For example, in late medieval Italian city-states, rulers and citizens saw the city as a central focus for the country-side it ruled, to the extent that rural areas were practically ignored.[32] The predominant mode of visual depiction of these city-states – bird's-eye views rather than town plans – both reflected and supported this notion. A plan shows the street layout on a geometrically equivalent scale (in theory at least), while a bird's-eye view emphasizes the centrality of the city by also showing, in extremely minimized form, the surrounding countryside.[33] Bird's-eye depictions remained popular in Italian city-states and elsewhere well into the sixteenth century, often in a mix with Ptolemaic map types.[34]

The portolan chart tradition of maritime navigational cartography also serves as an interesting contrast to the Ptolemaic map. The difference between political depiction on portolan charts and that on early modern Ptolemaic maps and atlases is particularly important, since portolan charts are often seen as a precursor to modern mapping, both in their reasonably accurate coastal outlines and in their occasional depiction of political authority claims.[35] Yet the differences are in fact great. Chartmakers sometimes placed flags, bearing the coat of arms or other symbol of a particular ruler, on towns or inside the territory of a state. (See Figure 3.2.) Although a flag may claim or represent political authority, it does so in a single-point-outward fashion: authority is clearly asserted over a city or point location, but only vaguely claimed over surrounding areas (unlike the use of discrete boundaries between spaces where authority is claimed over the entire inscribed area). Furthermore, flags were often more decorative than useful for navigators seeking to know exactly what ruler was in charge of a particular

---

[32] Martines 1979.

[33] A purposefully exaggerated version of the same effect is offered by the famous 1976 *New Yorker* magazine cover, "View of the World from 9th Avenue."

[34] Schulz 1987. For example, Philip II of Spain initiated two mapping projects of peninsular Spain: a collection of unified-scale regional maps and a series of bird's-eye views of Iberian cities. Only the latter was ever displayed publicly (Mundy 1996).

[35] Brotton, for example, writes that portolan charts used "symbolics of territorial possession (graphically articulated in the flags which define territorial sovereignty across its surface)" (1997: 55). Yet, as is discussed immediately below, the use of flags to depict territorial authority does not define that authority "across its surface" in the modern fashion, but rather as a center-focused point of strong authority radiating – and weakening – outward.

port they were approaching. For example, even into the fifteenth and sixteenth centuries, charts were rarely updated for Ottoman conquests of formerly Christian-controlled ports.[36] Rather than representing political changes, these maps instead remained oriented toward their primary purpose: shipboard navigation. All of these medieval cartographic techniques differentiated among diverse places visually, rather than treating space as a homogeneous expanse.

Within the Ptolemaic mapping tradition that accelerated in the late fifteenth century, on the other hand, the world came to be depicted as a collection of homogeneous spaces separated by lines. Yet the historical sequence – first, drawing divisions as discrete lines between spatial expanses on maps and, second, implementing political boundaries as linear on the ground – demonstrates that cartography did not simply follow existing practices but instead anticipated and shaped changes in political rule.

The increasing trend during the sixteenth and seventeenth centuries of drawing linear boundaries on maps has been well documented by James Akerman:

Whereas only 45 percent of the maps in Ortelius's *Theatrum* (1570) had boundaries, 62 percent of those in a Hondius edition of Gerard Mercator's *Atlas* of 1616 were marked with boundaries; 79 percent of those in the Blaeus' *Theatre du monde, ou nouvel atlas* (1644); and 98 percent of those in Nocalas Sanson's *Les Cartes générales de toutes les provinces de France* (1658–[59]). Thereafter large format world atlases typically had 90 percent or more of their maps showing boundaries.[37]

My own search through Joan Blaeu's 1665 *Atlas Maior* found that every map depicted color-coded linear boundaries – and this in one of the most voluminous, coveted, and expensive printed atlases of the seventeenth century.[38] During the later 1600s "graded boundary marks" were also increasingly used to distinguish between larger and smaller political divisions.[39]

These linearly defined spaces were then often filled with color, like today's political maps. Since maps could not be printed effectively

[handwritten margin note: Increase in use of boundary lines.]

---

[36] Astengo 2007; Campbell 1987: 401.   [37] Akerman 1995: 141.
[38] This was based on a search through a published reprint of the 1665 edition: Taschen and van der Krogt 2006.
[39] Akerman 1995: 141.

in color until the nineteenth century, color was added by hand after printing. Nonetheless, the coloring of printed maps was standardized, particularly for atlases, which were often colored before binding.[40] Other maps were printed with explicit instructions on where and how color should be added, and even the wealthy purchasers of maps got involved: adding color to maps became "an accepted genteel pastime."[41] Furthermore, color was often used to illustrate or suggest political differences. For example, a 1726 instruction manual on creating and coloring maps stated, "Color should serve only the informative purpose of emphasizing the administrative, religious, ethnic, and other divisions of a country."[42] This instruction exemplifies the notion that divisions of the human world – political, religious, or otherwise – can be best illustrated by homogeneous coloring of bounded spaces.

The particular way in which color was used with boundaries on maps in early modern Europe further emphasized the importance of these linear divisions. The coloring was often not completely uniform throughout the territory: the colors filling the different territorial units were made stronger at the boundary, thereby highlighting the boundary-focused nature of this depiction. For example, a seventeenth-century manual recommended that "[t]he boundaries of provinces and the seacoast are to be emphasized by graded area washes, darkest along the line symbol."[43] Not only is territory homogenized within the boundaries, but the identity of the political unit – defined in opposition to its neighbors' identities – is emphasized and made strongest at the boundary itself.

Considering the added difficulty and cost of coloring printed maps, why would mapmakers produce so many colored maps? The answer lies in the importance of aesthetic beauty to the appeal of cartography in early modern Europe, particularly in the appeal to rich commercial and governmental elites. Even as early as the late sixteenth century, Ortelius' "use of color was also influenced by the growing public demand for beautiful maps."[44] In the mid seventeenth century, the *Atlas Maior* of Joan Blaeu offers a key example of the emphasis on cartographic beauty. All the maps in this multi-volume work are fully colored, for good reason:

[40] Koeman 1970.   [41] Akerman 1995; Ehrensvärd 1987: 134.
[42] Ehrensvärd 1987: 138.   [43] Ehrensvärd 1987: 135.
[44] Ehrensvärd 1987: 137.

The display-loving European aristocracy ... showed a marked preference of the large six-volume atlases of Blaeu and Janssonius over the smaller, but scientifically superior French atlases ... It was rather the superb typography, the beauty of the six hundred hand-colored maps, and notably the unrivaled size that made the atlas desirable.[45]

In the eighteenth century, the extremely accurate and expensive cartography of Enlightenment projects such as the Cassini survey of France was overshadowed commercially by the continuing emphasis on maps as beautiful consumer objects, a large part of whose appeal was in the coloring. Robert de Vaugondy, a major French commercial map publisher of the 1700s, focused his efforts on the beauty of his maps rather than on their scientific accuracy. For example, his printing house made expensive changes to the calligraphy of place names but did not bother to make corrections based on the latest geographic discoveries.[46]

This depiction of color-filled, bounded spaces on maps might be interpreted as a case where maps were simply reflecting the progressively more linear and territorial boundaries between centralizing early modern states. However, the boundaries – and many of the units – depicted on these increasingly detailed and systematized maps in fact did not reflect the actual political arrangements on the ground. Instead, maps depicted linearly bounded, exclusively territorial states *before* such states existed, and thus provided part of the ideational architecture for the eventual consolidation of modern statehood. This "inaccuracy" took a number of forms, including the elision of regions of complex authority structures in favor of uniform territorial depiction, the visual linearization of boundaries that were anything but clear-cut in reality, and the unclear distinction between internal and external boundaries.

For example, consider the depiction of "Italia" and "Germania" on early modern maps of Europe. (See Figure 4.2.) Prior to their respective political unifications in the nineteenth century, both these areas were understood at most as distinct cultural regions, defined as such by the humanist focus on classical divisions of the Roman world.[47] But on the contemporary early modern maps of Europe, these two politically heterogeneous regions were depicted as equivalent to increasingly unified entities such as France, Spain, or England. A similar pattern is

[45] Koeman 1970: 32, 41.   [46] Pedley 1984: 56.   [47] Akerman 1984.

Figure 4.2 Map of Europe, Willem Blaeu, published *c.* 1644–55

Note: This map is from the Latin edition of Joan Blaeu's *Theatrum Orbis Terrarum*.

apparent in map labeling, with an equivalent type style and size being used to label all entities, whether relatively unified (France or England) or not (Italy or Germany).

The anachronistic reading of early modern maps as accurately representative of the political organization of Europe extends beyond Italy and Germany, and also pertains to the depiction of other polities. For example, far too often the existence of entities called "France" and "Spain" in the medieval or early modern period leads modern observers to assume that these polities were identical to the territorial and centralized states of the nineteenth century – in basic character if not in exact borders or extent. Thus maps from the early modern period depicting bounded, homogeneous territorial entities are read as representations of political reality, when the truth is otherwise. Boundaries in early modern Europe were not linear on the ground. Instead, they involved extensive overlaps, enclaves, and non-territorial complexities across broad frontier zones, through at least the late eighteenth century.[48]

Finally, in spite of the increasing depiction of clear, discrete divisions between political entities, the distinction remained unclear in practice between an external "international" boundary and an internal "provincial" boundary. This makes it even more difficult to argue that the boundary lines drawn so carefully on these maps accurately depicted political arrangements on the ground. For example, in the *Germania* volume of Blaeu's 1665 *Atlas Maior*, all of the maps contain carefully engraved linear boundaries, which were subsequently hand-colored before the atlas was sold. Yet the nature of the units distinguished by these boundaries is unclear. For example, the units depicted on the map of the entire region of "Germania" do not match those on the maps of smaller areas (such as the "Circle of Westphalia"), even though the visual symbolism of color-coded, linearly divided units is the same.[49]

The anachronism of the boundary-defined spaces drawn on early modern maps raises the question of why mapmakers would depict bounded territorial units that did not exist at the time – and that they could not know would become real centuries later. One answer is that "such inconsistencies show that map-makers did not intend to depict

---

[48] Sahlins 1990.
[49] Reprinted in Taschen and van der Krogt 2006: vol. III, part 1, 58–61.

contemporary political units."[50] This is certainly one possibility, not easily dismissed considering the awkwardly anachronistic, inconsistent nature of many of the boundaries drawn on these maps.

Yet there is evidence that mapmakers were very interested in depicting political arrangements, and that it was the *medium* of commercially printed Ptolemaic mapping and the related worldview of mapmakers that drove this depiction of the world as a collection of homogeneous, linearly bounded territories. For example, some mapmakers made clear their intention to help readers understand the political world they lived in. The text of the Mercator–Hondius–Janssonius atlas of 1639–42 explicitly states that in addition to depicting historical information, maps have "a more recommendable purpose, which is to know about the political State."[51] Additionally, the general shape given to the unit labeled "Germania" on sixteenth-century maps reveals that cartographers were most probably attempting to approximate the boundaries of the Holy Roman Empire – a political, though amorphous, entity – rather than simply the area of German language or cultural influence.[52]

Another piece of evidence that points toward a desire to depict political authority on maps is the treatment by early modern mapmakers of non-European parts of the world. While the New World of the Americas was often depicted as empty – and its coastal outline unclear for several centuries after Columbus – other parts of the world were often filled in with invented political units. For example, Nicolas Sanson's 1655 map of Africa shows a continent filled with imagined features. In particular, the map labels and draws clean linear boundaries between imaginary political territories that fill the continent (each labeled as a different *regnum*, or kingdom). These entities are clearly invented by the mapmaker: "The regional system on Sanson's African maps seems partly political, but their dubious association with actual polities suggests that Sanson's obsession with hierarchy seems here more *an expression of his working method* than of political structure."[53] This tradition continued into the early eighteenth century, as the leading French cartographer Guillaume Delisle printed a map of

---

[50] Biggs 1999: 393; see also Akerman 1984.
[51] Quoted in Pelletier 1998: 45.   [52] "A Corpus of Maps" 1993.
[53] Akerman 1995: 141; emphasis added.

Africa that similarly shows imaginary kingdoms divided by discrete boundaries.[54]

In contrast to the nineteenth-century practice of intentionally leaving unexplored regions blank,[55] this early modern approach of filling in unknown spaces with political delineations illustrates that mapmakers were ready to draw linear boundaries even when they knew that such lines – and the homogeneous territorial units defined by them – were anything but "accurate." Furthermore, the labeling of imaginary territorial regions in Africa as *regna* indicates their political character, rather than just being meant as names for geographic or cultural areas.

Several factors played a role in the mapmakers' knowing depiction of inaccurate political divisions, both outside Europe and within it, factors related to the character and context of early modern Ptolemaic mapping. First, finding an accurate way to depict the pre-modern form of territorial authority (over a series of places, potentially overlapping and shared), particularly on a map covering a large area such as the entire continent of Europe, was a challenging task. With the prevalent techniques of printing maps (first using woodblocks and later copperplate engraving), drawing a linear boundary was actually easy, and it required a minimum of expensive labeling to depict territorial authority. Coloring in those delineated spaces was the next logical step – further encouraged by the market demand for decorative maps – and once again it provided an easy visual way to differentiate areas for map users.

Second, while the techniques and market pressures of cartographic production favored the use of linear boundaries and color-coded political units, so too did the spatial grammar constructed by Ptolemaic maps. This factor was particularly strong in the case of the cartographers who spent their lives – and earned their livelihoods – creating maps based on the Ptolemaic grid. While attitudes among Europeans in general, and even among the educated ruling elite, may have shifted only

---

[54] Black 2002: 31; see also Schilder 1979. Many of these maps also reveal the popular idea that kingdoms should be defined by "natural frontiers," such as mountain ranges or rivers: the imaginary "kingdoms" of the African continent are delineated by equally imaginary chains of mountains, rather than just by dashed boundary lines.

[55] Bassett 1994.

slowly toward the understanding of space and territoriality as geometric and homogeneous, mapmakers would be among the first to internalize such a view as they produced maps that operationalized it.[56]

We can also see the effect of the new mapmaking techniques in how maps of a popular subject were transformed: European maps of the Holy Land, or Palestine. The Holy Land remained one of the most frequent subjects for printed maps in the sixteenth and seventeenth centuries, but the way in which biblical lands and events were depicted reveals the impact of Ptolemaic techniques. While medieval maps of religious space (including *mappaemundi* as well as regional maps) showed pilgrimage routes, key towns such as Jerusalem, and images of biblical events, early modern maps of the region used the visual language of Ptolemaic mapping. In particular, many mapmakers attempted to draw boundaries between the areas ruled by the twelve historical tribes of Israel. These tribal areas were presented as homogeneous territorial entities, in spite of the fact that the mapmakers had extremely limited information on what the boundaries of these territories might have been. The new visual grammar of mapmaking had no other way to depict political authority.

Until at least the late eighteenth century, the exact details of linear territorial divisions remained inconsistent in maps just as they remained unclear or unimplemented on the ground. Nonetheless, whether the exact placement of those boundaries was clear or not, the key constitutive *definition* of political authority as linear, geometric, and homogeneous on maps was consolidated. For example, James Akerman argues that, after 1648:

The French standardized the appearance of boundaries and regional names, but this does not mean that they applied them in a modern fashion ... Faced with many meaningful schemes for dividing Europe, seventeenth-century French mapmakers gave none primacy. All had equal value in their intelligence of the world. Nothing could prove more strongly that the mental process of dividing Europe had yet to settle on the principle of territorial sovereignty.[57]

---

[56] As Padrón 2002 notes with regard to the adoption of a modern notion of geometric space in early modern Spain: intellectual and political elites came to see the world in this way long before the majority of the population did.

[57] Akerman 1984: 90–91.

Note, however, that this passage misses the key transformation that has already occurred, which in fact does represent the consolidation of "the principle of territorial sovereignty" in the visual language of maps: namely, all of the different "regional schemes" for dividing Europe politically on a map involved drawing lines to divide homogeneous spaces. That is, all of the maps represent the endpoint of the transformation of the image of territorial authority, predating the implementation of territorial boundaries in practice.

These trends in the depiction of boundaries, their character, and the wide readership of such maps combined to create the conditions necessary to drive a change in the ideas held by European rulers about political authority. The timing, once again, indicates that maps and their depiction of discretely bounded political entities were not epiphenomenal to this process. Linear boundaries were firmly entrenched in the visual language of maps more than a century before ideas about political authority, let alone practices, followed suit. This language of mapping, built on linear divisions between homogeneous spaces, changed the terms of interaction among rulers, as well as the relationship between rulers and their subjects. Thus, although the increasing centralization of rule was driven by a variety of factors – many unrelated to mapping – the *form* that this centralization took was fundamentally shaped by the effect of cartography on ideas about political authority and organization.

In addition, the fact that depictions in maps were inaccurate representations of political practices did not undermine their influence on rulers' ideas – even though rulers certainly understood the divergence between their realms as they were represented by maps and as they existed on the ground.[58] The cartographically driven changes occurred in the deep grammar of political authority, not in the surface discussion of which ruler could claim what territory. (Chapter 6 explores this process in terms of the negotiation and content of major peace treaties, illustrating the ways in which mapping and cartographic ideas reshaped this essential point of interaction.)

Furthermore, the relationship between map depictions and the conception of territorial political authority as homogeneous and geometric

---

[58] This is similar to the way in which fictional accounts – even when known to be fictional – can have a strong influence on actors' political beliefs. See, for example, Strange and Leung 1999.

is more complex than merely a story of mapmakers dictating how map users would come to understand the world. Mapmakers were motivated to draw linear divisions and to color in the resulting spaces because the purchasing public demanded beautiful objects – and the first several centuries of modern mapping saw private cartography predominant. Even when official cartography began to accelerate, government-employed cartographers also produced maps for the private market, and major state-sponsored mapping projects such as that of the Cassini family in France were also sustained by private patronage.[59]

Mapmakers thus did not necessarily – and probably did not in fact – aim to promote the understanding of political space as geometric and homogeneous. Instead, it is inherent in the nature of Ptolemaic cartography, upon which these mapmakers had staked their intellectual and commercial fortunes, that space be treated geometrically: the coordinate system of latitude and longitude, applied to all points on the earth's surface, favors this conception. The effect on ideas of territorial political authority – homogenizing the medieval collection of places into a geometric expanse – was, in a sense, an unintended by-product of the visual language of maps and the commercial market for them in the early modern period. Once the modern conception of territoriality became hegemonic, however, maps with states colored homogeneously appeared to be the only natural way to depict the world, as we continue to see in maps today.

The elimination of non-territorial authorities

While politics in the European late Middle Ages involved the coexistence of territorial and non-territorial political authorities, the modern international system is structured by the exclusive use of territoriality to define political actors and units. The massive increase in the production and use of Ptolemaic maps in Europe delegitimated, and thereby undermined, the non-territorial authorities present at the beginning of the early modern period. As people came to understand the world increasingly in terms of these maps, ideas about political authority that were not depicted in them – or could not be depicted in them – lost their normative basis and were gradually eliminated as acceptable

[59] Petto 2007; Vigneras 1962.

foundations for political authority. The delegitimation of non-territorial authorities merged with other pressures toward standardization that favored centralized territorial rule over medieval complexity.[60] The effects of cartography were not intentional on the part of the private commercial producers of maps in early modern Europe, since they had no direct interest in reshaping political authority. Yet their work provided the ideational impetus and later the normative tools for rulers and subjects to reimagine their political relationships in an exclusively territorial fashion.

During the early modern period, as mapping became a popular means of depicting and understanding the world, the ways in which political authority was portrayed on maps increasingly shaped actors' political ideas, and hence their political practices. Early modern mapping depicted territorial authority and did so almost exclusively in the linearly bounded, homogeneously colored fashion discussed above, instilling in map users a sense that this was the only legitimate way of understanding the political world, particularly as rulers and subjects increased their use of maps. This dynamic is both parallel to and distinct from the transformation of territoriality: while the latter was primarily a process whereby the very ability to imagine the political world as composed of territorially exclusive units was made possible by Ptolemaic maps and their character, the elimination of non-territorial authorities involved the undermining of existing ideas by that same mapping technology and its widespread use.

Although this argument specifically concerns the inability to depict non-territorial authorities on Ptolemaic maps, mapping in general is fundamentally ill-suited for depicting – and hence understanding – non-territorial authorities. After all, such forms of authority are by definition non-spatial, and maps inherently involve spatial depiction. Consider, for example, the possibility of depicting on a map a feudal system of rule, based on personal bonds. How would this network of relations be depicted spatially? The lords and vassals could be placed on a map and then connected by lines representing their authority relations, creating a network diagram overlay for a territorial map. Yet what would be the particular use of such a depiction? In this system of rule, the persons involved are often mobile, and thus the spatial dimension is far less important or fixed than their relationships and

---

[60] See, for example, Spruyt 1994.

resources (such as obligations in terms of military service or protection). Furthermore, *why* would one want to map this system of authority relations? It is far easier to describe the relationships in words – which is, of course, exactly what medieval contemporaries did.

In short, it would have been difficult for early modern cartographers to map non-territorial authorities.[61] Yet one could conceive of ways of doing this, perhaps involving various color schemes, different types of engraved lines, or even non-linear depictions such as networks of relations – difficult, but not impossible, in other words. Whether it was possible or not, however, *contemporary cartographers did not depict non-territorial authorities on their maps.* The resulting absence shaped how European rulers and subjects conceived of the political world, making the authority relations that were not depicted on the increasingly popular mapping medium less legitimate and eventually less tenable. Furthermore, earlier types of maps that had depicted non-territorial relations (such as *mappaemundi* with their spiritual organization) disappeared as grid-based maps became the dominant visual depiction of the world.

Early modern mapmakers did not consciously aim toward the elimination of certain types of authority or toward the promotion of a particular form of territoriality. Yet they did actively address the problem of depicting the complexity of early modern authority structures. The character of their mapping techniques – based on Ptolemy's graticule and commercial printing technologies – shaped their response to this complexity, driving mapmakers toward the geometric simplification of complex overlapping authorities and the depiction of all political structures as territorial.

This process is evident in the increasing depiction of discrete boundaries and homogeneously colored-in spaces on commercially produced maps and atlases from the late sixteenth century onward (as detailed above). Not only do maps with linear boundaries tend to simplify the complexity of early modern territorial authorities, but the increasing proportion of maps containing such boundary lines undermined the legitimacy of the authority structures *not* depicted in them at all. For example, in the maps of Germania from Blaeu's *Atlas Maior* of 1665 discussed above, the careful delineation and color-coding of exclusive territories elides the continuing presence of imperial judicial structures

61   Black 1997b: 125.

and complex overlapping authorities. The quantitative increase in map production during the early modern period changed maps from being merely one among several possible means of describing political authority (and hence of understanding and claiming that authority) to being the *primary* means of understanding the world and, thus, the nature of the world's political structures. The consolidation of a visual language of linearly bounded and color-coded political spaces undermined the legitimacy of non-territorial authorities at the same time that it transformed territorial authority.

The territorialization of rule

These changes in the authoritative basis for rule created an exclusively territorial form of political identity and organization, which immediately made certain actions possible or more easily achieved. The repertoire of tools available to rulers expanded, because, for example, maps could delineate boundaries with increasing precision and cartographic ideas of authority could assert claims from afar. Yet the impact on political practices went even further: the new ideas also restructured the very identities of political actors. Specifically, the increasingly *territorial* nature of state identity yielded a new set of interests and goals, based around the notions of territorial exclusivity, continuity, and security. In order to achieve these new goals, actors invented or adopted new practices, such as the demarcation of linear boundaries on the ground and the active administration of territory circumscribed by such lines. In other words, the newly dominant ideas about political authority – and the cartographic techniques that brought those ideas to the fore – both enabled and legitimized particular political practices related to territorial rule.

Then, as the boundaries on maps were eventually turned into boundaries on the ground, the international system took on the form we are familiar with today: sovereign states, separated by discrete divisions and allowing no outside authority to be asserted within their boundaries. The key element in the territorialization of political actors, therefore, is the way in which the transformed ideas about political authority were implemented in political practices and thus imposed on and manifested in the material world. This construction of cartographic states, which accelerated in the late eighteenth century, was thus simultaneously institutional and material, involving both the

New tools means new political goals!

creation of new, centralized institutions of rule and the imposition of physical divisions on the landscape.[62] The territorialization of rule not only built upon the ideational changes driven by mapping but also followed numerous other incentives for centralization and bureaucratization, yielding a fundamental transformation of how polities were organized internally and externally.

The process of constructing the new political structures followed a general, if uneven and contested, trajectory. Frontier zones filled with enclaves and overlaps were "rationalized," or made linear, territorializing the state actors involved in international politics. This involved processes of fortification, internal homogenization and infrastructural development, and finally boundary demarcation. Cartography was an integral part of this process, although the visual language of maps preceded the implementation of territoriality by several centuries – in other words, existing customary authority structures within Europe were not immediately supplanted by map-based ideas.[63] Once the ideational foundations of those traditional authorities were undermined by maps and their effects, however, old authorities were actively eliminated by centralizing powers. Often this involved the implicit collusion of ostensibly hostile central rulers in order to eliminate marginal, non-territorial, or alternative authorities, using the new legitimizing tools offered by territorial exclusivity.

The territorialization of rule rested on a normative foundation provided both by maps and by the ideas they shaped. In the middle of the eighteenth century, ideas changed about how rule should be defined and operationalized. The Swiss philosopher Emerich de Vattel, for example, wrote in the 1750s: "It is necessary to mark clearly and with precision the boundaries of territories."[64] This was one of the first and most influential statements of the importance of boundary linearization. The ideas of territorial exclusivity were thus applied directly to boundary delimitation and demarcation, often using mapping as a tool. This progression from ideas to implementation took place throughout Europe:

A fruitful cooperation between political theory and geographic practice ensued. Legists emphasized the territorial integrity of the state and the

---

[62] Mukerji 1997: 257.   [63] Black 2002: 34.
[64] Quoted in Sahlins 1989: 93; also discussed in Prescott 1987.

overlapping and ambiguous sovereignties of traditional frontier regions became intolerable ... Cartographers contributed to this process by perfecting symbolic indications to manifest this development in political theory. Ill-defined frontier regions were superseded by fixed border lines on maps.[65]

The ideas created by mapping drove this linearization, and subsequently maps served as an important tool for the implementation of new divisions between states: "Maps also performed a leading role in the numerous treaties that tried to geographically simplify the boundaries between sovereign states, whereby states exchanged villages, deleted enclaves, and attempted to improve communication networks."[66] Thus, during the late eighteenth century, treaty-making began to involve cartography directly in the implementation of territorial exclusivity (as will be discussed in Chapter 6). This was subsequently implemented in boundary demarcations and other projects of material infrastructure along borders.

The three partitions of Poland, in 1772, 1793, and 1795, illustrate the shift toward a purely territorial form of rule at the end of the eighteenth century. In a series of trilateral agreements, Austria, Prussia, and Russia divided up Polish territory among themselves, eventually erasing Poland from the map. Yet there is a difference between the 1772 partition and those that came two decades later. In the first partition, ideas of territorial exclusivity coexisted along with traditional forms of authority over jurisdictions. For example, the claims in 1772 were justified by extensive searches in official archives for rights and titles to the lands being taken from Poland.[67] The second and third partitions, on the other hand, were effected without those traditional justifications. The divisions in the 1790s were also defined in more geographic and cartographic terms, and they were less carefully described in treaty texts. Finally, while individual properties that cut across the boundaries in 1772 were allowed to remain unchanged, in the final partition of 1795, landowners were forced to choose a state of residence and to divide their property so that no holding would cross the new linear boundaries.

The exclusively territorial nature of the partitions is also reflected in the demand by the powers that Poland agree to the cessions in territorial

[65] Solon 1984: 95.   [66] Pelletier 1998: 56.   [67] Lukowski 1999: 81.

terms. After the first partition, "Poland formally renounced all claims
to all the territories it had ceded, as well as any other territories to
which it might have any claims ... On paper at least, all claims and
feudal connexions were neatly severed."[68] The renunciation of non-
territorial forms of authority is a hallmark of the implementation of
exclusive territoriality within Europe. Similarly, the partitions involved
the delimitation and eventual demarcation of new boundaries, instead
of the simple transfer of existing jurisdictions that had characterized
earlier centuries' territorial exchanges.[69] These characteristics of the
Polish partitions were shared by the settlements throughout Europe
that followed the Napoleonic wars, as new divisions and entities were
drawn on a purely territorial basis. (See Chapter 6 for a detailed discussion of the 1814–15 treaties.)

     Thus, in the nineteenth century, maps finally "accurately" reflected
political practices – but only because cartography itself had shaped
those practices by changing actors' ideas about the legitimate form
of authority. Indeed, when one compares a seventeenth-century map
such as one from Blaeu's 1640 atlas (Figure 4.2) with nearly any map
produced after the early nineteenth century, the images look very similar in character, if not in the exact placement of linear boundaries.
Yet the lines on a map today are expected to represent actual political
divisions on the ground – demarcated and administered by territorial
states – while those on the seventeenth-century map do not and are
not expected to do so. This is not a case of mapmaking simply getting
more "accurate" through more careful surveying, mapping, or printing
techniques. Instead, the political practices of states followed the linearization of boundaries on maps when rulers effected linear divisions in
practice, at which point maps finally *did* represent political reality.

     In the nineteenth century, this sense of the geometric territoriality
of political authority was so strong that it was projected backward
onto history, in the form of contemporary historical maps and atlases
depicting linear boundaries where none had existed (a tradition in historical mapping that continues today).[70] As in the case of nineteenth-
century historiography's anachronistic projection of contemporary
states onto medieval Europe – and the resulting assumption that territorial states had always existed – our notion that political authority

---

[68] Lukowski 1999: 91.   [69] Evans 1992 : 492.   [70] Black 1997a: 27.

has always been understood as linearly divided originated in these historical atlases from the nineteenth century.

This centuries-long progression from the initial depiction of linearly defined territorial entities to their final implementation in the practices of European states has implications for how we understand the creation of boundaries. The standard conceptualization of boundary-making involves three steps: (1) *allocation* or *identification* of the linear boundary by both parties; (2) the exact *delimitation* of the boundary in a treaty or other agreement; and (3) *demarcation* of the boundary on the ground, usually with physical boundary markers of some kind.[71] Yet the discussion above suggests that an important step precedes these: the *constitution of the idea of linear boundaries* through mapping. Only after the idea of linear boundaries separating homogeneous political territories has been constituted and supported by mapping can the actual allocation, delimitation, and demarcation of boundaries begin.

The hegemony of cartographic territory

In early modern Europe, mapping was integral to the transformation of ideas of political authority and the resulting practices of rule. This effect began during a period in which most mapping was produced privately, not by official state institutions or even under state patronage. Any argument that maps depicted territorial authority because rulers wished to promote that idea is undercut by the chronology and character of early modern mapping. Of course, maps often reflected the interests or demands of politically, economically, or culturally powerful persons. Yet this appeared in the content of the maps and their subject matter, not in their fundamental geometric structure and visual grammar.

The hegemony of this cartographic form of territoriality persists today. The narrowing of the repertoire of acceptable bases for political authority has been so thorough that territoriality has invaded almost all elements of modern political discourse. The character of modern nationalism, for example, reflects this fixation on territory. Although nations are defined as collections of persons, linked by some imagined set of shared characteristics or experiences, these communities

---

[71] Giddens 1985: 120; Prescott 1987: 13.

are nonetheless understood and operationalized territorially, often in the form of a cartographic image of a national territory.[72] In the nineteenth-century growth of mass nationalism as a new political force, the recently consolidated territorial state was transformed into the territorial *nation*-state, in a process that filled the institutional and material container of the state with new nationalist content. Thanks to the hegemony of Ptolemaic cartography as the exclusive means of depicting space and political authority – and the resulting territorialization of rule – other forms of political organization or community, divorced from territoriality, became untenable.

In other words, any return to the "mapless society" of the European Middle Ages would be impossible – we could not understand such a non-cartographic environment.[73] Modern mapping and its geometric understanding of political authority dominate how nearly all societies today interact with their world. The hegemonic power of this particular set of ideas and tools – which represents merely one among many possibilities – is explained by a number of factors, some intrinsic to modern cartography and others the result of contingent events, ideas, and processes.

One characteristic of Ptolemaic mapping that favors its worldwide adoption is the way in which it has a "movable center" rather than a central focus dictated by the mapping technique (as *mappaemundi*, for example, center on Jerusalem).[74] Although modern cartography and geometric space were predominantly Western inventions, they can be adopted – and have been adopted – by actors anywhere on the globe. By equalizing all points on the grid, the modern view of space can, paradoxically, fit with any society's understanding of its putative centrality in the world. The example of sixteenth-century Jesuit missionary Matteo Ricci in China (discussed in Chapter 3) illustrates the mobility of the center of the map: his second world map, while equally based on the fundamentally novel coordinate grid, was acceptable to Chinese elites because of its centering on their realm. If Ricci had tried to introduce a medieval *mappamundi* to the Chinese imperial court, there would have been no way within the map's structure to recenter the image on China. Additionally, the most sophisticated means for creating local-scale maps in the early

[handwritten margin note: movable center]

---

[72] Anderson 1991; Krishna 1996; Thongchai 1994.
[73] Harley 2001: 165.   [74] Mignolo 1995: ch. 5.

modern period – triangulation-based surveying – could also begin at any zero point and expand outward, again making it possible for any point on the earth's surface to be the origin and ostensible center of the map (seen in the remeasured map of France discussed in Chapter 1, which is centered on Paris; see Figure 1.1).

We can thus also see the appeal and adaptability of early modern cartography – as well as its power to shape rulers' political ideas and practices – in the impact of mapping on non-Western cultures. For example, the Qing emperors of early modern China, to whom Ricci and later missionaries presented Ptolemaic mapping techniques, utilized these newly available tools to consolidate their rule. Just as in Europe, however, the new means of gathering and storing information did more than provide an improved governing technique: maps changed what rulers saw as the legitimate form of political rule and also promoted a new view of how their realms fit into the rest of the world. The common language of grid-based mapping gave any ruler the same "awareness of their own kingdom's position as one country located on a finite globe."[75]

A further illustration is provided by nineteenth-century Siam, which saw the introduction of Western geography into education and statecraft (as discussed in Chapter 3). At the same time, colonial powers in neighboring territories tried to impose Western notions of boundaries on the still-independent polity. Boundaries had not been the focus of pre-modern ideas of political authority in the region, because power had been conceived as radiating outward from a center of control and dissipating in a loosely defined frontier zone. The Siamese focus on centers clashed with the increasing incursions by Western powers: "The British attempt to demarcate the boundary [between Siam and Burma] induced confrontations between different concepts of political space. This confrontation, however, went unrecognized by both sides because they used words that seemed to denote the same thing."[76] Eventually, however, Western maps and ideas were adopted by Siamese elites, who used the new tools to negotiate more effectively with the British and French. In a matter of decades, territorial authority was transformed from a sense of loose control over differentiated places, defined from the center outward, to an understanding – based

[75] Hostetler 2001: 74.   [76] Thongchai 1994: 79.

on modern mapping – of authority as homogeneous, exclusive, and delineated by clearly defined boundaries.[77]

For the ruling elite in Bangkok, these ideas and practices offered a new tool of power, "a new mechanism of overlordship in terms of force, administration, and boundary demarcation and mapping" to use against marginal areas and tributary states.[78] Instead of allowing central control to fade toward the frontiers, this emphasis led to a new permanent military presence on the boundaries. Traditional notions of political authority, focusing on the center rather than the periphery, had allowed marginal areas to be shared or even given up without invoking the perception of a significant loss. By the late nineteenth century, however, "Many incidents [of conflict with neighbors] … took place in areas which would have been ignored had the premodern geographical ideas prevailed."[79] The imposition of central control along the newly implemented linear boundary, together with the new importance placed on such peripheral areas, meant that the actors who lost out the most were the marginal polities that had formerly paid tribute to, but been largely independent of, rulers in Bangkok. Just as in Europe, centralization was given both new tools and a new character by the visual grammar of modern mapping techniques, and the resulting homogenization of territorial claims simultaneously allowed for increased centralization and domination by those who made use of these tools.

Modern mapping and its concomitant view of space are thus acceptable to any and all actors, no matter their geographic position, since this technological discourse simultaneously equalizes all locations and allows each society to perceive itself as being at the center. In other words, modern mapping gains its hegemonic power not because it immediately places one group or set of interests above another but because Ptolemaic cartography has the "ability to involve varied interest groups in a single discourse"[80] – the discourse of political interest defined in homogeneously territorial terms. Even as different actors argue in favor of a particular center (or a particular boundary placement), they have

---

[77] This process of adopting Western ideas of linear political boundaries was not limited to Siam, of course. For example, under British imperialism, boundaries within India underwent a complete redefinition: "In a major conceptual reversal, boundaries were no longer vague axes of dispute (frontiers) between core areas of Indian polities but were configured as the means whereby those core areas were now defined" (Edney 1997: 333).

[78] Thongchai 1994: 101.   [79] Thongchai 1994: 111.

[80] Kivelson 1999: 84.

all implicitly agreed to the fundamental structure of graticule-based cartography and hence have adopted the same understanding of space and political territory. (This will be particularly apparent in the discussion of treaty negotiation and texts in Chapter 6.)

In addition to these inherent characteristics of grid-based mapping that encouraged its global adoption, there are also many reasons for the eventual dominance of geometric space that were contingent features of the historical context of early modern Europe. In the most general sense, the changes involved in the shift to modern cartography and the modern view of space formed part of the social, technological, and political changes that together constitute the transition to modernity. For example, early developments in Ptolemaic cartography dovetailed with the Renaissance combination of new learning with classical authorities. Later, cartographic developments and the geometricization of space mirrored general trends of the scientific revolution and the Enlightenment, seen, for example, in the obsession with complex geometric fortification designs and in the culture of quantification and measurement.[81] Unlike other ways of depicting space – particularly earlier, non-Ptolemaic visual means such as itinerary maps, portolan charts, or schematic diagrams – modern maps were built around the ideas of consistent scale and careful measurement of position and distance. Eighteenth-century "mathematical cartography," seen in state-sponsored survey projects, thus offered a means of unifying disparate mapping traditions and practices within the cultural discourse of the time.[82]

The increasingly geometric view of space was also driven by its close links to those in power, especially certain European rulers who, both using maps and being influenced by them, came to understand space abstractly and to conceive of authority in territorial terms. This applied particularly to the colonial expansion of European powers, which coincided historically with the cartographic revolution. The subsequent growth of European travel, commerce, and knowledge created fundamentally novel demands for maps as a means of understanding and claiming new territories. The important role played by these events outside Europe in shaping the European – and eventually global – state system is the subject of the next chapter.

---

[81] Both of which were closely linked to mapping. See Frängsmyr *et al.* 1990; Headrick 2000; Lynn 2003: 119.

[82] Edney 1993: 61.

5 | New World mapping and colonial reflection

Almost any seventeenth- or eighteenth-century map of America reveals the absolute faith Europeans of all religious persuasions had in the authority of the cartographic grid. Monarchs laid claim to lands solely on the basis of abstract latitudes and longitudes. Troops were sent to fight and die for boundaries that had no visible landmarks, only abstract mathematical existence.[1]

The European expansion of commercial activity and political power that began with the late fifteenth-century Iberian voyages to both east and west was tied closely to cartographic developments. These links went well beyond simply using maps in navigation – as the passage quoted above makes clear, new mapping techniques were central to how European political actors supported their claims to new territories, trade routes, or commercial privileges. Moreover, the interactions of European colonial powers in this new arena of competition were a key driver of the early modern shift from overlapping territorial and non-territorial authorities to territorial exclusivity.

It was the need to divide, claim, and assign dominion over the unknown spaces of the New World that drove the first use of the abstract mathematical and geometric methods that were newly available for understanding and claiming territories. The ostensibly empty spaces of the Americas – and "discoveries" in other non-European parts of the world – could be comprehended, negotiated over, and competed for *only* by using an abstract conception of space built on mathematical cartography. The novel requirements of making extra-European political claims demanded new authoritative practices by colonial powers, practices that were made manifest immediately in linear territorial divisions between spatial expanses. This abstraction of space in the colonial realm had effects in Europe itself: the

[1] Edgerton 1987: 46.

cartographic tools – and spatial understandings – first used elsewl
were later applied within European metropoles as well.

In other words, certain fundamental features of modern states and
international politics originated in the actions of European polities
and rulers *outside* Europe rather than within it. Technological innovations built on Ptolemaic mapping made the geometric division of territory possible, and the colonial expansion to the Americas made the
use of these novel ideas and techniques of rule necessary. Indeed, the
combination of these mutual dynamics – a supply of new tools and a
demand for their use – led to the emergence of our global system of
sovereign states.

Typically, sovereign statehood and international relations have been
characterized as a collection of ideas, norms, and practices that developed within Europe and were subsequently imposed on, or adopted
by, other parts of the globe during and after the period of European
colonialism. While this does describe a part of the story (as the previous chapters have shown with regard to mapping technologies and
their political effects), it ignores the constitutive importance of ideas
and techniques of rule that developed as part of European expansion,
rather than prior to it.[2]

Instead, I argue that certain practices and ideas fundamental to modern states and international relations appeared first in the colonial world,
albeit in the interactions of European polities operating there, and only
later were applied to intra-European political structures. This process I
label *colonial reflection*, because it involves the reflection of techniques

[2] The edited volume by Bull and Watson on *The Expansion of International
Society* offers an influential example of the conventional view. This collection
sees the practices of statehood spreading outward through colonialism and
adopted by new states as they are "allowed" into the system in the twentieth
century. Although they note that "[t]he evolution of the European system
of interstate relations and the expansion of Europe across the globe were
simultaneous processes, which influenced and affected each other" (Bull and
Watson 1984: 6–7), the analysis finds little influence on state formation from
colonial expansion, instead focusing on the expansion of the system to include
new actors. This emphasizes diplomatic practices and thus leads to a focus on
the inclusion of new actors in events such as multilateral conferences: "One
way of charting the evolution of a universal international society is to trace
the widening representation of non-European states at these conferences" (Bull
and Watson 1984: 121). By focusing exclusively on the formal relations among
political units, this approach ignores the possibility that those units may change
in fundamental character, rather than merely in number or identity.

Modernity does not 'just' emerge from Europe.

used first in colonial areas onto European internal political arrangements.[3] Many of these practices and ideas were implemented as a conscious response to the perceived novelty of extra-European expansion.
Therefore, the historically contingent process of European colonialism –
particularly in the New World of the Americas – was a key factor shaping
the development of European states and the international system.

The importance of colonial practices to later European political
developments has been noted by other studies, none of which, however, focuses on the shift to exclusive territoriality as a foundation
for modern statehood. For example, Hannah Arendt sees the origins
of twentieth-century totalitarianism in the racism and expansionism
inherent in nineteenth-century imperialism. Colonial practices eventually made their appearance within Europe in a "boomerang effect," to
the shock of a society of states accustomed to more "civilized" forms of
conflict among themselves.[4] Benedict Anderson's influential argument
about the construction of nations as "imagined communities" rests on
a similar logic. He contends that modern nationalism appeared first in
America, not in Europe:

> Out of the American welter came these imagined realities: nation-states,
> republican institutions, common citizenships, popular sovereignty, national
> flags and anthems, etc. ... In effect, by the second decade of the nineteenth
> century, if not earlier, a "model" of "the" independent national state was
> available for pirating.[5]

The fact that this aspect of Anderson's argument is often overlooked
reveals how deeply ingrained our notions of the European origins of
modernity are. The integral part played by extra-European events,
actors, or practices – particularly cartographic tools and ideas – needs to
be incorporated into our understanding of modern state formation.[6]

---

[3] This concept is partially inspired by, but distinct from, Michael Taussig's notion
of a "colonial mirror which reflects back onto the colonists the barbarity of
their own social relations, but as imputed to the savage or evil figures they wish
to colonize" (Taussig 1984: 495).

[4] Arendt 1966. Keene (2002) notes a similar process of importing colonial ideas,
particularly regarding the justification for war as a means of defending or
spreading "civilization."

[5] Anderson 1991: 81.

[6] This also applies to how we understand the origins of modernity more
generally. See, for example, Hostetler 2001 and Raj 2000.

While these existing theories focus predominantly on nineteenth-century developments, a process of colonial reflection also occurred in the first colonial age of the sixteenth and seventeenth centuries, fundamentally shaping the origins of territorial states. For example, Edmundo O'Gorman notes that the initial Columbian encounter and the subsequent "invention" of America as a New World by Europeans not only altered their understanding of the heretofore unknown parts of the world, but also reconstructed their conception of the world as a whole and the place of Europe within it.[7] Carl Schmitt echoes this point, arguing explicitly that the encounter with America "initiated an internal European struggle for this new world that, in turn, led to a new spatial order of the earth with new divisions."[8] Others have also noted the importance of the first wave of European colonial expansion to the formation of political modernity and international law.[9]

In particular, the sixteenth-century Spanish conquest of Amerindian civilizations – which were difficult to fit into the conventional categorization of peoples either as Christians or as known enemies of Christendom – brought up questions with implications not only for the position of New World possessions but also for the fundamental basis for political life within Europe as well.[10] In debates following the Spanish conquest – including one called by Charles V at Valladolid specifically to discuss the legitimacy of his New World possessions – the participants understood the potential repercussions of their arguments: "The jurists and theologians were acutely aware that any political theory used to legitimize in this way the conquest of the territories of non-Christian rulers could just as easily be used by Christian rulers against each other."[11] The declared justifications of conquest were fundamental to the later development of modern political theory as well as to political rule and the discipline of International Relations.[12]

Territorial statehood, whose origins are examined in this book, is part of the larger universe of ways in which colonial ideas and

---

[7] O'Gorman 1961.
[8] Schmitt 2003 [1974]: 87. See also Steinberg (2009) on the importance of the early modern division between spaces of state control on land and spaces outside state control on the oceans.
[9] Anghie 2004; Bhambra 2007; Muldoon 1999.
[10] Fernández-Santamaria 1977; Jahn 1999, 2000; Pagden 1995.
[11] Pagden 1995: 47–48; see also Fernández-Santamaria 1977: 58.
[12] Jahn 1999, 2000.

practices restructured European politics. The shift to exclusive territoriality appeared first in European expansion into, and political
competition over, the New World. These ideas were later applied to
European interactions, creating by the nineteenth century the hegemonic ideal of political organization represented by the territorial
state. Although this parallels some of the effects of colonial expansion in earlier eras – such as the *Reconquista* on the Iberian peninsula
or the medieval Germanic push into Eastern Europe[13] – New World
colonialism and its effects were fundamentally different. In the earlier
periods of expansion, newly conquered territories were incorporated
using traditional means of asserting rule, albeit applied to new areas.
From the fifteenth century onward, colonial powers had a new set of
tools available – Ptolemaic cartography and its ideational resources –
making it possible to assert claims from afar without detailed knowledge of the territory or peoples in question. The resulting character
of colonial expansion, and its eventual impact on European political
practices, was therefore new.

The rest of this chapter explores this dynamic further, examining
the demand for new cartographic technologies and ideas in colonial
expansion to the New World, the reflection of these practices back
onto European spaces, and, finally, the active imposition of cartographic territoriality on most of the globe during the second phase of
European imperialism.

New World, new mapping, new territories

The expansion of European political and economic activities to areas
outside Europe, and particularly to the New World of the Americas,
involved some of the first uses of the new tools – and ideas – of Ptolemaic
cartography. These recent innovations in mapping were less integral to
the logistical requirements of travel and navigation and more important, rather, to the ways in which Europeans came to understand and to
make claims to previously unknown spaces.

Navigational maps such as portolan charts had been used on ships for
several centuries by the time of the Iberian voyages of the late fifteenth

---

[13] Bartlett (1993), for example, argues that the politics and culture of the late
Middle Ages resulted from internal and external expansionism. See also
Barkawi (2010: 330) for a related point regarding institutional innovations in
Norman England.

century. In the era of European expansion, these nautical way-finding tools continued to be an important part of navigational technology, along with simple astronomical observation and written directions. The mapping of oceanic voyages and discoveries thus quickly captured the attention of the governments of Portugal and Spain, both of which created institutions for consolidating, managing, and securing cartographic knowledge: the Casa da Mina in Lisbon and the Casa de la Contratación in Seville. This represented a significant step toward government control of information and a new type of government activity: "Portugal and Spain were the first nations to attempt to construct spaces within which to accumulate and regulate all geographical knowledge."[14] In particular, both institutions were meant to create, update, and keep secret "master maps" of their respective overseas empires. These maps would then be used to create accurate navigational charts for pilots.[15]

Yet this type of map use represented only a small part of the role of cartography in colonial expansion. Beyond using maps for the practical needs of navigation – and keeping secure that kind of information from political rivals – European governments also used maps both to lay claim to and to gain information about their own colonial possessions, particularly in the Americas. Governments used maps as "weapons of imperialism," by claiming land ahead of actual conquest and legitimizing conquest during and after the fact. With Ptolemaic cartography and the geometric view of space that it implied, "the world could be carved up on paper" as never before.[16] Maps were used in this revolutionary capacity from the very beginning of the colonial era in the late fifteenth century, reshaping the evolving ideas and practices of political rule into the purely territorial form we see today.

The interaction between colonial expansion and cartography was complex, as the extension of European awareness and conquest actually created a *demand* for the use of the modern tools of spatial abstraction represented by Ptolemaic mapping. Maps were useful for achieving imperial goals, and imperial expansion simultaneously drove the increased use of mapping and the cartographic division of political territories. The previously unknown spaces of the New World required an abstract conception of space in order to be comprehended, explored, and claimed.

---

[14] Turnbull 1996: 7. [15] Sandman 2007: 1104. [16] Harley 2001: 57, 59.

After their "discovery" and increasing exploration in the 1490s and early 1500s, the Americas were not easily incorporated into European geographic and cosmological thinking. In particular, there was confusion among European rulers and intellectuals as to whether the territories encountered were parts of Asia (as Columbus believed) or an entirely unknown land. It was not until fifteen years after Columbus' first voyage that clear and widely influential statements were made that the "New World" was indeed "new."[17] Among these statements were world maps depicting America as a distinct continent separated by oceans from both Asia and Europe, such as the 1507 wall-sized map of the world by Martin Waldseemüller showing a very narrow – but freestanding – South American continent (Figure 5.1).

Ptolemaic mapping, in fact, offered a particularly useful means of integrating these and other discoveries into the existing knowledge and belief structure of Europeans, which was built on classical and medieval authorities: "[T]he graticule offered the flexibility of assimilating and integrating ancient authority [that is, Ptolemy] with empirical discovery."[18] The encounter with lands completely unknown to the ancients – whose texts were still seen as authoritative in most fields of knowledge – could be incorporated into the grid system described by Ptolemy in spite of his complete ignorance of these places. This incorporation was made possible by the Ptolemaic graticule and would have been impossible without it: medieval traditions of mapping did not portray the unknown as abstract "empty" spaces to be filled in as discoveries were made.

The evolution of medieval *mappaemundi* during the fifteenth century illustrates this difference. For example, a world map by Fra Mauro of Venice (Figure 5.2), *c.* 1450, offers a much more geographically accurate depiction of Europe than did *mappaemundi* of preceding centuries (such as that shown in Figure 3.1). Yet with its continuing use of Jerusalem as the center of focus, and the absence of any graticule indicating that this image includes only half of the spherical earth, there is no space available on Fra Mauro's map for the insertion of newly discovered continents. For the *mappamundi* tradition, the map structure itself precludes the addition of new continents.[19] Grid-based world maps, on the other hand, illustrate the usefulness of the new

---

[17] O'Gorman 1961.   [18] Cosgrove 2001: 107.   [19] Cosgrove 1992.

Figure 5.1 World map, Martin Waldseemüller, 1507

techniques, as the Ptolemaic graticule made it possible to insert *whatever* landmass the mapmaker believed to exist in a particular location defined by coordinates. The 360 degrees of longitude enabled a Ptolemaic map to encompass the whole globe, known and unknown, in one image. (Compare Figure 5.1 and Figure 5.2.)

The perception of the Americas as a completely New World, previously unknown to contemporary Europeans as well as to classical authors, fostered an understanding of the continent as a space empty of the kinds of specific places, with moral or human characteristics, that defined the known *orbis terrarum*. "The emerging new world did not appear as a new enemy, but as *free space*, as an area open to European occupation and expansion."[20] This perception of emptiness demanded a new way of understanding space and making political claims, a way provided by the cartographic tools of Ptolemaic mapping and the linear division of political control. The colonization of the Americas thus created a break with previous practices of political expansion:

Old World conquest before the Age of Exploration involved subduing and establishing suzerainty over older and resident agricultural populations. It did not involve displacing them entirely, even when these populations were thought by their conquerors to be inferior.[21]

In the Old World, where recognized authority structures existed, an invader could conquer a people by claiming the same authority that the previous ruler had held – whether that authority was defined on a territorial or personal basis. In the New World, the absence of recognized authority structures meant that these were, in effect, "spaces without places," requiring a different means for claiming authority.

The political implications of this difference appeared immediately after Columbus returned to Spain. Although the nature of the lands encountered was unclear (and would remain so for at least a decade), the Spanish monarchs wished to secure their claims no matter what the geographic facts turned out to be:

The Crown's reaction is governed by one primary interest: to ensure possession and juridical rights on whatever it was that Columbus had found ... With equal haste, the Crown started negotiations to obtain a legal title from

---

[20] Schmitt 2003: 87.   [21] Sack 1986: 87–88.

Figure 5.2 *Mappamundi*, Fra Mauro, *c.* 1450
Note: The map has been reoriented to put north at the top (it is originally presented with south at the top).

the Holy See. Here, also, the question of what the lands might be was not uppermost: the urgent thing was to insure juridical lordship over them.[22]

The geographic uncertainty of the discoveries, whether a new continent or a part of the known world, had to be circumvented, as the monarchs wished to assert their political claim in any case. Columbus' traditional means of asserting authority on the spot – as he declared, "by proclamation made and with the royal standard unfurled"[23] – was an insufficient basis for claiming a poorly understood territory.

[22] O'Gorman 1961: 81   [23] Quoted in Greenblatt 1991: 52.

Instead, the most effective means for making a claim over the unknown emerged from the new techniques of Ptolemaic cartography. In particular, the Ptolemaic grid built on celestial coordinates supplied the means required for the linear division of the world, resulting in the new practice of "global linear thinking" among European political actors.[24]

This new approach becomes evident, first, in a series of Papal Bulls in 1493 and, second, in the 1494 Treaty of Tordesillas, which was a direct agreement between Spain and Portugal without the involvement of the pope.[25] As a result, Spain was allotted all newly discovered territories west of a line drawn in the Atlantic Ocean, and Portugal apportioned those to the east. In essence, this reflected the respective directions that explorers from each country had already been traveling, and the agreement was thus meant to legitimate their claims versus each other, as well as versus other European powers.[26] The importance of Tordesillas was not so much in the details of the line dividing the two empires (the exact location of which was unobtainable and ignored[27]), but instead in the very idea of using a geometric division to assign political authority: "For the first time in history an abstract geometric system had been used to define a vast – global – area of control."[28]

In the evolution of these linear divisions, cartography was involved not only in the form of geometric demarcations but also in cases in which cartographers directly participated in political negotiations. For example, in the 1520s Spain and Portugal began negotiations to resolve where on the opposite side of the globe the Tordesillas line fell, and thereby to determine where the already agreed-upon division of global control between Portugal and Spain was located.[29] In the 1524 negotiations, "Each country was to be represented by nine official delegates,

---

[24] Schmitt 2003: 87–88.

[25] As O'Gorman points out, the two monarchies left the papacy out of the discussion because "the Holy See would not grant sovereignty over the Ocean either to Spain or to Portugal" (1961: 156–57).

[26] These were merely the first among many linear political divisions effected in the extra-European world. Others took the form of "amity lines," drawn to divide the part of the world where peace treaties or truces between European powers held from other areas were fighting, raiding, or privateering could continue. For example, in 1634 Richelieu forbade French attacks on Spanish or Portuguese vessels above the Tropic of Cancer while explicitly allowing them beyond that line. See Schmitt 2003: 92–93.

[27] Sandman 2007: 1108.   [28] Sack 1986: 132.

[29] Brotton 1997: ch. 4; Sandman 2007.

consisting of three lawyers, three cosmographers, and three pilots."[30] The pilots represented the practical knowledge of maritime navigation, while the cosmographers were present as savants of the still relatively new Ptolemaic understanding of the world. The resolution of the issue with the Treaty of Saragossa in 1529 was a strictly political decision, since a technical cartographic solution was made impossible by the lack of accurate longitude readings. Yet the agreement reached by Spain and Portugal nonetheless demonstrates the power of the cartographic idea of territoriality: the agreement was made under the illusion that a cartographic line had actually been drawn as a basis for the division, as this was the acceptable means of settling claims over extra-European spaces.

Building on these initial divisions, during the first two centuries of European colonialism, maps came to be used increasingly by colonial powers. The Spanish crown, for example, made several attempts to gain geographical information about its New World possessions, using methods that included written questionnaires, requests for various types of maps, instructions for celestial observations, and government-commissioned survey-based mapping.[31] The most successful was a standardized questionnaire distributed in the 1570s, the responses to which are known as the *relaciones geográficas*.[32] The fifty-question survey contained three explicit requests for maps, drawings, or charts. The response from colonial officials, though extensive, was predominantly in the form of textual material rather than maps. In addition, many of the maps that were returned were sketched town plans, and the few regional maps were so unclear and vague that "such maps provided somewhat less accurate location patterns than textual data on directions and distances."[33] The types of maps submitted were predominantly in the itinerary-based tradition of the European Middle Ages, treating direction and distance schematically,[34] or were drawn by indigenous painters using a mixture of European and native visual traditions.[35] This reveals both the limited penetration of the cartographic view of the world in the late sixteenth century (among, for example, provincial officials who were uninterested in mapping their domains in the Ptolemaic fashion) and, simultaneously, the extent to which

[30] Vigneras 1962: 77.   [31] Edwards 1969; Mundy 1996.
[32] Cline 1964; Edwards 1969; Mundy 1996.
[33] Edwards 1969: 27.   [34] Padrón 2004: 77.   [35] Mundy 1996: ch. 4.

officials in Spain had absorbed this view. The latter were unaware of
how their request for maps would be differently interpreted by local
officials in the Americas.[36]

The newly popular grid-based map techniques were put to use, however, for the promotion of colonial interests rather than as direct tools
of government. Dutch colonial officials, for example, used maps as persuasive devices to increase their prestige and legitimacy: they "considered maps and topographic paintings effective vehicles to promote their
activities and to establish their historic role."[37] In England, when the first
major proposals for colonial ventures appeared during the Elizabethan
age, maps were used rhetorically by advocates, both to "visualize their
goals" and to convince the rich and powerful of their cause.[38]

During the seventeenth century, however, maps came to be seen as
important resources for ruling colonial possessions, and thus the control of map production became a central goal of many governments.
For example, the Dutch States General granted cartographic monop-
olies to the West India and East India companies in the first half of
the 1600s. Maps came to be "viewed as an aid to clarify political,
military, economic, cultural, and administrative particularities in order
to make sound decisions," rather than just as promotional tools.[39]
Similarly, the growing English colonial claims of the seventeenth century made increasing use of maps and cartographic ideas. Even when
English claims to New World territory involved "the 'legal cartographies' of charters and grants" rather than maps per se,[40] many of these
documents based their authority claims on the *ideas* of geometric,
Ptolemaic cartography: lines of latitude or longitude. For example, the
1606 charter of Virginia delineated the colony as being all land on the
Atlantic coast "between four and thirty Degrees of Northerly Latitude
from the Equinoctial Line, and five and forty Degrees of the same
Latitude."[41] Charters for other colonies followed similar patterns.[42]

---

[36] Padrón 2002: 39.   [37] Zandvliet 2007: 1458.
[38] Baldwin 2007: 1757.   [39] Zandvliet 2007: 1445.
[40] Baldwin 2007: 1765.
[41] http://avalon.law.yale.edu/17th_century/va01.asp.
[42] Sack 1986: 134. Although many of the claims in the New World also
   incorporated older feudal notions of control, the form that the latter took
   illustrates the particular requirements of making claims in the New World:
   "the type of land tenure they most often stipulated was modeled after ... the
   least feudally encumbered system of land tenure" of England (Sack 1986: 137).

The cartographic basis for large territorial claims in colonial charters was eventually succeeded by the imposition of survey-based property mapping as a key element in delineating and assigning colonial lands to settlers.[43]

The extensive use of maps and cartographic delineations of political authority in European colonial expansion and competition evinces some of the clearest and earliest examples of political action and interaction being structured by cartographic tools. The attempt to make claims to political authority in the Americas demanded a new form of territoriality, founded on linear divisions and homogeneous expanses of space. As interactions in the colonial world rapidly took on cartographic characteristics – in both the practices of rule and the imaginations of rulers – it helped drive the eventual transformation of interaction, authority, and the interstate system *within* Europe as well. In short, European expansion not only demanded mapping; it also legitimated mapping as a useful tool for understanding the world as a whole, thereby reshaping territoriality and undermining non-territorial forms of authority.

Reflection and consolidation of territoriality

Ideas and practices first implemented in the colonial world were later applied to interactions within Europe, and were imported because of their extensive use and usefulness in colonial rule. Then, once this territorial ideal was fully implemented within and among European states in the early nineteenth century, later waves of imperial expansion were even more fundamentally shaped by the cartographic form of political rule, leading to the imposition of linear divisions and territorial authority over nearly the entire globe.

The homogenization and geometricization of space in the New World was complex, far beyond being yet another example of European colonial powers imposing their understandings on conquered peoples and spaces. Within Europe during this period, space was still predominantly perceived in the medieval fashion, as a collection of unique places related by human experiences. It was only *after* the geometric view of space had been imposed and established in the New World that

---

[43] Kain and Baigent 1992: ch. 8.

this same conception came to be applied to the European continent, homogenizing that space as well. The internal logic of this grid-based view of space, in fact, dictated that it would eventually be applied to European space: the graticule, as a whole-globe covering grid, decreed that if it was applied to the understanding of any part of the world, it could be applied to all of the world. European space, however, had long been understood in a different fashion – as a collection of unique places – and therefore the application of geometric space to Europe did not occur overnight. Rather, it progressed in a piecemeal fashion, leading up to the post-Revolutionary territorialization of rule.

This reflection of the geometric view of space back onto Europe can be seen in the adoption of cartographic techniques that enable and enforce such an understanding, first in the Americas and then subsequently in Europe. For example, the earliest governmental institutions created to generate, collect, and keep secret cartographic information were the Portuguese and Spanish organizations for managing their empires, created by the early sixteenth century. Cartographic institutions for mapping European states internally only appeared later. Furthermore, the Spanish *relaciones geográficas*, originally used to request information about colonies, were subsequently applied to information-gathering within peninsular Spain.[44] Thus key steps toward bureaucratization, an integral part of the development of the modern state, were responses to the novelty of making claims to the New World and only later reflected back onto rule within European territories as well.

In practices as well as in ideas, therefore, the colonial application of Ptolemaic space preceded – and suggested – the subsequent conceptualization of European space as geometric as well. This dynamic culminated in the creation of the United States as an independent entity and potential model, built on an exclusively territorial, rationally designed foundation. "The American system of government established between 1776 and 1789 may have been the first to conceive of its sub-units, the states, as generic territories – all alike in their form and place in government."[45] This involved the active implementation of Enlightenment ideals of rationalization to a degree that was still unheard of within Europe.[46]

---

[44] Cline 1964.   [45] Sack 1986: 149.
[46] Onuf and Onuf 1993: 3.

Essential to this rationalization of space in the United States were mapping projects, oriented both externally and internally. Externally, this was evident in the lengthy, map-focused negotiations over the delimitation of the boundary between Canada and the United States. Internally, efforts by the newly independent United States to survey and organize its western territories were based on the coordinate grid and took on a particularly geometric character. Thomas Jefferson proposed dividing the land according to a Ptolemaic grid of latitude and longitude, as well as imposing a strictly decimal system, reflecting the Enlightenment ideal of rational geometric division. Although the plan actually implemented was different (and relied on more traditional measures), the idea of a grid-based division still formed the fundamental basis for the system of townships and property ownership in the American Midwest.[47]

Then, in the late eighteenth century and particularly in the post-Napoleonic settlements, rulers territorialized political practices within Europe, often using the institutions and ideas of the Americas as a model. The partitions of Poland, for example, imposed New World practices in the Old World. These agreements between Prussia, Russia, and Austria at the end of the eighteenth century involved increasingly territorial divisions of Polish territory, against the wishes of the local population. The linear division by European actors of territory inhabited by people not consulted in the process had of course begun with Tordesillas and then continued throughout the era of European colonialism. In fact, the parallel was not entirely lost on the participants: after his officials had difficulty gathering geographic information within Poland, Emperor Joseph II of Austria wrote: "I don't believe that even among the Iroquois and the Hottentots such ridiculous things occur."[48] The imposition of colonial practices in Poland required the demotion of the Polish people to the status of indigenous subjects of European colonial rule.

In the decades that followed, Napoleon's conquest itself represented a "vast experiment with colonialism within Europe," during which complex traditional authorities either were directly eliminated or were undermined by their collaboration with the French.[49] In 1814–15, therefore, Europe itself presented something of a blank slate – upon

---

[47] Hielbron 1990; King 1996: 68–69; Linklater 2002.
[48] Evans 1992: 492.   [49] Schroeder 1994: 391.

which the post-Napoleonic settlement was drawn in purely territorial terms. Many of the novel institutional arrangements of the United
States, including its territorial foundation of rule, were seen as successful innovations by post-Napoleonic statesmen and were imitated
in the new order.[50] (The relevant treaties are examined in the next
chapter.)

In sum, the transformation of political authority within Europe
followed the technical and ideational developments of Ptolemaic cartography and their implementation in the previously unknown spaces
of the New World. Although the attempt to claim and control these
new spaces demanded this novel understanding of political authority, within Europe the extensive knowledge of territory and the longstanding traditional authorities claimed over it resisted such demands.
Instead, it was the shift in the ideas Europeans had about space in general – and the reinforcement offered by the use and usefulness of maps
and map-based political authority in the New World – that eventually
helped drive a change in intra-European ideas and practices. Both the
geometric nature of modern territoriality and the elimination of non-
territorial authorities thus appeared first in the colonial world and
were reflected back onto Europe only later.

The eventual hegemony of territorial authority within Europe provides an explanation for the fundamentally cartographic nature of
later colonial expansion, particularly during the race for empires in
the nineteenth century. This later period can be read to support the
conventional narrative regarding the active imposition of European
ideas on non-European subject peoples, a narrative that has made it
easy to miss the very different dynamic of sixteenth- and seventeenth-
century colonial rule. While the first phase of European colonialism
made some use of maps for exploration, legitimacy, and rule, it was the
later European imperialism of the eighteenth and nineteenth centuries
that saw an even more dominant role for mapping as a tool of colonial
expansion and authority.

This dynamic is clear in Britain's mapping projects in India, as well
as in its efforts to assert direct rule on the subcontinent. The Great
Trigonometrical Survey undertaken during the nineteenth century lent
both practical and rhetorical support to colonial rule: mapping helped
"make Britain understand its conquests, while in addition helping to

---

[50] Onuf and Onuf 1993: 219.

legitimate the British presence."[51] This legitimation was based on the ideal of an advanced European civilization being inherently superior to indigenous cultures. "For the British in India, the measurement and observation inherent to each act of surveying represented *science*. By measuring the land, by imposing European science and rationality on the Indian landscape, the British distinguished themselves from the Indians."[52] In short, the British conquerors were rational, scientific, and liberal, while the Indians were irrational, mystical, and despotic. This rhetoric existed in spite of the fact that the "scientific" ideal on which British cartography rested – exact measurement through direct observation by trigonometric survey – was impossible to achieve over all of the subcontinent because of technical and logistical obstacles that were never overcome.[53]

The British also pursued local-level projects, as administrative mapping actively tried to "rationalize" existing jurisdictions, creating linear boundaries where there had been only vague distinctions between areas.[54] This imposition of discrete divisions between jurisdictions closely resembles the process that occurred within Europe, beginning in the eighteenth century. The effects of British mapping were long-lasting and deep: "The geographical rhetoric of British India was so effective that India had become a real entity for both British imperialists and Indian nationalists alike."[55] The political structure of the subcontinent still reflects this construction of a unified Indian geopolitical space.

Similar cartographic techniques were applied to the division of Africa among colonial powers in the nineteenth century. The practical use of maps was well established by this post-Enlightenment period, and hence African expeditions included mapmakers in their number.[56] In addition, maps were used to promote expansion back in Europe, particularly through the contemporary practice of depicting unknown areas as blank spaces on maps (as opposed to earlier practices of extrapolating or outright inventing geographical information for unknown areas). "Evidence from the late nineteenth century indicates that map readers interpreted blank spaces as areas open for exploration and ultimately colonization. Rather than interpreting

---

[51] Black 2002: 29. [52] Edney 1997: 32. [53] Edney 1997: 17.
[54] Michael 2007. [55] Edney 1997: 15. See also Raj 2000.
[56] Bassett 1994: 319.

them as the limits of knowledge of African geography ... imperialists presumed that the empty spaces were empty and awaiting colonists."[57] Filling in those "blanks" on a map came to represent a means of claiming authority over colonial space. The famous Berlin Conference of 1884–85 thus represented not the first example of carving up Africa on paper, but rather the culmination of a trend occurring throughout the nineteenth century.

By the end of the century, map-based claims to territory had become an official means of settling imperial rivalries: "maps produced by surveyors formed part of the documentary evidence needed to claim protectorates by the procedures agreed to at the Berlin Conference."[58] This led to conflict as much as to cooperation, however, as both official and unofficial maps often created disagreements about the extent of colonial claims or left unclear where boundaries would actually fall on the ground.[59] As is well documented, these often arbitrary divisions have continued to structure African politics well after independence, both within countries and, internationally, between them.[60]

Thus nineteenth-century colonial empires, though hierarchically organized internally, were built on the same ideal of geometric territorial divisions and exhaustive claims to authority that were being implemented within Europe, but that had originally been innovations in the New World rather than the Old.[61]

The ideal of territorial exclusivity as the basis for political organization drove the process of implementing territorial statehood within Europe, and that very implementation strengthened the ideal. By the middle of the twentieth century, then, newly created postcolonial states were born into an international system where the ideal of territorial exclusivity was firmly consolidated, making it possible for these ostensibly weak political entities to be constituted and in some cases fully

---

[57] Bassett 1994: 334.   [58] Bassett 1994: 321.

[59] See Bassett 1994: 325 and Seligman 1995.

[60] Herbst 2000; Jackson 1990.

[61] The nineteenth-century extraterritorial concessions to European powers in China offer a contrasting model of colonial rule, as authority was held over particular persons rather than strictly delineated spaces. This was, however, understood as the exception to the ideal colonial form of direct territorial rule. See Kayaoglu 2007.

supported by this ideal. Moreover, as will be discussed in Chapter 8, the strength of this idea also made it impossible for new political units to be constituted by any other notion of political authority.

The contours of this shift to exclusively cartographic forms of rule become particularly evident when we look at the goals, techniques, and results of interstate negotiation among early modern European rulers. The next chapter addresses exactly this, revealing the gradual – and generally inadvertent – transformation of the deep grammar of authority and the resulting changes in political practices, driven in significant part by cartography.

6 | Peace treaties and political transformation

Mr Raudot begs you to remove from your plate the dots that you have put in to mark the limits of Louisiana, California, New Mexico, etc. The court does not agree to the limits assigned by geographers, yet foreign nations use our maps against us when we discuss important questions with them.

Père Jean Bobé, chaplain at Versailles, 1715[1]

This request, made following the publication in 1714 of a world map by French cartographer Guillaume Delisle, reveals the emerging influence of mapmaking over early modern diplomacy. The map showed expansive French claims in the New World, much to the chagrin of Antoine-Denis Raudot, a member of the inner circle of the French minister of the navy. The minister feared that, even in a commercially produced map, boundaries drawn too far in France's favor would aggravate other states. In other words, even though officials did not plan to use this map – or perhaps any map – to resolve territorial conflicts, they feared that *others would do so*, hence making such maps important shapers of the conditions within which negotiations would take place. Cartography, in short, imposed constraints on the behavior of political actors.

Treaty negotiations and texts – the focus of this chapter – reveal the key role played by mapping in driving and implementing the transformation of ideas about political authority. During the early modern period, maps were increasingly used in international negotiations, giving new shape to the immediate and long-range goals of the actors involved. This, in turn, led to observable changes both in the negotiating strategies of rulers and in the treaties that resulted, providing an analytical link between broad changes in political ideas and the implementation of those new ideas in the material practices of rule.

---

[1] Quoted in Petto 2007: 104.

Negotiations, treaties, and political authority

Throughout the early modern period, diplomats increasingly used maps, both in formulating foreign policy and in actual negotiations. Yet this trend's major effect on political behavior and outcomes became evident not with the initial use of maps in the sixteenth century but with the full consolidation of map-based political territoriality in the eighteenth century and thereafter. This diplomatic use of maps involved a two-way process: not only did mapmakers shape diplomats' perceptions of their world by depicting it in a particular way, but diplomats also increasingly demanded maps with political content, thereby reinforcing the trend among cartographers toward mapping the world in political terms.[2] Yet the manner in which mapmakers responded to this demand – filling their maps with linear divisions between homogeneous spatial entities – did not reflect any specific requests by diplomats. Instead, it was determined by the dominant visual language of early modern mapping.

The texts that resulted from these increasingly cartographic negotiations serve as key indicators of the ideas about political authority held by rulers and their representatives. While treaties are – and always have been – regarded as agreements that can be broken, they nonetheless reveal some of the dominant political conceptions of their time. Whether or not rulers plan to abide by an agreement, the negotiation and signing of that agreement exposes the fundamental ideas held by actors about what they are negotiating over.[3] In particular, the way in which political authority is exchanged, transferred, claimed, or captured reveals norms about authority, even if both sides do not agree on the specifics of who gets what. Questions central to this investigation include: was the exchange made in terms of territory, or something else? If territory was discussed, how was it defined and then passed from one ruler to another? What was the role of maps or cartographic language in the implementation of a peace settlement?

In early modern Europe treaties represented a crystallization of shared norms about political rule and negotiation. The language used in claims and counterclaims reflected the deep grammar of political

---

[2] Black 1997b: 127–28.
[3] Krasner 2001: 34. Also see Lesaffer 2004 on the importance of peace treaties to the development of international law.

authority, the fundamental structure within which rulers contested immediate political outcomes. Although diplomats and other political actors may have sometimes aimed consciously to invent or implement new norms, practices, and institutions, there is a difference between, on the one hand, the issues and goals dealt with directly by diplomats and, on the other, the authoritative framework of territorial versus non-territorial rule. Negotiators were almost always concerned with immediate issues and goals, but they were rarely aware of how their negotiated settlements manifested a transformation in this fundamental framework of rule.[4] In fact, constitutive norms of authority – which shifted only slowly – structured how political actors approached more immediate strategic or tactical issues.

The evolution of the French–Spanish border in the Pyrenees offers an illustration of the complex way in which ideas underlying treaties interacted with political events and structures. Although the 1659 treaty included the agreement that the boundary should follow the "natural frontier" of the mountains, several centuries passed before this boundary was actually delineated and demarcated on the ground (discussed further below). This might appear to indicate that the treaty was disregarded by the relevant actors in their pursuit of political interests. In fact, however, the language in the 1659 treaty influenced how actors pursued their goals in the frontier region – territorial expansion, military defense, and internal administrative reform – meaning that the treaty anticipated later political structures that made the linear boundary real.[5] Thus the language of that treaty was an important determinant of later changes in political practices and institutions.

This chapter details the ways in which maps and map-based political authority claims came to be directly involved in international negotiation. These key examples exhibit the continuing non-cartographic nature of negotiations through the seventeenth century and then the rapid adoption of cartographic tools and ideas in the late eighteenth century. Changing practices led to new institutional outcomes in how peace settlements were made: treaty texts reveal an increasingly territorial focus and a shift from claiming a series of places to delineating boundaries between homogeneous spaces. These trends, which appeared

---

[4] John Ruggie frames this difference by contrasting "constitutive," "configurative," and "positional" wars (Ruggie 1993: 162–63).
[5] Sahlins 1989. See especially pp. 62–63.

in New World claims before their application within Europe, constituted a key step in the transformation of the international system.

This progression is demonstrated by examining the following representative treaties: Arras, 1435; Cateau-Cambrésis, 1559; Westphalia, 1648; the Pyrenees, 1659; Utrecht, 1713; Vienna and Paris, 1814–15; and Versailles, 1919.[6] Each case reveals the prevalent contemporary ideas about political authority, and thus the collection as a whole demonstrates the early modern transformation of territoriality.

The Congress of Arras, 1435

In negotiations during the European Middle Ages, whether it was in formulating goals, negotiating particulars, or implementing an agreement after signing, maps were almost never used. Although proving that diplomats brought no maps to the 1435 Congress of Arras is impossible, the absence of mapping as a negotiating tool is supported by the fact that an entire book-length study of this meeting makes no mention of the use of maps by diplomats, mediators, or rulers.[7] We also know from historical studies of cartography that maps were exceedingly rare in this pre-print era and that the form that maps took would be relatively useless for detailed negotiations.

The negotiations in 1435 among the English king, the French king, and the duke of Burgundy – which yielded no settlement between England and France but did result in an agreement between Burgundy and France, shifting Burgundy's allegiance from England to France – illustrate the medieval notion of territorial authority over a listed series of places. The unsuccessful negotiations between England and France involved demands for control over towns, listed as a series of places and not defined as a homogeneous territory.[8] In the agreement between Burgundy and France, "express mention is made of the

---

[6] These treaties have been chosen for two reasons: first, their illustrative value in demonstrating the transformation in the ideas of political authority; and, second, the central place they have been given in traditional narratives of the historical development of the state system. The latter allows these cases to reveal clearly the ways in which the conventional understanding of historical international relations has been based on a misunderstanding of the actual ideas and practices of different eras. The passages selected for discussion below are representative of language used throughout the treaties.

[7] Dickinson 1955.   [8] Dickinson 1955: 148.

cession of Mâcon, Auxerre, Péronne, Montdidier, Roye, and Bar" as a series of towns, not as delineated spatial areas.[9] In short, the negotiations and treaty demonstrate the medieval notion of spatial authority and its complete dissociation from mapping and homogeneous territoriality. Furthermore, these negotiations involved more than the mere exchange of towns. With non-territorial forms of authority still strong, the question of homage also arose, with the French king in particular demanding homage from the English monarch.[10] Personal feudal relations, thus, continued to be important to the negotiating parties.

Peace of Cateau-Cambrésis, 1559

In 1558–59, France, Spain, and England met to negotiate an end to the Italian wars that had begun at the end of the preceding century. These meetings, which took place at Cercamp and Le Cateau, occurred at the beginning of the early modern growth in the production and use of maps. In spite of sporadic references to maps in the negotiations, however, the forms of authority – both territorial and non-territorial – continued to reflect medieval notions of political control over people and places.

In the several treaties that resulted from these meetings, territorial trades and cessions were still noted in the form of lists of towns. For example, Article 11 of the French–Spanish treaty stated: "The King of Spain shall restore to the King of France S. Quentin, Le Catelet and Ham, with their dependencies."[11] In another example of the continuing relevance of medieval ideas of territoriality, negotiations over control of parts of Piedmont included a proposal by the duke of Savoy to receive several towns; "the towns were, however, not to include all the territory surrounding them."[12] This agreement also illustrates the persistence of non-territorial authorities, as, for example, Section 13 mandated an equal division of revenues from a newly created diocese.[13] Such overlapping jurisdictional divisions did not line up with territorial boundaries, even as territory was traded as a series of places at the same time. The pre-modern, unmapped view of political authority lived on into the sixteenth century, even in agreements at the highest level among the most powerful – and culturally central – polities of Europe.

---

[9] Dickinson 1955: 166.   [10] Dickinson 1955: 150, 167.
[11] Russell 1986: 243.   [12] Russell 1986: 159.   [13] Russell 1986: 202.

Additionally, map use was by no means consolidated as the norm in international negotiation practices. In the discussions over Piedmont, for example, the French "brought out their map and measured out what their King wanted, looking at the map again and again, while Alva and Granvelle [the Spanish negotiators] pretended not to follow."[14] The fact that the cartographic evidence presented by one side could be dismissed by the other – through confusion real or feigned – illustrates the difference between mid-sixteenth-century practices and those of the late 1700s onward, discussed below: in the later period, maps would be the center of negotiations for all parties.

The Treaties of Westphalia, 1648

Contrary to the conventional narrative in International Relations about the innovative and transformative nature of 1648, the treaties signed at Münster and Osnabrück contained little if any change in the deep grammar of political authority. Territory continued to be understood in the medieval fashion, as a series of differentiated places. Additionally, these treaties contained numerous references to "rights" and "privileges" associated with those places, referring to jurisdictional or non-territorial notions of authority, which continued to be asserted in the mid seventeenth century. In the negotiations among diplomats, the same pattern was evident: non-territorial and place-focused territorial authority dominated, as none of the discussions was made with the language or tools of modern geometric territoriality. This is all the more surprising, given that rulers had been using maps for a century or more and had been making purely geometric political claims in the New World since the 1490s. At Westphalia, in short, older notions of rule remained dominant, and new ideas were not implemented.[15]

One close study of the French negotiations over Alsace reveals this pattern clearly.[16] Although one goal for French leaders was to gain

---

[14] Russell 1986: 159.
[15] This could be in part due to the fact that these treaties were more concerned with the internal politics of the Holy Roman Empire than with any larger European settlement (Nexon 2009: ch. 8). Whatever the intended scope of the negotiations, however, the fundamental ideas about the form of political authority are still revealed in the treaties.
[16] Croxton 1999.

control over all of Alsace, the manner in which their negotiating strategy was formed and negotiations undertaken reveals that "all of Alsace" was not defined geometrically or even geographically, but juridically. Maps appear not to have been used by the French, either in the negotiations or in preparations for them, and all discussions were textual, focusing on the description of the various jurisdictions that made up the province. In fact, the complexity of the juridical composition of Alsace was so great that most actors involved had limited or contradictory notions of what they were negotiating over.[17] Had they attempted to implement an exclusively cartographic notion of territorial authority, this confusion would have been avoided: the geographic limits of the territory could have been discussed without regard to the juridical complexities inside those lines.

The resulting treaties reveal the same complexity of political claims. For example, in Article LXXVI of the Treaty of Münster, after listing a series of Alsatian towns to be under the control of the French crown, the following text appeared:

Item, All the Vassals, Subjects, People, Towns, Boroughs, Castles, Houses, Fortresses, Woods, Coppices, Gold or Silver Mines, Minerals, Rivers, Brooks, Pastures; and in a word, all the Rights, Regales and Appurtenances, without any reserve, shall belong to the most Christian King, and shall be for ever incorporated with the Kingdom of *France*.[18]

While this yielded the result of giving control over basically the entire disputed territory to the French crown – and hence sounds similar to the modern notion of exclusive and complete sovereignty over territory – in fact it demonstrates the persistent strength of the medieval notion of territorial authority. Every aspect of the towns concerned had to be explicitly named; it was not yet sufficient simply to delineate a certain spatial area and thereby claim authority over it, and hence over all that went on within it.

In other words, any given place had a related group of non-territorial rights, jurisdictions, and resources that, if they were to be included, had to be named. For example, in the list of possessions to be returned to Austria the following passage appeared:

[17] Croxton 1999: 98, 238ff.   [18] Israel 1967: 31.

Item, The County of *Hawenstein*, the *Black Forest*, the *Upper* and *Lower Brisgaw*, and the Towns situate therein, appertaining of Antient Right to the House of *Austria*, viz. *Neuburg, Friburg, Edingen, Renzingen, Waldkirch, Willingen, Bruenlingen*, with all their Territorys; as also, the Monasterys, Abbys, Prelacys, Deaconrys, Knight-Fees, Commanderships, with all their Bayliwicks, Baronys, Castles, Fortresses, Countys, Barons, Nobles, Vassals, Men, Subjects, Rivers, Brooks, Forests, Woods, and all the Regales, Rights, Jurisdictions, Fiefs and Patronages, and all other things belonging to the Sovereign Right of Territory, and to the Patrimony of the House of *Austria*, in all that Country.[19]

Although the authority was mentioned as a list of places "with all their Territorys," this had to be followed by a careful listing of all the associated personal and jurisdictional authorities – otherwise these might have been considered *not* to have been granted. In later centuries, no such inclusion would be necessary, after the cartographically shaped understanding of territory supplanted these other forms of political authority.

The treaty included many other passages that discussed feudal concepts such as fiefs or vassalage. For example, referring to several German princes, "these Vassals shall be bound to take an Oath of Fidelity to the Lord *Charles Lewis* [the Elector Palatine], and to his Successors, as their direct Lords, and to demand of him the renewing of their Fiefs" (Article XXVII).[20] This reflected the continuing strength of feudal, and hence non-territorial, claims to authority. The combination of feudal and territorial authority created overlapping claims to particular places – an outcome that would have been unacceptable to the parties involved if they had understood rule in terms of territorial statehood.[21]

Finally, the continuing absence of cartographic or geographic language is particularly notable in these documents. There was no discussion of delineating territorial claims or exchanges by the use of linear boundaries, mapped features, or "natural frontier" divisions. The complexity of the passages above demonstrates that it was not yet acceptable simply to describe the geographic limits of a territorial claim and

---

[19] Article LXXXVIII; Israel 1967: 35.
[20] Israel 1967: 16.
[21] See, for example, Article LI, which grants one party a number of "Dependencys … within or without his Territorys" (Israel 1967: 23).

leave it at that – all of the detailed particulars of the territory had to be named for authority to be exchanged. Therefore, in terms of ideas and practices of political rule, the Westphalian settlement shows very little change from the medieval form of authority. Without the consolidation of the modern form of territoriality, what emerges out of 1648 is not the modern international system composed of sovereign states – or even a nascent form of statehood – but instead a continuingly complex organization of jurisdictions, territories, and persons. Westphalia was anything but the founding moment of modern international relations.

Treaty of the Pyrenees, 1659

In the 1650s the rulers of Spain and France began negotiations to resolve the outstanding issues surrounding their boundary in the Pyrenees mountains, as well as authority over parts of the Low Countries. The negotiations leading up to the 1659 treaty demonstrated little in the way of political practices or authority being directly structured by mapping. For example, the chief French minister, Mazarin, "appears to have first consulted a map only after three weeks of discussions."[22] Considering the absence of map use in negotiation, it is hardly surprising that, in the effort to implement the boundary in the Pyrenees, the traditional notions of jurisdictions and place-focused territoriality prevailed.[23]

The treaty itself illustrates this complexity. For example, the portion of the text dealing with the Low Countries reflects the medieval notion of authority over places rather than over space:

It hath been concluded and agreed, concerning the Low Countrys, that the Lord most Christian King shall remain seiz'd, and shall effectually enjoy the Places, Towns, Countrys and Castles, Dominions, Lands and Lordships following. *First*, Within the County of *Artois*, the Town and City of *Arras*, and the Government and Bayliwick thereof; *Hesdin*, and the Bayliwick thereof ...[24]

Once again, the understanding of territorial authority as being held over a collection of places was clear, as was the continuing need to list verbally the aspects of authority that were being asserted.

[22] Sahlins 1989: 39.   [23] Sahlins 1989.   [24] Israel 1967: 66.

Yet this treaty also saw the introduction of a geographic division of Spain and France along the "natural frontier" of the Pyrenees mountains. This principle was introduced in the following passage: "the *Pyrenean* Mountain, which antiently had divided the Gauls from *Spain*, should also make henceforth the division of both the said Kingdoms."[25] This statement was of course ambiguous, particularly given the vague geographic knowledge of the time, so it was followed by: "And that the said Division might be concluded, Commissioners shall be presently appointed on both sides, who shall together, bona fide, declare which are the *Pyrenean* Mountains, which according to the tenor of this Article, ought hereafter to divide both Kingdoms, and shall mark the limits they ought to have."[26]

In spite of this geographically focused language, in order to effect the division on the ground, the older notion of authority over a series of places had to be invoked, in practice as well as in official language. First, the above text was followed by discussion of border counties and who possessed what: "the Lord Most Christian King shall remain in possession, and shall effectually enjoy the whole County and Viquery of *Roussillon*, and the County and Viquery of *Conflans*, the Countrys, Towns, Places, Castles, Boroughs, Villages and Places which make up the said Counties and Viqueries."[27] Furthermore, without direct recourse to mutually agreed-upon maps (something which would appear in later centuries), using the mountains to divide the countries did little to prevent future conflict, since the two sides had different ideas about the relevant topography.[28] Hence the need to resort to older practices of naming towns and associated places for actually achieving a division of the mountain region.

Yet the introduction of the novel idea of dividing France and Spain by using the natural frontier of the Pyrenees did begin a shift away from the use of non-territorial authorities. For example, Article XLIII of the treaty explicitly removed the feudal obligations of Spanish subjects on the French side of the boundary, and vice versa:

The said Lord the Catholick King [of Spain] doth declare, will and intend, that the said Men, Vassals, Subjects [on the French side of the Pyrenees] ... be and remain quitted and absol'v from henceforth and for ever, of the Faith,

---

[25] Israel 1967: 70.   [26] Israel 1967: 71.
[27] Israel 1967: 71.   [28] Sahlins 1989: 43.

Homages, Service and Oath of Fidelity, all and every of them may have made unto him, and to his Predecessors the Catholick Kings; and withal, of all Obedience, Subjection and Vassalage, which therefore they might owe unto him: Willing that the said Faith, Homage and Oath of Fidelity, remain void and of none effect, as if they had never been done or taken.[29]

The implementation of this agreement, however, once again reflected the resilience of non-territorial notions of authority. In fact, after 1659, "The commissioners used the word 'delimitation' and claimed to seek the 'line of division,' but they resorted to ideas of 'jurisdiction' and 'dependency' when dividing up the villages."[30] These non-territorial authorities remained practical and legitimate solutions to the difficulty of dividing control in this frontier region.

Treaty of Utrecht, 1713

In the negotiations ending the War of the Spanish Succession, a wide range of issues emerged, including the separation of the crowns of France and Spain, territorial cessions within Europe, and competing claims in the Americas. The territorial settlements reveal the continuing divergence between how authority was asserted within European space and how it was claimed in the New World from afar.

Like earlier treaties, European territorial settlements were made by listing places to be handed over, as well as their attendant rights and properties. For example, Spain's cession of Gibraltar to Britain took the following form:

The Catholic King does hereby, for himself, his Heirs and Successors, yield to the Crown of Great Britain, the full and entire Propriety of the Town and Castle of Gibraltar, together with the Port, Fortifications, and Forts thereunto belonging; and he gives up the said Propriety, to be held and enjoyed absolutely, with all manner of Right for ever, without any Exception or Impediment whatsoever.[31]

Similar language was used with regard to the transfer of the Kingdom of Sicily to Savoy.[32] As with earlier texts, what is particularly noticeable

---

[29] Israel 1967: 73–74.   [30] Sahlins 1989: 6–7.
[31] Israel 1967: 223.   [32] Israel 1967: 227.

is the absence of cartographic language or the commissioning of surveyors or maps.

Yet in the negotiations themselves, maps were used as a form of supporting evidence for claims and as a means of agreeing to particular divisions of authority.[33] This marked a significant shift. For example, in response to the proposal that France give up some of its frontier territory in the Alps, the French diplomat Colbert de Torcy wrote the following to his British counterpart Bollingbroke in 1712: "Take the trouble, Sir, to examine only the map of the country, and judge if His Majesty could, with any sort of security to his provinces, grant such pretensions?"[34] Whether such an argument was convincing is a separate question, but the invocation of cartographic evidence suggests the increasing legitimacy of map-based political claims. Yet these ideas were not included in the resulting treaty documents; territorial authority continued to be asserted over places and jurisdictions rather than over geographic spaces.

In the negotiations between France and Britain regarding New World colonies, on the other hand, the effect of map use was clear. Maps were used, in fact, as mutually acceptable tools of territorial negotiation:

In December 1712 the French plenipotentiaries sent the king a British map with a British proposal for a boundary between Canada and British territory to the north of it ... A boundary between Canada and Acadia was also marked ... Accordingly, the king returned the British map to Utrecht with a slightly variant northern boundary. Noting that French and British maps often differed, he also sent a mémoire from Pontchartrain outlining the pros and cons of having the boundary pass through specific points.[35]

Although the map was accompanied on its return by a textual description of some points of contention, the negotiations were nonetheless fundamentally structured by the use of a map. This was not the case of one side plying the other with cartographic evidence, but rather an example of both parties using a single cartographic tool to come to an agreement.

---

[33] Black 1999: 65.   [34] Quoted in Osiander 1994: 145.
[35] Miquelon 2001: 666.

The resulting treaty text, then, offers a particularly illustrative example of the continuing divergence between colonial and intra-European ideas about territorial political authority. Unlike the place-focused transfers within Europe, territorial adjustments to New World possessions took the form of geographic descriptions of spaces. For example, the treaty between Britain and France contained the following concerning North America:

The said most Christian King shall restore to the Kingdom and Queen of *Great Britain*, to be possessed in full Right for ever, the Bay and Straits of *Hudson*, together with all Lands, Seas, Sea-Coasts, Rivers, and Places situate in the said Bay and Straits, and which belong thereunto, no Tracts of Land or of Sea being excepted, which are at present possessed by the Subjects of *France* ... But it is agreed on both sides, to determine within a Year, by Commissarys to be forthwith named by each Party, the Limits which are to be fixed between the said Bay of *Hudson* and the Places appertaining to the *French*; which Limits both the *British* and *French* Subjects shall be wholly forbid to pass over, or thereby to go to each other by Sea or by Land. The same Commissarys shall also have Orders to describe and settle, in like manner, the Boundarys between the other *British* and *French* Colonys in those parts.[36]

This practice of establishing boundary commissions after the treaty to survey the relevant territory and to implement the linear division on the ground would become common within Europe only a century later, in 1815.

Conflict in the New World could take such a territorial and cartographic form because of the perception that the continent was relatively empty: "As understood at Utrecht, the empire was also abstract – a simulacrum constructed from dispatches, maps, and theory. Having none of the obduracy of a real world, it was especially amenable to colonialist 'remapping' that seemed rational and realistic."[37] The abstract understanding of these territories made them easily divisible on maps from far away, but the implementation of these divisions proved to be very problematic. Although it is not clear exactly what map was used in the French–British negotiations, all of the probable candidates were commercially produced British maps, filled with the

[36] Article X; Israel 1967: 207–8.   [37] Miquelon 2001: 654.

geographic inaccuracies inherent in early modern "armchair" cartography of distant places.[38] Thus, when it came to implementing the boundaries on the ground, those map divisions that had been easily agreed to from afar became controversial in practice and, in fact, yielded no agreement until further warfare pushed the French out of the region altogether in 1763.

Later eighteenth century

While the Treaty of Utrecht continued to demonstrate the presence of medieval notions of territorial authority within Europe – as places were exchanged in a listing, without any cartographic delineation – the century following would witness the transformation of this aspect of international interaction. In French foreign policy, for example, "The preparation of maps as part of treaty making had been exceptional before 1715; it became routine by 1789," particularly after the institutionalization of mapping in a dedicated office within the ministry of foreign affairs in 1775.[39]

International agreements demonstrated the growing trend as well. While the 1748 Treaty of Aix-la-Chapelle restored the status quo from before the War of Austrian Succession by listing places to be handed back (e.g. Article VI),[40] the treaties involved in the partition of Poland among Austria, Prussia, and Russia in the 1770s through 1790s began to include cartographic delineation of territory of the kind seen extensively at Vienna in 1814–15. In fact, the third partition (in 1795) included both types of territorial language: the listing of "lands, cities, districts and other domains" to be claimed and the division of land using linear demarcations (Articles I and II).[41]

Yet the process was not a simple story of maps being increasingly useful tools of negotiation. In fact, as cartography came to be seen as essential in the second half of the eighteenth century, the inaccuracy of some maps made implementing territorial settlements more difficult rather than easier. For example, in the first partition of Poland, an erroneous map led to problems: "On Giovanni Zannoni's map of Poland, published in January 1772 and used to mark out the Partition, the eastern boundary of the Austrian share was to run along the river

---

[38] Miquelon 2001.   [39] Konvitz 1987: 33, 35.
[40] Israel 1967: 274.   [41] Israel 1967: 422.

Podgórze. But the map was wrong: there was no such river."[42] The use of maps in spite of these difficulties reveals that whether maps served their functional purpose well or ill was not a central concern: no matter their practical limitations, they had come to be understood as essential.

In North America, the ambiguity of the Utrecht settlement between Britain and France led to decades of controversy over exactly where the divisions between the two powers' colonies fell. Significantly, this conflict often took the form of arguments directly concerning maps and the divisions depicted in them. As with many aspects of carto-graphic technology and use, the problematic character of maps served as a source of conflict among European powers first in the colonial world.

This cartographic controversy began immediately following the agreements at Utrecht. Because the French saw mapping as "a means of declaring territorial legitimacy in the face of English encroachments," maps were produced by French cartographer Guillaume Delisle to solidify political claims.[43] Even privately produced maps could be con-troversial – as illustrated by this chapter's epigraph. Similarly, when the Vaugondy family of French mapmakers published a commercial map that showed extensive French territories, the mere fact that the publication was dedicated to a prominent French government minister prompted British officials to accuse their counterparts of making new claims. The publication of another Delisle map also led to boundary disputes and even a direct appeal by the governor of New York "decry-ing the impertinence of the French."[44] Instead of merely complaining, however, the British responded in this case with maps of their own.[45] Maps, in short, were used by each side to try to secure or extend its opposing territorial claims.

Maps were, however, sometimes forced upon political actors in spite of the fact that they preferred not to rely on them. English bound-ary commissioners, for example, wrote the following in an official memorandum:

[M]aps are from the Nature of them a very slight Evidence, Geographers often lay them down upon incorrect Surveys, copying the Mistakes of one

---

[42] Lukowski 1999: 89.   [43] Petto 2007: 100, 106.
[44] Petto 2007: 105.   [45] Reinhartz 1997: 41.

another; and if the Surveys be correct, the Maps taken from them, tho' they may show true Position of a Country ... can never determine the Limits of a Territory.[46]

And yet maps continued to be used by negotiators in the New World.

All of this furor over the depiction of boundaries on maps of the New World – even unofficial ones – occurred during a period in which maps of Europe depicting wildly inaccurate boundaries raised no controversy. As claims in the Americas were made solely on the basis of cartographically depicted territorial exclusivity, however, a map of the New World was politically threatening in a way that maps of Europe were not. In the Old World, traditional notions of territory and jurisdiction continued to form much of the basis of political organization, making maps less of a challenge to existing authority claims.

This explicitly cartographic definition of rule in the Americas was further cemented in the foundation of the newly independent United States – particularly in the 1783 Treaty of Paris that established the boundaries of the new nation. Article II of this treaty established the northern boundary of the United States, using geographic designations ("along the middle of said river") as well as purely geometric ideas, including the 45th parallel.[47] Once again, one of the first independent states to be defined in such cartographic terms was not on the European continent but in the New World where novel technologies, ideas, and practices prevailed.

The Congress of Vienna and the Treaties of Paris, 1814–1815

The series of negotiations and treaties ending the Napoleonic wars consolidated the transformation of the way in which European rulers operationalized territorial political authority. In sharp contrast to the preceding century, territory was divided linearly, with those lines of division described in careful geographic and cartographic terms. Authority was now defined entirely by its boundaries, and places *within* those boundaries were implicitly claimed; no longer did all towns, rights, and jurisdictions have to be explicitly listed.

[46] Petto 2007: 108.   [47] Israel 1967: 346–47.

In the treaty signed at the Congress of Vienna, for example, the redivision of the Duchy of Warsaw among Austria, Prussia, and Russia was effected in an entirely linear fashion:

That part of the Duchy of Warsaw which His Majesty the King of Prussia shall possess in full sovereignty and property, for himself, his heirs, and successors, under the title of the Grand Duchy of Posen, shall be comprised within the following line: – Proceeding from the frontier of East Prussia to the village of Neuhoff ... from thence shall be drawn a line ...[48]

Two features of this text stand out. First is the clear linear nature of the division. This was understood so geometrically that part of the boundary was drawn by "a semi-circular territory measured by the distance" from one town to another.[49] Second, the Prussian King was assigned this territory "in full sovereignty" based *solely* on the delineation of its boundaries – no list of towns or rights was necessary.

Furthermore, even when places were listed in the old style, this listing was no longer sufficient, and the exact territorial delimitation also had to be included. For example, Article VI of the Vienna treaty declared, "The Town of Cracow, with its Territory, is declared to be for ever a Free, Independent, and strictly Neutral City, under the Protection of Austria, Russia, and Prussia."[50] A century earlier, this simple declaration would have been sufficient – the place had been named, and all the related rights and jurisdictions would have been included. In 1815, however, territorial authority was no longer defined from the center outward, and thus the exact boundaries of this neutral entity had to be delineated. Therefore, Article VII stated, "[t]he territory of the Free Town of Cracow shall have for its frontier upon the left bank of the Vistula a line," and then proceeded to describe carefully the placement of that line.[51] Spatial authority could only be claimed geometrically, defined by boundaries, not by a listing of places.

Moreover, these descriptions of boundary lines, although textual in nature, were really not comprehensible without maps, used either for reference or to inscribe the linear divisions onto them. Previous forms of territorial cessions as lists did not require maps to make sense, and in fact maps might have made many of those divisions appear illogical

---

[48] Article II; Israel 1967: 520.   [49] Israel 1967: 521.
[50] Israel 1967: 522.   [51] Israel 1967: 522.

in terms of territorial continuity.[52] At Vienna, territorial authority was understood so geometrically and visually that maps were directly mandated by the treaties. For example, the first Peace of Paris (1814) declared the following concerning the boundaries of France:

[T]here shall be named, by each of the States bordering on France, Commissioners who shall proceed, conjointly with French Commissioners, to the delineation of the respective Boundaries. As soon as the Commissioners shall have performed their task, maps shall be drawn, signed by the respective Commissioners, and posts shall be placed to point out the reciprocal boundaries.[53]

This passage reveals both the explicit demand for the mapping of the boundaries and the instruction to implement that boundary in practice, by placing boundary markers on the ground.

Beyond drawing a line on existing maps, some articles from these treaties demanded an actual survey in order to create detailed maps that did not yet exist. For example, Section I of the second treaty of Paris declared:

The thalweg [deepest channel] of the Rhine shall form the boundary between France and the States of Germany, but the property of the islands shall remain in perpetuity, as it shall be fixed by a new survey of the course of that river, and continue unchanged whatever variations that course may undergo in the lapse of time. Commissioners shall be named on both sides, by the high contracting parties, within the space of three months, to proceed upon the said survey.[54]

Thus maps were not only referenced but actively created in the treaty-making process.

These treaties also removed the remaining non-territorial authority structures from European international politics. From this point on, whatever fell within the boundaries as described fell within the territorial rule of one party. The linear boundary circumscribed the territorial claim completely, while the spatial homogeneity within those lines obscured other forms of authority. Remaining non-territorial authorities, such as feudal rights or privileges, were actively removed

[52] Hale 1971: 52.   [53] Section III; Israel 1967: 505.
[54] Israel 1967: 579.

or waived by the signing parties. For example, on the Swiss cantons the Vienna treaty stated that "feudal rights and tithes cannot be re-established."[55] Concerning the boundary of Saxony with Prussia, the Vienna treaty contained the following exemplary passage:

His Majesty the King of Prussia and His Majesty the King of Saxony ... renounce, each on his own part, and reciprocally in favor of one another, all feudal rights or pretensions which they might exercise or might have exercised beyond the frontiers fixed by the present Treaty.[56]

The process is clear: the linear boundaries so carefully drawn in the text – and to be inscribed on maps – were used to eliminate non-territorial authorities.

The negotiations and treaties from 1814–15 reveal the impact of centuries of map use on European rulers' notions of territorial political authority. No longer defined by a listing of claims over persons, jurisdictions, or places, authority was understood exclusively as a delineated geometric expanse, depicted visually in maps.

Treaty of Versailles, 1919

A century later, the treaty settlement after the First World War demonstrated that the cartographically inspired geometric territoriality seen in 1814–15 was fully consolidated as the only means of operationalizing political authority. In 1919 there were no more non-territorial authorities to renounce, let alone argue over, and the treaty thus dealt exclusively with the careful delineation of homogeneous territorial authority. In spite of fundamental differences between the two treaties in terms of the goals of the major powers – at Vienna, the restoration of the balance of power; at Versailles, the punishment of Germany or the implementation of self-determination – the post-Napoleonic territorial grammar of treaty-making persisted.

First, the language of the treaty, when discussing the drawing of new divisions within Europe, consistently used the phrase "a line to be fixed on the ground." For example, the delineation of the territory of the free city of Danzig (in Article 100) comprised a long description involving both geographic boundaries using rivers and purely cartographic lines

[55] Israel 1967: 554.   [56] Israel 1967: 527.

requiring demarcation on the ground.[57] Second, many linear divisions were described not only in terms of their relation to landmarks or cities but also with purely geometric directional headings and coordinates of latitude and longitude. For example, the delimitation East Prussia – the German enclave territory inside Poland – in Article 28 included the following text:

The boundaries of East Prussia ... will be determined as follows: from a point on the coast of the Baltic Sea about 1½ kilometres north of Probbernau church in a direction of about 159° East from true North: a line to be fixed on the ground for about 2 kilometres; thence in a straight line to the light at the bend of the Elbing Channel in approximately latitude 54° 19½′ North, longitude 19° 26′ East of Greenwich; thence to the easternmost mouth of the Nogat River at a bearing of approximately 209° East from true North ... [etc.].[58]

This type of boundary description remains common in treaties to this day.

Finally, while in 1814–15 maps had been commissioned to help delimit the boundaries described in the treaties, in 1919 maps were not only commissioned for that purpose but, in fact, were *included* in the treaty as attachments. For instance, Article 29 read:

The boundaries as described above are drawn in red on a one-in-a-million map which is annexed to the present Treaty ... In the case of any discrepancies between the text of the Treaty and this map or any other map which may be annexed, the text will be final.[59]

As with property lawsuits in most Western countries today, the text took precedence in the case of disputes.[60] This does not, however, mean that territorial authority was understood in the pre-modern, textually described fashion. In 1919 the authoritative text was not comprehensible without cartography: if a map were not immediately required, it was at least fundamental that a reader of this text understand the basic notions of modern mapping. Without that mindset, drawing boundary lines based on celestial coordinate location would be impossible.

---

[57] Israel 1967: 1338.   [58] Israel 1967: 1291.
[59] Israel 1967: 1292.   [60] Monmonier 1995: ch. 4.

In 1919, many of these cartographic divisions of authority – particularly those proposed by the US delegation – were aimed toward achieving a relatively new goal: establishing political units concomitant with the principle of national self-determination. Although the idealistic purpose of the American commission may have been novel, the means of promoting self-determination were structured by the hegemonic grammar of cartographically defined, territorially exclusive political authority. The Inquiry, as the US planning and negotiating effort was known, relied extensively on academics trained in history and geography and tried to draw "scientific" boundaries for new postwar nation-states. The delegation brought an extensive collection of maps and other material to Paris and produced a summary document for use by US negotiators. This "Black Book" contained extensive maps depicting the goals of the US delegation.[61] Although the placement of boundaries was controversial, the question of whether to draw boundaries – rather than using some other form of division – was never raised. Thus when the head of the Inquiry, Isaiah Bowman, talked about his work after the war, he noted, "Unfortunately, nations cannot be separated approximately. A boundary has to be here, not hereabouts."[62] In spite of the difficulties known to result from drawing linear boundaries to try to separate different national groups (and leaving aside the deeper problem of defining and distinguishing those groups to begin with), the chief negotiators and their advisors in 1919 were left with no other choice than to draw lines between territorial states.

Since 1919, further changes in the normative goals of international negotiation and settlement have not undermined the principle of territorial exclusivity but have, instead, provided new aims to be pursued using the techniques, tools, and ideas of map-based political authority.

The overall direction of the early modern shift in treaty language concerning political authority is clear: from a careful listing of jurisdictions, persons, and places with their attendant rights and resources to an equally careful delineation of geometrically defined expanses. The timing of the transformation contradicts the traditional IR narrative of "Westphalian" statehood: through the early eighteenth century, territorial exchanges were made without maps or cartographic

---

[61] Reisser 2012. See also Crampton 2006; Heffernan 2002.
[62] Quoted in Reisser 2012: 14.

language – in other words, without the territorial exclusivity that defines the modern state system. Moreover, the medieval form of territorial authority easily coexisted with non-territorial authorities – all of them could be listed together in one text, as was the case in major treaties well past 1648. With the modern form of linear, geometric, homogeneous territorial authority, however, it became more difficult to accommodate territorial and non-territorial authority types in the same document. In order to make international agreements work, non-territorial authorities were ignored and even directly renounced.

Thus, the culmination of the shift in ideas in the early nineteenth century represented a complete transformation of sovereign authority, as detailed in Chapter 2, from mixed to solely territorial and from overlapping to exclusive. Linear boundaries and homogeneous territory leave no place for overlap. The early nineteenth-century drive toward exclusivity, therefore, extended to places previously shared, such as bridges over rivers between political jurisdictions. The Second Treaty of Paris (1815), for example, stated that on the Rhine, "[o]ne half of the bridge between Strasburg and Kehl shall belong to France, and the other half to the Grand Duchy of Baden."[63] Nothing could be left undivided.

This fundamental transformation in ideas about political organization was not just about actors using a new (ideational and technological) tool to pursue their goals, such as territorial security or aggrandizement. Instead this process *created* those very goals – made them imaginable and appealing – and simultaneously made other types of political goals unimaginable or illegitimate. Sovereignty, after all, is both the norm that structures the rational pursuit of actors' interests (territorial expansion, self-preservation as an independent entity) and the norm that constitutes actors as territorial entities in the first place.[64] Moreover, as actors came to conceive of authority exclusively in territorial terms, they also found that pursuing goals based on those conceptions could be politically useful, both within their own polities and internationally. Cartography and other tools of territorial rule thus not only enable certain political practices and organizations; they also constitute those practices as conceivable or legitimate in the first place. The next chapter illustrates this mutual constitution of political and cartographic ideas and practices by closely examining the influential case of France.

---

[63] Article I; Israel 1967: 579.   [64] Parsons 2007: 30.

7 | Mapping the territorialization of France

We tend to think of territoriality as a state of mind, a way of feeling about a portion of land, but the territoriality that developed in seventeenth-century France was, first of all, a form of material practice, a way of acting on the land that helped to make it seem like France.[1]

Over the course of the seventeenth and eighteenth centuries, France was transformed from a complex realm, defined by a myriad of authority structures, into a sovereign state, ruled by centralized authority claims over a defined, delimited, and mapped territory. As the passage above suggests, this process was simultaneously institutional, ideational, and material. Examining this particularly influential case of territorialization reveals the close interplay between cartographic technologies, political ideas inspired by those technologies, and changing material practices of rule that built upon both. The mapped image of France produced in the sixteenth and seventeenth centuries reshaped how French kings and their advisors went about centralizing, standardizing, and consolidating their rule, culminating during the Revolution in the creation of one of the first exclusively territorial states in Europe. This history demonstrates the interaction between the territorializing impact of cartography and the early modern impetus toward centralization.

For a number of reasons, France is an especially useful case for close examination. First, French history serves as a representative example of the shift that occurred throughout Europe during the seventeenth, eighteenth, and nineteenth centuries: the replacement of overlapping territorial and non-territorial authorities – asserted over persons, places, and jurisdictions – with centralized territorial rule over a boundary-defined space. Second, not only does France represent

---

[1] Mukerji 1997: 9.

this overall trend, French territorialization also served as an influential model that was followed, implicitly or explicitly, by many rulers throughout Europe.[2] French practices, from major state mapping projects to the demarcation and administration of linear boundaries, were often imitated in other territorializing states. While some efforts in other states were nearly simultaneous with the French (in Sweden, for instance), many others followed upon the successful use of new cartographic tools by France (in Hapsburg Austria, for example). Third, because French history is well documented, it clearly reveals both the changes in state practices and the sources of those changes in new cartographic techniques and ideas.

Finally, the manner in which this well-established history of France has been constructed – predominantly in the nineteenth-century "national history" tradition – has created an anachronistic view of the political structure of early modern France, one that requires significant revision. Modern arrangements have been read backward into periods where they did not actually exist, resulting, for example, in an image of France as a unified, territorially discrete entity long before it had become one.[3] Because France served as an early and influential model for later practices in other polities, overturning the conventional narrative about French territorialization supports my argument that territorial states emerged significantly later that previously thought – only after the mid eighteenth century and not before.[4] Once this timing is established, the role played by sixteenth- and seventeenth-century mapping, both commercial and official, becomes clear.

What, then, was the actual course of territorialization in France? How did the medieval French polity – defined by a mix of personal and territorial authorities – become the centralized, territorial state of the Revolutionary period and after? Even in the fifteenth century,

---

[2] And, perhaps, beyond: see Hostetler 2001 on the parallel use of mapping and territorial consolidation in Qing China.

[3] Of course, not all historical studies of France read backwards in this way. Among the numerous revisionist accounts, Sahlins 1989 serves as an extremely useful source for my description of French political and cartographic ideas and practices. In much of the social science literature, however, these revisions have not been incorporated, leading to a persistently anachronistic understanding of early modern political forms.

[4] France therefore serves in some ways as a "least-likely" case for my argument; on this method see George and Bennett 2005: 120–23.

at the very end of the Middle Ages, France remained a polity of a fundamentally medieval type: a complex collection of diverse forms of rule over persons and places, heterogeneous internally and defined externally by loose control over frontiers. French kings and their ministers attempted to reshape this polity throughout the sixteenth, seventeenth, and eighteenth centuries, but the consolidation of France as a territorial entity defined by discrete boundaries and exclusive claims to rule within those lines did not take place until the middle of the eighteenth century and after. In other words, this transformation took significantly longer than we might expect and longer than has been traditionally ascribed. Furthermore, this process, which was often contested and sometimes temporarily reversed, involved the layering of new practices on top of old ones, rather than the immediate displacement of the earlier by the later.

Maps and other cartographic tools were integrally involved throughout this territorialization of rule, both as material objects that reshaped political ideas and as tools that enabled new assertions of authority and control. Combined with the drive toward centralization pursued by French rulers, the eventual result was the consolidation of a state defined entirely in territorial terms. The new, predominantly commercial, depictions of France in the sixteenth and early seventeenth centuries created new conditions of possibility for how French rulers thought about their realm, lending new strength to the notion of discrete boundaries around a homogeneous spatial territory. Subsequently, when rulers began to assert this transformed idea of rule through material practices (both at frontiers and internally), these practices included the commissioning of extensive, survey-based mapping projects to delineate, and thereby to claim, territory. Yet these government mapping projects built directly, if implicitly, on the foundation provided by a century of commercial mapping, making use of the visual grammar of geometric cartography and even improving on the medium's ability to achieve its ideal: the accurate depiction of space as a measured surface. Thus, these new official maps enabled the delineation of territorial boundaries to a degree of precision previously unavailable, but they did so only because earlier mapping had made hegemonic this particular way of defining and asserting authority. This chapter will track these interrelated changes in mapping and political rule in France, from the medieval kingdom to the post-Revolutionary state.

Mapping France, territorializing French rule

In the Middle Ages, France was a typical medieval polity, defined by complex and varied forms of rule. This "mosaic state, made up of many pieces," was held together only loosely by central authority.[5] Even as late as the fifteenth century, the legacy of feudalism meant that much of the French king's authority was based on personal ties, or bonds conceptualized as personal ties, between ruler and ruled. These ties of vassalage were complex and often led to situations of overlapping authority between different lords, preventing the king from exercising the kind of centralized authority that would appear later. Yet France was nonetheless understood as a single political entity – at least in theory – even if it took on a form fundamentally different from that of a modern state. In short, France was an assemblage of diverse pieces rather than having a single unified structure.[6]

Medieval French kings understood and operationalized their rule through the use of techniques and tools that allowed for and reflected this complexity in political ideas and practices. During the Middle Ages, French rulers predominantly gathered and recorded information about their realm through written surveys. These "inventories" appeared at least as early as the beginning of the thirteenth century and became standardized by the early fourteenth century into extensive and thorough archives. This approach persisted into the following century, as Louis XI (r. 1461–83), for example, even "set out himself in order to satisfy his thirst for knowledge" about the lands and peoples under his rule.[7] This kind of firsthand observation was very different from the later use of maps as tools for gathering and processing information: maps made it dramatically easier to rule from afar, without direct knowledge of the territory. Yet listing domains, places, and vassals in textual surveys did allow for the complexity of the traditional forms of authority that French kings had gathered, because all could be listed together.

On the other hand, visual means for the depiction or assertion of authority claims were used only rarely. When they were used, the resulting images differed fundamentally from later maps. For example,

[5] Strayer 1970: 53.
[6] Bloch 1961: 425. See also Duby 1968; Finer 1997; Mitteis 1975; and Sahlins 1989.
[7] Revel 1991: 137.

a manuscript about French dynastic genealogy and legitimacy from *c.*
1460 contains a map about which the scribe writes: "This image contains all of the realm of France."[8] (See Figure 7.1.) The image depicts
the French kingdom schematically, with the dominant features on the
map being a large number of cities and towns marked in relation to
each other generally and with no features shown in between. This is
an essentially place-focused notion of authority, asserted over towns
themselves rather than over the spatial expanse within which towns
are located. Similarly, France itself takes on the appearance of an island,
floating independent of any neighboring realms, rather than appearing as a discretely bounded entity defined by borders of mutual exclusion with other states. Nonetheless, "[i]t is clear … that the scribe's
intentions were to articulate a coherent and persuasive expression of a
unified, bountiful, and independent French kingdom and to record an
explicit statement of defiance against the English."[9] This kind of propagandistic use of a map is a common feature of all periods of cartography, but the image nonetheless reveals the fundamental grammar of
rule at the time. In short, the map is a visual list and thus fits well with
the complexity of medieval authority types, as any and all claims over
places can be drawn without regard to their geographic complexity.[10]

Mapping, of course, changed radically in the late fifteenth century.
Ptolemy's *Geography* was translated, printed, and widely distributed,
with many copies containing maps drawn with the geometric grid of
latitude and longitude rather than using the schematic basis of medieval cartography (as discussed in Chapter 3). Thus, for example, the
first "modern" map of France was published in a 1480 edition of
Ptolemy.[11] As was the case with the rest of the European continent,
during the sixteenth century France was mapped by commercial printers and mapmakers.

French rulers began to use maps in the late fifteenth century,
although, as was the case throughout Europe, this use remained limited. For example, when King Charles VIII of France (r. 1483–98) used
maps of the Alpine passes to aid in his invasion of the Italian peninsula

---

[8] Translation by Serchuk (2006: 143).
[9] Serchuk 2006: 134.
[10] As can be seen in efforts in historical atlases today to show the extent of
French medieval rule using the modern cartographic grammar of discretely
bounded spaces – the results are bizarre patchwork quilts of territories.
[11] Pelletier 2007: 1480.

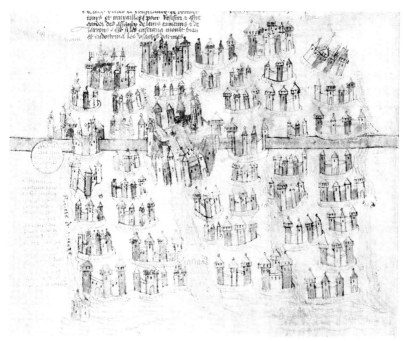

Figure 7.1 Manuscript map of France, *c.* 1460

in 1495 – often cited as an example of "modern" map use – what made
the maps useful were the extensive textual annotations they contained.
Even in the middle of the sixteenth century, when Catherine de' Medici
asked Nicolas de Nicolay, a royal geographer, for a "detailed description of the kingdom," no map of the whole kingdom was ever produced – the project was terminated with only two provinces mapped.[12]
By the time of the reign of Henry IV (r. 1589–1610), some official
cartographic efforts were underway. For example, the *ingénieurs du
roi* not only mapped the fortifications they designed, but also created
maps of the countryside. Such maps were significant: "These came to
influence the way in which many generations of French people 'saw'
their country."[13]

Yet even these efforts were far from centralized and standardized in
the way that mapping would become a century later. The work of the

---

[12] Buisseret 1992b: 106; Pelletier 2007: 1485, 1503.
[13] Buisseret 2007a: 1513.

ingénieurs du roi never culminated in a standardized representation of the entire realm – nor were their regional mapping projects intended to do so.[14] In other words, "Most of the sixteenth-century regional maps of France were made for different reasons by men of different education and background and were not intended to cover the whole kingdom."[15] The kind of centralized mapping that we are familiar with today would appear only much later.

Nonetheless, although official mapmaking was sporadic, the mapping of France by commercial printers took off in the sixteenth century. These depictions created a fundamentally new image of French territory – an image that would become influential on rulers' ideas and practices. Based on the Ptolemaic grid of latitude and longitude and using the developing techniques of printing and coloring, France as it appeared on maps of this period came to resemble a homogeneous territorial entity defined by discrete divisions and analogous to all other mapped territories. This shift in visual representation occurred over the course of the sixteenth century. In 1525, for example, Oronce Fine published what was probably the first map of France made by a French mapmaker. The map, explicitly described as "setting down the whole of Gaul," focused on the depiction of places – as medieval maps of France had done – but located those places in terms of their coordinate position on the geometric grid, that is, using the Ptolemaic innovation.[16] Although this map had inaccurate coordinates for many cities, it still fulfilled its purpose, which was to make a propagandistic statement of French territorial claims and ambitions.[17] Yet the map's failure to contain a clear depiction of linear boundaries surrounding France revealed the gradual layering of the new, geometric depiction and understanding of French territory over the medieval place-focused ideas.

With the rapid increase in commercial mapping during the sixteenth century, however, depictions of France were eventually transformed. Thus, the first atlases (published in the 1570s) had maps of Europe and France drawn according to the latitude–longitude grid, and they gradually adopted an increasing number of discrete boundary lines and homogeneously color-filled spaces.[18] We can see the transformed image of France in the 1595 *Atlas Cosmographicae*, by Gerhard

[14] Buisseret 2007a; Pelletier 2007: 1489.
[15] Pelletier 2007: 1489.   [16] De Dainville 1970: 52.
[17] Revel 1991: 149–50.   [18] Akerman 1995.

Figure 7.2 Atlas map of France, Gerhard Mercator, *Atlas Cosmographicae*, 1595

Mercator. Like other sixteenth-century atlases, this work contained a number of maps, drawn to a variety of scales, building on and superseding the maps discussed by Ptolemy. Figure 7.2 shows the map of France, labeled "Gallia." France is depicted as a homogeneous territory defined by linear geographic features (rivers and mountains) and filled in with a color that distinguishes it from surrounding territories. As with the other maps in this atlas, the image was built on the latitude–longitude grid but was preceded by a page containing a listed inventory of the places depicted on the map. Thus, like the 1525 map, this combination reveals a layering of place-focused and spatially defined notions of territory – but in this case, the image has clearly shifted toward homogeneous spatial depiction. And this shift would not be reversed, as maps continued along the path toward geometric measurement and accuracy.

This visual grammar made possible a reimagining of the French polity as a boundary-defined territory rather than as a mosaic of heterogeneous authorities. The effects of this type of image would later appear in the political ideas and practices of rulers and elites in France, but only gradually, because place-focused forms of rule proved to be remarkably resilient during the seventeenth century. Thus, at the end of the sixteenth century, France remained a political entity defined as much by jurisdictional sovereignties as by territory – even as contemporary maps showed a very different image. Furthermore, the form of territoriality being practiced involved authority over listed places rather than over delineated spaces. Yet the French polity had become more centralized since the late Middle Ages – the late sixteenth-century civil wars, for example, were contests over who would control the center, rather than conflicts among different peripheral actors.[19] Nonetheless, this increasingly centralized authority continued to be asserted, both internally and externally, over specific places, jurisdictions, and persons.[20]

Thus, although France would eventually emerge as one of the first fully territorialized states of Europe, this change took significantly longer than has often been argued. The seventeenth-century notion of frontier "rationalization" – a policy actively pursued by French kings and their advisors – was actually shaped by the persistently non-linear idea of territorial authority and was driven by practical military needs rather than new or changed norms. It was not until well into the eighteenth century and later that the idea of rationalization took on its modern form: eliminating overlaps and enclaves and demarcating linear boundaries. Centralization, in short, had long been a goal of French kings and their advisors, but it was only with the use of new cartographic tools and ideas that rulers were able to assert the territorially defined claim to direct rule that we now recognize as part of sovereign statehood.

With the increasing production of commercial and official maps depicting the world as a homogeneous surface during the early seventeenth century, we can observe the first stages of this transformation, as maps began to reshape how rule would come to be understood. Maps and their use, particularly governmental efforts to gather information

---

[19] Collins 1995: 22ff.   [20] Sahlins 1989.

about the peripheries of France, began to create the conditions of possibility for the exclusively territorial form of rule that would be put into practice later. The use of maps changed both the process and the product of official "surveying" and information-gathering. Mapping imposed a particular form of simplification and territorialization of authority claims, as a map could include only those types of claims that the visual grammar of early modern mapping allowed, a grammar fundamentally different from the medieval use of textual inventories of places, persons, and jurisdictions.

The work of Claude de Chastillon, a royal engineer, illustrates this process.[21] Sent in 1608 by the king to survey one of France's complex frontiers, Chastillon reported back to the crown both with a written description and with maps. While Chastillon's particular maps have been lost, David Buisseret has compared a contemporaneous map of the same frontier region against Chastillon's written description, positing that the map was likely based on Chastillon's surveying. Thus, Buisseret's comparison offers an opportunity to see how cartographers dealt with the complexity of political authority in frontier regions at the beginning of the seventeenth century:

The *château* of Passavant, he [Chastillon] says, belongs to Lorraine, though the town and wood are French. Baffled by the problem of distinguishing between these areas, our cartographer has drawn a little enclave, with a *château* in the south of it. At Martinvelle, three-quarters of a league from Passavant, all the hearths owe tax to the king of France; this village, according to Chastillon, was partially French and partially *lorrain*. On our map it is shown as lying in Lorraine. Selles, though west of the Saône, belonged to Franche-Comté according to Chastillon, and is so shown on the map. Vauvillers was a more difficult case, in dispute between France, Lorraine and Franche-Comté; the map shows it as lying some distance inside Franche-Comté.[22]

Chastillon's written description is able to capture each particular aspect of complex authority along this frontier, while the subsequent map is forced to simplify in order to make a readable, easily produced visual document. Overlapping or unclear claims are simply eliminated by placing the village in question inside the boundary line of one side

[21] Buisseret 1984a, 1984b.   [22] Buisseret 1984a: 78.

or by drawing an enclave around it. Yet even the pictured enclave represents a fundamentally exclusive and territorial notion of political authority, held over a boundary-defined space, rather than the complexity of existing practices.

In fact, those existing authorities are revealed by the criteria Chastillon listed in his effort to delineate the frontier:

Feudal Allegiance: to whom did the inhabitants of a given territory owe allegiance? This, of course, was established by taking sworn statements ... Fiscal Dependence: To whom had taxes been paid, and from what *greniers* had salt been bought? ... Judicial Dependence: Where were law-cases judged?[23]

All of these criteria represent fundamentally non-territorial forms of authority: personal feudal ties and jurisdictionally defined authorities. Yet the map that was drawn to depict the same information converted these non-territorial links to an image of territorial authority, and a discretely bounded one at that. The tendency of Ptolemaic cartography toward simplification and territorialization of political relations is operationalized in conversions such as these, performed whenever a map was produced to depict complex authority structures.[24]

Although this process illustrates the tendency toward map-driven simplification of territorial complexity in the *representation* of political authority, it did not lead immediately to the *implementation* of linear territoriality on the ground. On the contrary, the textual description of the complex and overlapping boundary – and not the simplified visual form that the boundary took in the map – was retained in official

---

[23] Buisseret 1984b: 104.

[24] While this may sound like an example of the "primitive" or "unscientific" nature of early modern cartography, this difficulty in depicting authorities or relations other than exclusive territoriality persists today. For example, Rekacewicz (2000) finds it nearly impossible to map African political theorist Achille Mbembe's conception of the continent that replaces traditional boundaries with "an unobstructed view, identifying regions or territories not in terms of their location but rather in terms of shifts in global politics and global economics that have had an impact on these regions" (703). Moreover, "The complexity of Mbembe's schema did not therefore allow for comprehensive visual representation. For example, the relations or forms of exchange between different regions, crucial aspects of the analysis, could not appear on the map without making the map overburdened and thus illegible" (704). Once again, complex relations and structures that can be described textually must be simplified in order to appear on a map.

records. Thus, the contention that this map serves as "an example of the way in which the theories of the political philosophers, concerning the nature of sovereignty and territorial control, came to be translated into reality on the ground"[25] overstates the case, anticipating practical developments that came only later. Drawing the map, simplifying the boundary into a line between two homogeneous spaces, was merely the *first* step toward implementation, not the last. Although these types of maps provided the ideational framework for that shift, this mapping project did not immediately change actual practices of internal administration or interaction with neighboring polities.

During the seventeenth century, in fact, the policies of frontier "rationalization" pursued by French kings and their advisors remained focused on authority and control over places rather than delineating discrete boundaries to define the extent of French rule. This involved a strategy of fortifying the frontiers of the kingdom and removing fortifications from the interior. For example, a memorandum of 1629 from Cardinal Richelieu to Louis XIII (r. 1610–43) after the capture of La Rochelle (a key internal stronghold of the Huguenots) contained the following: "All fortresses not on the frontier must be razed; we should keep only those at river crossings or which serve as a bridle to mutinous great towns. Those which are on the frontier must be properly fortified."[26] Similarly, Richelieu's *Political Testament* argues: "It is necessary to be deprived of common sense to be ignorant of how important it is to great states to have their frontiers well fortified."[27] Although these policies and recommendations have sometimes been read as efforts to make the boundaries of France linear, in fact they never go into any detail on the character of the borders. Both recommend merely that the frontiers – however defined – should be strongly defended. Compared with what happened in the following century when the idea took on a much more detailed form, this push toward frontier defense is not evidence of the linearization of territorial boundaries.

The long reign of Louis XIV (r. 1643–1715) witnessed a continuation of the trend toward fortification but, as in to the preceding period, did not involve the linearization of French boundaries. Thus Louis XIV's

---

[25] Buisseret 1984a: 78.
[26] Quoted in Bonney 1988: 9.
[27] Hill 1961: 120. Note that although the authorship of the *Political Testament* is uncertain, it was almost certainly written during this period.

expansionary foreign policy involved the growth of French territory without changing the way in which authority was asserted over places and persons. For example, although the 1659 Treaty of the Pyrenees established the idea of a linear boundary on the mountains, it did not lead to the actual implementation of such a boundary on the ground.[28] Louis XIV's policy toward the frontier with the Netherlands and the German territories also lacked any direct effort to implement linearly defined territorial authority. In many cases, Louis XIV actually promoted enclave-filled frontier zones in order to support his expansionist goals on these borders.[29] Thus, many of his annexations were in the form of fiefs or jurisdictions rather than linearly contained spaces.[30] For example, in the 1680s Louis set up "chambers of reunion," bodies created to find legal justifications for annexing territories and jurisdictions from neighboring principalities. In order to demand new territories, these annexations made use of the idea that any town had "dependencies," citing what were often dubious historical claims.[31] The ways in which frontier territories were subsequently annexed continued to reflect non-geometric ideas of territorial authority, as traditionally defined jurisdictions were passed unchanged from one ruler to another.[32] In addition, the military nature of these frontiers made claiming – and then having to defend – a clear line of division impractical, since it would have been more difficult than defending towns or forts.[33]

The career of Sébastien Le Prestre, Seigneur de Vauban, France's chief military engineer in the late seventeenth century, also serves to illustrate the complexity of the actual process of frontier rationalization. Vauban was closely involved in French military strategy, planning, and fortification construction. In this capacity, he proposed that France's frontiers be converted into a *pré carré*, a term for a "dueling ground" that "connotes a regularly shaped arena of well-defined perimeters."[34] Vauban wanted this "squaring off" to be a primary goal of French military strategy.[35] More specifically, Vauban proposed a double series

---

[28] Sahlins 1989.   [29] Black 1997b: 123.
[30] Febvre 1973: 214.   [31] Black 1999: 45.
[32] Miquelon 2001: 672–73.   [33] Sahlins 1989: 65.
[34] Hebbert and Rothrock 1990: 41.
[35] Lynn 1999: 75. The primacy of this goal to Vauban is made clear by the fact that he was apparently "baffled" when peace negotiations were sometimes completed without making gains toward rationalized frontiers (Hebbert and Rothrock 1990: 57).

of fortifications along France's frontiers, particularly those that were less easily defended due to geography. This would be combined with continuing efforts to eliminate all fortresses internal to France as well as those fortifications held well beyond the French frontiers.[36]

The conventional assessment of Vauban sees him as driving a process of active and conscious rationalization of France's frontiers, making them both more linearly defined and more strongly fortified. This would appear to represent a significant step toward the material implementation of linearly bounded territorial authority. Yet the fortification strategy actually executed by Vauban reveals that his efforts had little to do with implementing new ideas of exclusive territoriality and were driven instead by purely practical military needs. To modern observers who have internalized the "rationality" of linearly bounded territory, the very idea of "rationalizing" frontiers implies linearity. To a practical military planner of the seventeenth century like Vauban, however, rationalization simply implied making the kingdom more defensible and lowering the expense of securing territorial gains.

Vauban's writings advocating the double line of fortifications make no reference to notions of territory or sovereignty in itself; he is, instead, entirely focused on the practical defensibility of the kingdom (and especially the cities within it) through the use of fortified points. For example, Vauban briefly proposed fortifying Paris itself, due to its cultural, economic, and political importance to the kingdom.[37] For Vauban, the problem with such a construction was not that it contradicted a notion of internal territorial homogeneity (by focusing on the center rather than the boundaries), but rather that it was impractical. Thus both his ends (protection of Paris and other major cities) and his means (forts and fortified towns in frontier zones) were *place-focused* rather than imagined in terms of linearly defined spatial expanses.

Although France's frontiers remained zones of military conflict and overlap, Louis XIV's reign did mark the beginning of territorialization internally, particularly in the activities of Jean-Baptiste Colbert, the minister of finance from 1665 to 1683. Colbert considered the centralization and rationalization of the complexities of the French state to be a key goal.[38] One project that Colbert initiated was a significantly

---

[36] Hebbert and Rothrock 1990: 142–43.
[37] Hebbert and Rothrock 1990: 188.
[38] Yet this was a goal towards which Colbert could make only limited progress. As one scholar notes, he "could only reform, not destroy, the internal tolls

more central role for mapping – and map production – in the internal administration of France.[39] Thus, while Louis XIV's rule continued over a collection of places in practice, in terms of the official depictions of his rule we see the shift toward geometric ideas represented by the visual grammar of mapping. Yet these mapping efforts were only a first step toward linearization – the *depiction* of rule as exclusively territorial and linearly bounded – and were part of the cause, not the effect, of the later implementation of linear rule. During the seventeenth century, mapping consistently showed an image that anticipated later linear boundaries rather than the military complexities of existing frontier zones.[40]

Under the direction of Colbert and his successors, the production of maps by official agencies became central to statecraft. Yet this government-sponsored mapping was built on the foundation provided by non-governmental mapping and technical innovations from the preceding two centuries. In other words, when advisors to Louis XIV commissioned exhaustive survey-based maps of the realm (as discussed below), this was merely the latest link in a long chain of ideational and material changes. In the sixteenth century, printed maps and atlases showed a new image of the world, including France in particular, as homogeneous space defined by linear divisions, and knowable through scientific measurement and mapping. This, in turn, created demands for continued technological improvements, but *in a particular direction*, that is, improvements oriented toward more accurate geometric measurement and recording. The innovations in geometric surveying techniques that followed were specifically designed to allow for extremely accurate measurement and mapping of space, including the linking together of close-in, survey-based measurements with the mapping of entire regions. It was at this point in the process that the mapping project discussed below appears – in other words, even the very desire to measure France in this particular way had been created by the preceding century, or more, of map use and the ideational change that grew out of it.

so pernicious to commerce. He also failed in his efforts to introduce some regional standardization into the system of weights and measures" (Collins 1995: 92).

[39] This was just one part of Colbert's larger project of putting scientific projects to work for the better administration of France. See Soll 2009.

[40] Sahlins 1989.

In the 1660s, Colbert began to include mapping in his efforts at internal reform. Soon after entering his office, Colbert realized that

he had no maps that could help him with two investigations he deemed of paramount importance: the visualization of the complex and overlapping administrative divisions of France (that were in dire need of simplification), and a thorough and accurate assessment of the kingdoms' income, necessary for economic and tax reforms. These two concerns were expressed in an inquiry circulated in 1663–64.[41]

This led, first, to a request that regional authorities send in all the maps that could be gathered depicting their domains, which were then to be collated by Nicolas Sanson, the royal geographer. During the preceding decades, Sanson had undertaken similar though unsuccessful efforts to collate existing sources into a single, legible guide for the king and his ministers.[42]

Thanks to the unsatisfactory level of accuracy in this kind of mapping, however, Colbert began looking into the production of maps covering all of France based on firsthand observation. To this end, in the late 1660s he commissioned Jean-Dominique Cassini, an established astronomer and cartographer, to create a survey-based series of maps of the entire realm, initiating a mapping project that ultimately spanned multiple generations.[43] From the beginning, this project was intended to correct the inaccuracies and inconsistencies of previous maps by conducting triangulation-based observational surveys of the entire realm. The theoretical tools for this approach had been established by the 1620s, but the funding, knowledge, and accurate instrumentation required came together only in the 1660s with the Cassini project. One of the first results of this new approach was the production of the map, discussed in Chapter 1, comparing the accurate coastal outline of France to that of Sanson's maps (see Figure 1.1).[44]

It took nearly eighty years for the first complete set of maps of France to be published, with the country covered by eighteen equivalently

---

[41] Pelletier 1998: 44.   [42] Konvitz 1987: 2; Pelletier 2007.
[43] Konvitz 1987; Turnbull 1996.
[44] In fact, the map comparing the two outlines was published in 1693, illustrating the persistent importance of commercial map production, even in the case of an officially commissioned project. Petto 2007: 7, 57.

scaled sheets. Although such an extensive process would have been slow in any case, the project was also delayed by numerous setbacks. For one, official funding for the required fieldwork disappeared for several decades, only reappearing in the 1730s when the government realized it needed more complete maps for public works and infrastructure projects. Also, surveyors were sometimes treated hostilely by peasants and local authorities, often out of fear that more information in the government's hands would lead to more taxes.[45] Additionally, while this fundamentally geometric survey of France was ongoing, different forms of surveying persisted in other official projects. For example, in 1708 the regional estates of Burgundy commissioned Guillaume Delisle to map their region, but the request was phrased in terms of places, rights, and obligations. Just as in the case of Chastillon a century earlier, however, the map ended up recording political relations in a discretely bounded territorial fashion that failed to reflect the full complexity of existing political rule on the ground.[46]

When the Cassini project's eighteen sheets were finally published in 1744, it represented the first successful effort to map an entire realm using direct observation and surveying. The territory of France had thus become a mapped and measured expanse, to which the king could lay a claim based on the most scientific form of information-gathering of the day. (Figure 7.3 shows the triangulation involved in measuring the major axes of France.) The importance of this achievement was not lost on contemporaries: "People who never saw even a portion of the Cassini survey nonetheless knew that France had been mapped in unprecedented detail and accuracy. The Cassini map represented the conquest of space through measurement."[47] When the French government began a new, more detailed survey only four years later – growing out of the army's desire for greater accuracy for military planning – other rulers throughout Europe took up similar projects and pursued them in the decades that followed (as discussed in Chapter 4).

During the early eighteenth century, rule by the French crown was still understood and operationalized predominantly in terms of persons and jurisdictions, rather than territory.[48] With the growing availability and use of tools such as the Cassini maps, however, the ideational impetus and material instruments for a more territorial form of rule

---

[45] Konvitz 1987: 14.   [46] Petrella 2009.
[47] Konvitz 1987: 21.   [48] Sahlins 1989: 78.

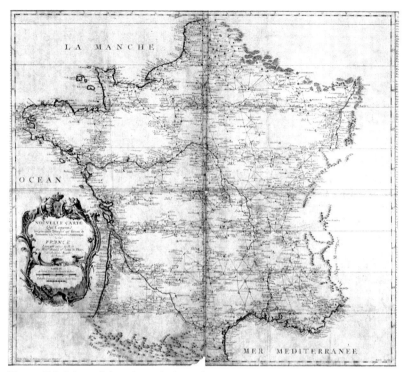

Figure 7.3 Map of the triangulation of France, *c.* 1744

were in place. Thus, for example, the first efforts to linearize the complex portions of the frontier in the Pyrenees came in the 1730s, when Spanish officials surveyed frontier areas for property taxation. In this process, they attempted to draw a straight-line division that cut across existing properties and jurisdictions.[49] While this new line failed to be implemented, it did represent an early example of a trend often to be repeated later: detailed surveying combined with international boundary demarcation.

In the second half of the eighteenth century, then, the "rationalization" of the frontiers of France took on a new form, shaped by the depiction of rule as linear and homogeneous in maps. This also marked a shift away from Louis XIV's expansive foreign policy of the preceding century, as late eighteenth-century French rulers and ministers

---

[49] Sahlins 1989: 85–86.

focused instead on maintaining the status quo, trying to solidify the advances Louis XIV had made.[50] Linear borders, as depicted by mapping, offered a means to accomplish this goal. Only in this period – after the first Cassini project was completed and published – were efforts made to implement linear boundaries and exclusive territoriality on the ground. Maps, in other words, provided both the impetus and the tools for territorialization, which had come to be understood as essential to the longstanding goal of centralizing rule in the hands of the king and his advisors.

The primary institutional form that this new goal and practice of linearization took was the treaty-making activity of the French foreign ministry, "which in the second part of the eighteenth century developed a coherent policy of 'establishing and fixing the limits of the kingdom'."[51] Thus the 1770s and 1780s saw a number of treaties signed with France's neighbors, both to clarify control over remaining zonal frontiers – by making boundaries linear – and to eliminate enclaves. Linear boundaries were explicitly operationalized in terms of territorial exclusivity, as compensations were proposed for property owners who held possessions that crossed the new boundaries.[52] This would leave no property divided by a newly demarcated boundary, thus implementing linear territoriality in actual property relations on the ground. The use of maps was closely tied to the execution of these treaties.[53]

Furthermore, the implementation of some linear boundaries, such as that in the Pyrenees between France and Spain, was an integral part of the central government's efforts at *internal* control, specifically in response to concerns about smuggling.[54] In this sense the process was an agreement between centralizing governments (Spanish and French) rather than an imposition by one side on the other. This occurred during a period of relative peace and cooperation between the two states and thus suggests that the linearization of boundaries had little to do with military needs or changes in offensive or defensive capabilities.

The Revolutionary period saw the further imposition of territorial authority in France, in particular in the internal reorganization

---

[50] Black 1997b: 125–26.   [51] Sahlins 1989: 93.
[52] Sahlins 1989: 95.   [53] Pelletier 1998: 56.
[54] Sahlins 1989: 89–91.

of political administration. The old regime had been plagued with internal tariffs, divisions, and administrative confusion: "In France, at least 1,500 internal river tolls were estimated to exist in 1789, for all Colbert's attempts at elimination."[55] Ideas had been proposed before the Revolution for more "rational" internal divisions of France, based on geographic and even geometric notions. For example, in 1780 the geographer Robert de Hesseln "proposed that France be divided into nine regions each in the shape of a square; each region would in turn be divided into nine subunits, each of which would be further subdivided into nine small squares."[56] Although this radically geometric plan was not adopted, such suggestions were influential in the 1790 reorganization of France into *départements*, which emphasized equal area (defined in terms of travel time) but not rectilinear shape. In this successful internal rationalization we can see the impact of the influential example presented by the newly created United States of America – a fundamentally novel and territorial form of political organization that offered a laboratory for Enlightenment notions of rational rule, later imitated within Europe when opportunities arose. Thus, with the French Revolution's focus on "abolishing privilege as the basis of private and administrative law," the French government could implement this more homogeneous form of territoriality internally – though not without resistance, particularly in peripheral areas and along frontiers.[57]

With this rationalized, territorial form of rule – internal and external – came a new focus on the inviolability of French "national" territory. Thus, in the late 1790s, the Directory refused foreign-ministry requests to trade territories with other powers, overturning what had been a common practice under the Old Regime. Territory had, by this point, been redefined and remeasured as a geometric expanse and then given the additional weight of national identity. As the Directory wrote, "The patrie is an indivisible property, and a Frenchman cannot allow it to be taken away."[58] Maps of French territory likewise became the jealously guarded possessions of the Revolutionary government. The second Cassini survey project, begun in the late 1740s, had mapped most of France by 1789 and was planned as a published

[55] Evans 1992: 482–83.   [56] Konvitz 1990: 4.
[57] Sahlins 1989: 168–70.
[58] Quoted and translated by Sahlins (1989: 190).

series of maps, just as the first Cassini project had been. The surveys and master maps were quickly seized after the Revolution, however, because the newly territorialized national identity required that this territory – and its accurate representation – be controlled by the state. The territorial state that had been consolidated only at the end of the eighteenth century was thus given a new national identity, making any threat to that territory a threat against the French nation itself.

France, in short, did undergo the traditionally ascribed transition from a complex medieval polity with zonal frontiers to a modern territorial state with linear boundaries, but it did so through a far more contested and uneven process than is usually assumed by scholars. Thanks to mapping and its impact, rationalization of the frontiers changed in meaning between Vauban's fortification plans of the late 1600s and the push toward linearization in the late 1700s. By the time of the Revolution and the Napoleonic expansion, therefore, the French state had developed a territorial ideal that could be imitated by, or imposed on, other parts of Europe. Within France, Napoleon pursued further policies of territorialization and rationalization of rule, such as the 1804 initiation of a land property survey in order to implement a uniform land tax.[59]

Napoleon's rule, then, set the stage for the wholesale redrawing of boundaries in the 1814–15 settlements, in which divisions not only were moved but in many cases were delineated as discrete territorial boundaries for the first time (as seen in Chapter 6). Along some frontiers, however, the process took even longer: in the Pyrenees, for example, the treaties of 1814–15 did not delimit boundaries. Instead, commissions were established in the 1850s to implement a linear division. As with many previous boundary-demarcation efforts, the commissioners ran up against the common problem of "the 'signification' of the descriptions – the relation between the text and the terrain."[60] The commissioners resolved the complexities by drawing linear boundaries, including many straight lines that cut across existing properties, and attempted to base the new boundaries on recent, rather than ancient, historical claims. Their main goal, however, was "eradicating local struggles" rather than determining the most historically or geographically well-founded claims.[61] These new boundaries were then marked with an established number and placement of

[59] Sahlins 1989: 254.   [60] Sahlins 1989: 252.   [61] Sahlins 1989: 247.

boundary stones, thereby imposing the abstract linearity of post-Revolutionary French boundaries on one of the country's last remaining complex jurisdictional frontiers.

In the nineteenth century, therefore, France became the exclusively territorial political entity that we recognize as the norm today. Boundaries were discrete and linear, demarcated and administered by the state and understood to separate the exclusive sovereign authority of France from that of each of its neighbors. Again, however, this transformation took significantly longer than has usually been posited by scholars, culminating at the time of the post-Napoleonic settlement rather than during the rule of Louis XIV, let alone earlier. Mapping and related techniques were fundamental to this change and in more ways than simply as tools to accomplish predetermined goals. The available cartographic techniques made territorialization legitimate, desirable, *and* possible. Thus, the argument that "innovations in map-making contributed to efforts to re-order the nation's political structure during the Revolution"[62] applies both to the material tools available and to the ideational structure that underlay efforts at territorialization. Mapping of an earlier period – particularly the popular atlases and maps of the late sixteenth and early seventeenth centuries – helped create the demand for further improvements in surveying and mapping. These improved techniques then made it possible for Jean-Dominique Cassini and his successors to provide French kings with the geometrically accurate representations of their kingdom that they desired. With these tools available, then, authority could be – and, it was felt, *should* be – asserted over a clearly delineated territorial realm.

Some movement toward this desired end is evident in the late eighteenth century, but the culmination and consolidation of these interlinked ideas and practices came only with the French Revolution. Before the Revolution had given rulers the ability to overturn traditional and customary practices and authorities, new efforts to delineate boundaries or rationalize administration were often resisted successfully or at best were layered on top of existing arrangements rather than displacing them outright. Only with the crisis and upheaval of the Revolution and the Napoleonic period could the old ideas be superseded entirely.

[62] Konvitz 1990: 3.

Crisis and upheaval, however, were not unique to the nineteenth century. The impact of today's technological, economic, and social changes may yield another period in which broad political transformation becomes possible. The next chapter thus takes up this question, linking the theoretical implications of this historical study to the possibility for fundamental change in international politics today.

8 | *The cartographic state today*

The publication of maps of India depicting incorrect boundaries of the country indirectly questions the frontiers and challenges the territorial integrity of the nation. This is a criminal offence which is punishable with imprisonment.

Official notice published by the Survey of India, 1992[1]

The deep connection between mapped images and political authority examined in this book is by no means an exclusively historical phenomenon. As the epigraph above reveals, in the late twentieth century, states continued to attempt to assert control over how their territories were mapped – with "incorrect" maps seen as a threat to the very identity of the nation. These efforts to control cartography extend from issues of map content to attempts to dictate who is allowed to map the state's territory. The latter issue, in fact, is probably becoming increasingly important to governments, thanks to the ways in which map creation and distribution are escaping their grasp.

Although the first two centuries of early modern cartography were dominated by private or semi-private map production – with important consequences for the character and influence of maps – by the nineteenth century, major state institutions had come to dominate mapping. State-sponsored projects such as the Cassini maps in France, the Ordnance Survey in Great Britain, or the United States Geological Survey often provided the most detailed maps with the most extensive coverage. These projects, of course, gave states direct control over how their territories were mapped. Beginning in the last two decades of the twentieth century, however, the rapid adoption of digital mapping technologies coincided with a decline in state expenditures on general-purpose civilian cartography, resulting in a significant and continuing shift back toward private map production. This shift has

---

[1] Reproduced and discussed in Krishna 1996: 203–4.

accentuated the conflict between governments and mapmakers. In 2011, for example, disagreements between the Chinese government and companies providing online maps (such as Google) revealed that the web-based expansion of coverage and accessibility has merely transformed, not eliminated, such conflicts.[2]

Mapping, in other words, continues to be fundamentally tied to political ideas and practices as closely as in the period examined in this book. Simultaneously, mapping is undergoing its most all-encompassing change in techniques and uses since the early modern cartographic revolution. Thus, unlike the cartographic conflicts of the nineteenth and twentieth centuries – which can be thought of as positional disagreements over, for example, where boundaries should be drawn – today's technological shifts are potentially leading to conflicts of a more constitutive nature. Since the 1980s, the digitization of map production, distribution, and use has dramatically expanded the questions of what it means to map the world, who is involved in that mapping, and how and by whom maps are used. These fundamental changes may be creating the conditions of possibility for new ideas, practices, and institutions, particularly related to territorial political claims and conflicts.

This concluding chapter thus considers some of the broader theoretical and empirical implications for today of the historical study in the preceding chapters. The book has shown that maps were key drivers of the complex, centuries-long emergence of territorial statehood. These technologies fundamentally changed how actors thought about political space, authority, and organization, thereby shaping the fundamental structure of modern international relations: states claiming exclusive rule over discretely bounded territories. Mapping altered how rulers went about competing with one another – politically and militarily – and how they pursued policies aimed at centralizing authority in their own hands. Thus the drive toward centralization, a near-permanent feature of early modern politics, was given its particularly territorial character by cartography. Contrary to the importance conventionally accorded to 1648, however, it was only in the post-1815 settlements that this form of territoriality was fully implemented in the political practices of European rulers. The territorial structure of politics has been so hegemonic that it has remained relatively unchallenged

[2] Fletcher 2011.

from the early nineteenth century onward, in spite of the multitude of changes to other fundamental political ideas and goals. As Chapter 6 notes with regard to the differences – and similarities – between the 1814–15 and 1919 settlements, exclusively territorial rule could be directed toward new or altered goals without changing its fundamental structure.

The resilience of territorial statehood can also be seen in the decolonization and independence movements of the second half of the twentieth century. Describing postcolonial states as "juridical" rather than "empirical" states, or as "quasi-states,"[3] not only illustrates the divergence of these political entities from the expected norm of strong statehood (that is, the ability to assert control within territorial borders); it also reveals the particular aspect of sovereignty that maintains them as independent entities: the ideal of externally recognized, territorially exclusive, linearly bounded states. These political units could only become viable after the implementation of territorial exclusivity had made this ideal the hegemonic norm of international society.

Territorial exclusivity formed both the ideational framework of postcolonial statehood and an effective tool of government for postcolonial rulers. Decision-makers in newly independent states took advantage of the legitimacy of cartographic territoriality to consolidate their rule within the often arbitrary boundaries drawn by colonial powers. In many cases this was an active decision by postcolonial elites, not simply an unthinking habit, and it was a conscious response to the circumstances in which rulers of newly independent states found themselves.[4] Agreements among newly independent states exhibit this focus on static boundaries and the recognition of territorial exclusivity, even in the absence of effective control. For example, a declaration from the 1964 meeting of the Organization of African Unity on "boundary disputes among African states" affirms that "all Member States pledge themselves to respect the borders existing on their achievement of national independence."[5] The choice to honor existing boundaries and thus to adopt the European model of territorial statehood was debated at the time – and continues to be challenged by proposals to redraw or eliminate boundaries – but the hegemony of this particular form of territorial rule in the mid twentieth-century international

[3] Jackson and Rosberg 1982; Jackson 1990.
[4] Badie 2000; Spruyt 2000.   [5] OAU 1964: 16[I].

system was difficult to resist.[6] This institutional isomorphism cannot be explained by rational interests alone but is instead the result of the dominance of cartographically constructed ideas, institutions, and practices of statehood.[7]

The next section considers what this book's argument suggests about our understanding of institutional change in general and about the field of International Relations as an academic discipline. Then the remainder of the chapter examines today's rapidly evolving cartographic technologies, suggesting some potential changes that these new techniques and uses may drive. Digital map creation, distribution, and use may very well represent the most significant transformation of maps – and thus, potentially, territorial political ideas and practices – since the emergence of the cartographic state in early modern Europe.

Technology, institutional change, and international relations

The hegemony of territorial statehood in the modern political world represents a fundamental transformation from the complex structure of authority and organization with which the early modern period began. This process – and particularly the way in which it unfolded – can give us new insights into the dynamics of institutional change in general, with implications for how to think about possible changes today as well as how we define International Relations as a field of study.

The process of institutional transformation in early modern Europe was extremely complex, involving recursive connections between technologies, ideas, and practices as well as the layering of new elements on top of old ones. Furthermore, because generational turnover is a key element in major ideational shifts, it can take centuries for the social and political impact of even revolutionary technological developments to become clear.[8] The process was also recursive: once mapping technology changed, this altered the maps in circulation and the

[6] Similar dynamics can be seen in the 1989–91 collapse of the Soviet empire – both internal and external – and the resulting adoption of existing boundaries to define newly independent territorial states. See Bunce 1999; Spruyt 2005: ch. 7; Wendt and Friedheim 1995.

[7] On the inability of a "logic of consequences" to explain the form of statehood, see Meyer *et al.* 1997.

[8] Deibert 1997.

view that actors held of political space. These changes, in turn, created new demands for mapping, in terms of both the kind of maps being produced (increasingly politically oriented) and the cartographic technologies pursued (aiming toward increasing accuracy of surveying and of coordinate-location measurement). The continuing development of the accuracy-focused "scientific" form of mapping, in turn, further consolidated the notion of political space as geometrically measurable, divisible, and claimable. Old ideas and practices are rarely replaced by new ones in a clean break with the past; instead the new are often layered on top of the old.[9] Thus cartographic territorial authority was only slowly built on top of the traditional notions of jurisdictionally defined authority. Finally, unintended consequences can be an essential element in political transformations: major changes can occur without any actual constituency favoring them. Mapmakers who drew linearly bounded, homogeneous political units (where in reality divisions remained unclear) had no intention of changing political structures but instead were primarily interested in selling maps in a commercial market. Political rulers who later implemented linear boundaries were not consciously innovating, but rather acting on their sense that linear boundaries were simply more "rational" than enclaves and overlaps.

Furthermore, although this book has argued throughout that the invention, dissemination, and use of Ptolemaic cartography were *necessary* for the emergence of territorial states, by no means were these technological developments *sufficient*. Many other concurrent processes and driving forces played significant roles. For example, the influence of Ptolemaic mapping was only possible because of the near-simultaneous printing revolution, represented by both the invention of the printing press and the rapid growth of a market for printed material, both written and visual. In addition, numerous other factors – political, economic, and social – favored the increasing centralization of rule within European polities, which was then molded by the territorialization of political authority into the powerful institutions of the sovereign territorial state. Finally, the contingent events following the European encounter with the New World played a large role in shaping the effect of cartography on political authority, as the demand for a new and useful means for making political claims proved influential in the eventual dominance of territorial exclusivity.

---

[9] As is pointed out about institutional change in general by Thelen (2003).

In fact, as Chapter 5 argues, many of the ideas and practices constituting the modern international system appeared first not in Europe, but in the actions and interactions of European actors in the Americas. This points toward a larger phenomenon: peripheries as sources of institutional innovation. Thus, in terms of possible changes in today's state system, we should not necessarily focus exclusively on the center, on the actions taken and ideas promoted by the most politically powerful actors. Instead, new ideas from the peripheries of the system may be applied at the center in unexpected or unintended ways.[10]

More broadly, this book has implications for the enterprise of studying "international" politics, that is, for the academic discipline of International Relations (IR).[11] This field predominantly trains scholars to examine the world in a particular way, with a focus on interactions among territorial states assumed to precede the analysis. The hegemony of cartographic ideas of political authority has not only shaped political practices and outcomes (i.e. leading to the dominance of territorial states in the world); it has also shaped how IR scholars have studied that world. Mapping and its ideational effects, in other words, have given a particularly territorial character to our theories, making it more difficult to incorporate non-territorial causal drivers, processes, and outcomes.

For example, one of the most active and long-running research programs in IR is the attempt to study the causes of interstate conflict through the statistical analysis of large datasets.[12] These analyses typically focus on the post-Napoleonic period, looking at the characteristics of states involved in military conflicts in order to draw generalizable conclusions about the particular conditions that are conducive to the outbreak of war. In a way, this makes perfect sense, particularly given the time frame adopted by these studies. After all, it was with

---

[10] Peripheries can be understood broadly here, including diverse possibilities such as new ideas or practices emerging from indigenous-rights struggles in the global South (Reyes and Kaufman 2011), competition over the Arctic in the wake of climate change (Gerhardt *et al.* 2010; Young 2009), or the politicization of orbital space (Duvall and Havercroft 2008).

[11] I would like to thank Daniel Nexon for pointing my thinking in this direction.

[12] The most influential example of this is the Correlates of War project: www. correlatesofwar.org. Note that there are ongoing efforts to include "non-state" actors in these datasets (such as with the Correlates of War project's "Extra-State War" data), but these remain secondary and typically operationalize non-territorial actors as entities comparable to states.

the post-Napoleonic settlements that territorial statehood was firmly consolidated as *the* legitimate form of political authority and organization, at least within Europe.[13] Yet this leaves out the possibility of understanding conflict in different eras, when territoriality of this particular type was not dominant and political actors were more varied in their fundamental characteristics – varied, that is, in ways not captured by standard variables such as territorial size, population, and so on.

In other words, territorial state boundaries have not only structured political outcomes over the past two centuries; they have also structured how knowledge about political and social outcomes is generated.[14] This is the "territorial trap" into which IR has fallen, implicitly ignoring any phenomena that do not fit within the territorial state narrative.[15] Even in the case of war, by focusing exclusively on disputes between states, we may be missing significant drivers of military conflict that are revealed only if we include change in institutional forms as a possible cause – or consequence – of war.[16] Thus, many IR studies that look at earlier historical periods (that is, before the consolidation of modern territoriality in the nineteenth century) may be asking the wrong questions because the territorial character of political organization is assumed rather than questioned.[17] This problem is replicated in more abstract approaches to examining the origins of the state, which again assume territoriality and then use that assumption to explain the other aspects of statehood (such as centralization or relative size).[18] Analyses of exceptions to the sovereign-state model could also be improved by reframing the questions to acknowledge that cartographic statehood, though dominant today, is not the only

[13] This is also not surprising, from the perspective of the intellectual heritage of IR theory: the traditional IR approach to history builds directly on the nineteenth-century "national history" approach. Many of these nineteenth-century historians projected the territorial state model of their time backwards into the early modern era. For a critique of this approach, see Smith 1999: ch. 6.

[14] Häkli 2001.

[15] Agnew 1994.

[16] Wimmer and Min 2006. Bishai 2004 also provides a useful critique, focusing on secession.

[17] This can be a particularly difficult problem in studies that use historical Geographic Information System (GIS) databases. Often such datasets assume that polities have always been defined by linear boundaries, in the same way that historical atlases have done since the nineteenth century.

[18] See, for one example, Wagner 2007.

possible form of political organization. Thus, instead of analyzing "violations" of an ideal-typical sovereign state model, it would be better to ask what the possible changes are to the authoritative basis for political organization.[19] This would allow our questions to be more open rather than being implicitly framed by a baseline defined by territorial statehood.

Therefore, when considering the possibility of international change today, it is more useful to avoid conceptualizing sovereignty or the state statically. Today's economic, social, and technological changes may lead to a transformation of the very constitutive basis of statehood and the state system. Thus, we should ask the following: is the foundational ideational structure of political organization being changed by new forms of territoriality, by the undermining of territoriality, or by new forms of non-territorial organization? Is such ideational change being implemented in practice? These key questions are difficult to answer so long as we continue to assume a fixed definition of sovereign statehood and merely question whether that is being violated, weakened, or supported.[20]

Digital cartographies and political transformation

One area in which asking the right questions can be very productive is the potential effect of today's digital cartography. New technologies and practices for making, distributing, displaying, and using maps may alter the ideational structure created by centuries of institutionalized mapmaking and map use. While pre-digital mapmaking was built upon standardization and the abstraction of human space onto the

---

[19] Many of the violations of sovereignty pointed out by scholars (by, among others, Cooley 2005; Krasner 1999, 2001; Lake 2009) are examples of de facto or even de jure authority relations between states and thus represent exceptions to the principle of sovereign equality. Yet these authority claims – and the admittedly more complex political relations that result – continue to be defined today in territorial terms, bounded by discrete divisions, and thus actually represent transformation *within* cartographic territoriality rather than changes *to* that ideal.

[20] Similarly, the extensive literature on globalization, which interrogates many aspects of the contemporary international system, benefits from the fact that many studies actually do focus on possible *changes* in the authoritative basis for political organization, rather than the dichotomous question of whether the state is "dead." See Agnew 2009.

printed Ptolemaic grid, computer-based map production and distribution offer the possibility of undermining the homogenization and
geometricization of space by breaking the constraints of the earlier
system. This could suggest new forms of territoriality or even undermine territoriality as we know it altogether, giving advocates of other
forms of authority the representational tools required to overcome
our tendency to see the political world as a color-coded, boundary-
filled map. Yet the implications of these rapidly changing technologies
remain ambiguous: digital maps and the representations they make
possible could be undermining the hegemonic ideal of the territorial
state, or they could be lending additional, albeit unintended, support
to that institution. The rest of this chapter examines these opposing
possibilities.

The innovations in cartography of the last several decades have
been some of the most substantial changes in mapping since the cartographic revolution of the early modern era. In fact, there are significant
similarities between these two periods of technological change – similarities that suggest the possibility of today's technologies being equally
transformative. Just as in the early modern period, mapping today falls
predominantly outside the control of political authorities at the same
time that new techniques are being developed and put to use. In the
intervening centuries, cartography was dominated by state efforts and
the work of large, centralized mapmaking institutions.[21] Today, radical
change in mapping may be creating the possibility of equally radical
political and social effects.

Analytically, there are two lines of investigation. First is the possibility of significant, long-term change in political ideas, identities, and
organization, similar to the earlier outcome examined in this book.
Could the use of new mapping tools transform, undermine, or replace
the territorial basis for political authority and thus transform the sovereign state? Such a fundamental change in the ideational structure of
political organization would be particularly difficult to observe as it
is occurring. Second is the possibility of more immediate, though less
far-reaching, effects on political outcomes. Are the new cartographic

---

[21] This is not to argue that mapping had no effect on worldviews in the
intervening centuries. See Henrikson (1975), for example, on the effect of mid-
twentieth-century polar-projection mapping on geopolitical views in the United
States.

tools making possible – or even encouraging – new or altered interactions among political actors? For example, interstate conflict or negotiation could be reshaped by the presence of new mapping tools, just as interactions in early modern Europe were restructured by the ubiquity of printed maps. In addition, the growing importance of non-state actors, organizations, and flows may be more easily mapped with the new cartographic tools, giving current challenges to state sovereignty additional legitimacy and power. The different levels at which these processes operate are closely linked, of course: historically, it was the extensive use of maps in short-term interactions that helped to drive a significant long-term shift in political ideas and practices. The following paragraphs examine these possibilities in detail, focusing on the potential impact of Geographic Information Systems and web-delivered digital mapping as two key contemporary cartographic technologies.

Geographic Information Systems, or GIS, encompass a set of computer technologies for gathering, storing, analyzing, and displaying spatially located data. While the general idea is quite broad, this technology typically takes the form of using either raster or vector data to create multi-layered maps showing particular variables, relationships, or dynamics. The possibility of creating a dynamic map, or a variety of maps from one dataset, suggests that this technology might enable far more complex displays of space and thus make possible equally complex spatial ideas – thereby altering notions of territorial authority or identity.

Although the technology was seen at first as a normatively neutral tool for geographic and social analysis – or as a tool for challenging existing hierarchical relationships – questions have since been raised about the constraints and incentives imposed by GIS software. GIS has been criticized for being too technologically driven, making it nearly impossible for people without extensive training to participate in the creation or analysis of these spatial datasets and maps. Thus, these technologies may offer new means for propping up existing social and political hierarchies, rather than opportunities for questioning social relationships.[22] Yet this debate has suffered from technological determinism on both sides, ignoring the socially embedded nature of any set of cartographic tools. Proponents of GIS tend to argue for a teleological

---

[22] Goodchild 2006; Pickles 1995.

march of progress, without acknowledging the impossibility of such technologies being socially neutral. Critics, on the other hand, have presented the harmful social effects of GIS as independent of any possibility of social control or restructuring. Instead, we should recognize the reciprocal relationship between a technology such as GIS and the societal norms and ideas that are constituted by that technology.[23]

When we take into account the potential for causal influence in both directions, therefore, more interesting analyses come to light. In particular, digital mapping has two contradictory, but equally plausible, effects on the territorial foundation of modern statehood and particularly on the emphasis typically placed on linear boundaries. For example, one potential innovation of computerized map production using GIS is the ability to create maps that are less focused on linear boundaries and existing political authorities, particularly in the display of social or demographic data. While a printed map of a particular phenomenon must take just one form – often coding something like literacy by country, which merely reinforces the linearly bounded modern notion of political space – a GIS-produced map could theoretically display the data in more complex ways. Yet the adoption of GIS has actually encouraged particular cartographic simplifications because the software makes certain types of maps much easier to create than others.[24] In other words, GIS technologies are fundamentally shaped by existing social ideas about space and how it is organized. For example, the maps built into GIS are still founded on the coordinate system of modern print mapping. Furthermore, the way in which digital technologies such as GIS spatially code the world actually "presupposes the existence of an *already* geo-coded world of house numbers, zip codes, and the like."[25] This "geo-coding" was largely implemented – and continues to be reinforced – by a combination of state action and private organizational initiative. Thus even new digital mapping technologies are built on centuries of geographic understanding, making it likely that they will be shaped by those ideas and will reinforce them going forward.

One effort to make GIS technology (and its outputs) representative of a broader set of actors and interests has been in the Popular Participation GIS (PPGIS) movement, which is an effort to make GIS

[23] Chrisman 2005.   [24] Crampton 2004.
[25] Rose-Redwood 2006: 470.

"more equitable, accessible, and empowering."[26] This has predominantly focused on increasing the involvement of non-technically-trained participants in creating GIS databases and maps, even if it does not actually make GIS software more accessible to untrained persons. The intention is to restructure the "power-knowledge" inherent in GIS and the maps produced by GIS away from control by the state. Many of these efforts, however, have fallen short of breaking down the technological barriers to entry into GIS use, and many of the PPGIS proposals have been more at the level of abstract or theoretical calls for participation than actual practical solutions.[27]

One area of digital mapping that has opened up to much wider participation, however, is web-based mapping (such as those provided by Google, Yahoo!, or Microsoft) and more sophisticated virtual globes such as Google Earth. Even in the brief period since the launching of some of these products, they have seen enormous public use. Google Earth, for example, was downloaded 350 million times in only its first three years (2005–8).[28] Furthermore, many of these digital maps have allowed for public participation in the form of so-called "mashups," in which users create additional information to be layered on top of the basic digital map base. These combinations of sophisticated but easy-to-use online mapping with user-created content may actually offer the first real possibility of achieving the goals of PPGIS. For example, in the wake of Hurricane Katrina, two individuals created a website that allowed anyone to place information or questions about particular locations hit by the hurricane on a Google Maps base. This website proved to be very useful for those trying to get information concerning their status and whereabouts out to relatives or authorities. One observer sees this mashup as a repeatable model of participatory digital mapping: "[A] technically minded agent builds a system that can be used by the non-technically minded to generate content out of their own data or local knowledge."[29]

This is just one example of the possibilities of "distributed mapping" systems, in which users define and create on-demand maps, with

[26] Miller 2006: 189.
[27] See, for a variety of views, Crampton 2010; Crampton and Krygier 2006; Dunn 2007; Miller 2006; Wood 2010.
[28] Google's "Lat-Long" blog: Chikai Ohazama, "Truly Global," 11 February 2008, http://google-latlong.blogspot.com/2008/02/truly-global.html.
[29] Miller 2006: 197. See also Wood 2010.

each particular map being ephemeral but the digital "mapping environment" being permanent.[30] Beyond enabling map users to generate the kinds of maps they need from a set source of geographic data, there are also "open-source" forms of mapping, in which users also are involved in creating the base cartographic layers as well as occasional content. One example is OpenStreetMap, which uses the Wikipedia-style approach of allowing users to create and edit the base street-map layer, thereby producing a public-domain web map – since commercial products are actually built on proprietary base-map layers.[31] There are many other ongoing efforts involving "volunteered geographic information," including non-profits such as Ushahidi.com, designed to allow for crowd-sourced mapping of disaster relief, protest movements, and the like. These projects have been made possible by the interactive nature of the "Web 2.0" model, as well as by the increasing availability of Global Positioning System (GPS) devices and broadband Internet access. Of course, while these open-source maps may not have some of the same potential issues of institutional bias as traditional mapmaking, they are subject to a different set of problems, those inherent in a system where the truth of claims is often simply asserted by volunteers "without citation, reference, or other authority."[32]

To many analysts, these developments imply the opening up of cartographic technology to the masses and hence the end, perhaps, of the tendency of mapping in the modern era to reinforce existing institutional and social hierarchies:

Maps are no longer imparted to us by a trained cadre of experts, but along with most other information we create them as needed ourselves ... Open-source mapping means that cartography is no longer in the hands of cartographers or GIScientists but the users.[33]

This optimistic reading of the impact of these new digital cartographic technologies can be convincing, particularly when the new techniques are compared against the mapping possibilities of even twenty years earlier. The open possibilities are evident, for example, in the ability to add layers to Google Earth and to remove them as well. Thus, linear

[30] Crampton 2003. For an overview, see Crampton 2010.
[31] See www.openstreetmap.org. For a discussion, see Crampton 2009.
[32] Goodchild 2007.
[33] Crampton and Krygier 2006: 15, 19.

national boundaries can be depicted in the traditional fashion, as a fundamental feature of the physical globe. By un-checking a single box, however, the user can make those disappear. Layers and filters created by users, furthermore, can add a wide variety of information, from displays of social or demographic variables to labels of specific points of interest. This can turn the static content of the system into dynamic content, all by drastically increasing user input and control.

Yet the participation and emancipatory potential of these technologies can easily be overstated. Everyday users can add content (provided they are sufficiently technologically savvy), and they can certainly change how they themselves view the map content that already exists. Yet these technological tools do not appear out of thin air but are created by technical experts with their own ideas and norms, even if no explicit agendas. The "default settings" on tools such as Google Earth are an inherent feature of any software product, no matter how adjustable the software is in skilled hands. Thus, what the maps look like when the program is first used – as well as the outer bounds of what can be changed on them – is determined in the same way that GIS or traditional mapmaking always has been shaped: by trained experts within established institutions.[34]

The most fundamental default setting of these online mapping tools, furthermore, is their foundation in the coordinate grid of latitude and longitude. GIS maps as well as online digital mappings all start with the geometric understanding of space, defined by a coordinate location on the surface of the earth. Even though virtual globes such as Google Earth no longer have to flatten the sphere into a map, they also treat space as a geometrically measurable expanse. Replacing abstract map images with satellite photography (as is possible with most of the online tools) merely moves one step closer to the Enlightenment ideal of a map being a perfect "mirror" to reality. While the tendency of printed maps towards linear (political) division and homogeneous (political) color-coding is reversed, at least potentially, the underlying spatial

---

[34] Efforts to map any number of features or phenomena, therefore, most easily take on the visual language of Google Maps: placing labeled "pins" on a readily available map or satellite image. For example, in the same way that early modern mapping gave religious mapping a new emphasis on delineation of the territories of the twelve tribes of Israel (see Chapter 4), maps of biblical history today can easily be made by labeling places mentioned in the Bible with pins. See, for example, www.biblemap.org.

understanding remains the same.[35] Furthermore, digital mappings often continue to use existing political divisions as their units of analysis because of the technical sophistication required to do otherwise.

Nonetheless, the ease with which complex layers and dynamic images are made with digital mapping tools removes some of the pressures toward abstraction and simplification that were inherent in print-based cartography. Furthermore, the geometric foundation of digital cartography is sometimes irrelevant to the goals of popular mappings, as for example, with the post-Katrina Google Maps mashup discussed above: "The 'standards and goals' of … participants had nothing to do with Cartesian coordinate systems and only as much attention to positional accuracy as would be required for rescuers to locate an intersection or a row of houses; all relative positions."[36] Thus the user-cartographers were not bound by Ptolemaic notions of accuracy but instead relied on a non-geometric route-finding approach because it better served their purposes. Yet the representational foundation for this, and for all other Google Map mashups or Google Earth layers, remains geometric. The grammar of mapping, in other words, remains unquestioned.

This persistence at the deepest level even in the newest cartographic techniques is also apparent in the case of so-called "indigenous" mapping projects. This term, though broad, encompasses many efforts to bring digital mapping tools to bear in order to assert the rights of indigenous groups to land, resources, or political autonomy.[37] Yet the use of these tools can actually undermine those rights by reinforcing the deep grammar of exclusive claims to geometrically defined territory – whether for political or economic purposes – rather than allowing for the possibility of other ways of operationalizing ownership

[35] Of course, the shift from measurement-based surveying to aerial or satellite imaging as the basis for mapping – a shift that, admittedly, was underway before the digital mapping revolution – does make mapping more representative of the *physical* geography of the world (natural features, etc.) rather than exclusively representative of the *measured* and *abstract* geography of the surveyor.

[36] Miller 2006: 196. Today's technologies may, in fact, be simultaneously encompassing both aspects of space: the abstract geometric space of grid-based mapping *and* the predominantly place-focused way in which the world is understood and interacted with on a daily basis (Curry 2005).

[37] For an example from Southeast Asia, see Roth 2009; for Central America, Wainwright and Bryan 2009.

and control. Since the maps are often explicitly created in order to assert claims against the state, this essentially forces those claimants to "speak the language" of the state, which in this case means traditional property delimitations within the neoliberal model of property rights.[38] One of the few circumstances in which maps are created with fundamentally non-geometric characteristics is the creation of "parish" maps in European villages, but these documents are asserting local cultural elements rather than making property claims – the latter, of course, being relatively secure in this context.[39]

Another potential avenue for the cartographic restructuring of ideas of political authority may exist in efforts to use new mapping tools to represent the network nature of the postmodern "space of flows."[40] After all, if linearly bounded states are losing their power or their functions in favor of global networks of transactions, effectively representing those networks could serve to undermine the common notion of the political world as a set of territorially exclusive states. In fact, new representations may be necessary:

Under these circumstances, the image of global social space as a complex mosaic of superimposed and interpenetrating nodes, levels, scales, and morphologies has become more appropriate than the traditional Cartesian model of homogenous, interlinked blocks of territory associated with the modern interstate system. New representations of sociospatial form are needed to analyze these emergent pluri-territorial, polycentric, and multiscalar geographies of globalization.[41]

These new representations may be needed, but are they possible? Can the complexity of the space of flows be represented in a way that both satisfactorily captures its dynamics and is comprehensible enough to influence societal norms or give shape to new ideas of sociopolitical space?

---

[38] Wainwright and Bryan 2009; Wood 2010. This is an excellent example of the continuing efforts of states to make their populations, territories, and resources "legible," even if in this case states are not actively imposing this themselves, but have instead set the terms of the debate in a language that demands a particular type of response or claim (Scott 1998: ch. 1).

[39] Wood 2010. As Crampton (2011: 7) argues, these and other examples (such as the crowd-sourced mappings discussed above) suggest that perhaps we should "expand our notion of indigenous" with regard to mapping.

[40] Castells 1996.   [41] Brenner 1999: 69.

Efforts to map aspects of global networks exist, particularly in relation to the Internet, but they are less than revolutionary in their depictions and, hence, in their implications. Maps are used to depict numerous aspects of the global computer network but tend to use one of two techniques: either layering network information (sometimes in three dimensions) over existing Ptolemaic maps or else creating complex non-geographic network diagrams of nodes, hubs, and links.[42] While these may capture many features of these networks, the former will do little to undermine existing conceptions of space, and the latter may be too abstract for building new notions of identity, community, or authority. After all, the very simplicity of early modern mapping was one of its most persuasive assets, just as simplicity and ease of comprehension remain among the most ideationally powerful features of today's political maps, with their clean linear boundaries and homogeneously colored spaces. Just as with efforts to map indigenous forms of authority or property, the digital mapping medium continues to force images – and thus ideas – into the pre-existing geometric spatial mold.

A separate line of inquiry concerns the use of these new tools, not by the general public, but by traditional international political actors, such as leaders and representatives of states. International negotiations, for example, have begun to make use of digital mapping technologies. At the 1995 Dayton negotiations to end the conflict in Bosnia, GIS and other computer-based mappings were used extensively. This relatively early use did see its share of problems – both with the relatively low-resolution technologies and with some negotiators who were resistant to moving away from their paper maps – but it represents the general trend toward using these digital tools.[43] The question remains, however, as to whether this will lead to any potential changes in the outcomes of negotiation, particularly at the level of the form of authority claims being discussed. In spite of the fact that these tools provide the possibility of visualizing more complex forms of political authority, digital maps, so far at least, have been used mainly to further efforts toward achieving traditional goals, such as drawing clear, undisputed linear boundaries between territorial jurisdictions.

---

[42] See, for example, Dodge and Kitchin 2001. For an analysis of the issues surrounding making maps of cyberspace, see Zook and Dodge 2009.
[43] Johnson 1999.

In the near term, however, there are two parallel but contradictory tendencies that may be among the outcomes shaped by digital mapping techniques: first, the destabilization of some settled boundaries as increasing exactitude reveals inconsistencies and reduces the range of politically useful ambiguity; and, second, the potential stabilization or settlement of divisions that previously were impossible to resolve. Both tendencies are the result of the same trend toward increasing accuracy and ease of use in mapping.

First, the technological trend toward increasing accuracy and reduced cost in location-finding and mapmaking may yield situations in which the previously existing "wiggle room" for resolving negotiations is no longer available. During the early modern period, many agreements on divisions of political claims were made in the face of great uncertainty or ambiguity regarding the actual divisions on the ground, a fact that made these resolutions easier, not harder, to achieve. For example, during the Spanish–Portuguese negotiations over the anti-meridian to the Tordesillas line (discussed in Chapter 5), the impossibility of determining the line technologically made a political agreement possible, as claims were traded without either side having to admit that they were giving away anything on their own side of the line. This dynamic persisted in early modern European peace settlements, as treaties were signed without having resolved the exact nature of the boundaries involved, allowing complex local solutions on frontiers to emerge that might have been impossible at the highest negotiating level. Today, as the technological ability to find one's position with pin-point accuracy and to reference it to detailed maps is increasingly available, the recourse to ambiguous but workable divisions becomes less available.

A countervailing trend, however, may enable effective bargaining over currently difficult divisions. The complexity of determining, mapping, and displaying information about spaces other than land surfaces – such as the oceans or underground resources – has made effective resolution and enforcement of agreements difficult. Yet with technologies for measuring and displaying detailed information becoming increasingly accurate and affordable, certain divisions may be more easily effected. Three-dimensional mapping of oceanic resources (both those in the water and those under the sea floor) or of underground resources are part of this, as is the ability of dynamic maps to display the dimension of time. Thus, spatial claims that are migratory in character (that is, a claim to a space during a certain, regular time period but not otherwise) can be easily displayed. Having easy and familiar means of presenting these patterns or data is essential, because most often the actors doing the negotiating are not personally at the forefront of technological use. With techniques for displaying the information in user-friendly formats, however, the negotiating parties need not be particularly technically proficient. This may end up making certain previously indivisible spaces or resources divisible in new ways.

Both potential trends are the result of the single tendency toward perfect geometric accuracy in spatial representations. Yet the outcomes could be very different: stable arrangements becoming unsettled or previously difficult settlements becoming easier. The possibility that new mapping technologies will disrupt status quo ideas and practices is only further increased as cartography moves more and more beyond the control of centralized states and other large institutions.

Beyond mapping, beyond the state?

The possible implications of digital mapping technologies, while extensive, are merely one potential avenue for the digital information technology revolution to restructure political ideas, identities, and practices. The possibility for change may actually be greater with non-cartographic technologies, since maps of all types are so inherently tied to spatial ideas and authorities – tied, in other words, to the territorial state.[44] The non-territorial actors, processes, and flows that result from globalization will become increasingly important regardless of whether or not they can be depicted in maps. Thus, the communication and organization possibilities of the Internet are one potential route for change having little to do with cartography. Cyberspace, for example, while subject to immense hyperbole, does in fact pose new questions concerning possibilities for novel political, social, and spatial arrangements. After all, if there is a fundamentally new form of "space" that is simultaneously experienced by people all over the globe but not explicitly located in any particular territory, this concept could have implications for political territoriality and authority.

The Internet provides means for new actors to emerge or for existing actors to find new tools and resources, including political actors

[44] Murphy 2012.

such as diaspora communities.[45] Criminals have also taken advantage of the global reach of the Internet, such as when hackers targeting people in Western countries locate themselves strategically in countries where they are unlikely to be prosecuted, such as Russia or Romania.[46] As one analyst puts it, "The issue is not jurisdictional conflict, but whether the basic idea of territorial jurisdiction is still relevant."[47] Of course, these criminals know that boundaries continue to matter, and thus consciously place themselves within the physical borders of non-prosecuting states. Boundaries that are so porous to cybercrime are still politically solid enough to make it difficult if not impossible for targeted states to prosecute the foreign offenders.

The networking possibilities of cyberspace have also recently developed into a massive presence of online social networks. These new forms of organization – within which technologically sophisticated people in many regions of the world spend much of their time and energy – suggest the theoretical possibility of forms of community that are utterly non-territorial and non-spatial, instead being based on person-to-person ties. Yet the persistent strength of socialization by the "schoolroom" map – literally during school but also afterwards in the media and elsewhere – may leave little room for complex, non-cartographic forms of identity, community, and authority to take hold.[48] After all, the very terminology of "cyberspace" illustrates the resilience of modern territoriality and the strength of spatial understandings of the world, evident in the predominantly spatial metaphors applied to this new realm.[49] And while the role played by social networking tools

---

[45] Newman and Paasi 1998; Sassen 2002.

[46] Gilman 2009.   [47] Kobrin 2001: 24.

[48] Migdal 2004. Particularly when compared to maps, social networks appear to have a very limited capacity to give members a sense of cohesive (political) community. This is not to deny that the tools of social network analysis could be used to study online social networks to come up with measures of centrality, groupings, etc. This has, of course, been done (e.g. Ellison *et al.* 2007). But these "objectively" measured characteristics of networks are often invisible to the people actually within them. While that invisibility may add strength to their structuring power, it does not lead to subjective perceptions of community. Thus members of those groupings will not necessarily see themselves as part of a cohesive group, even if network analysis can point out that they actually are. Since the potential changes I am examining here are built upon actors' ideas of new forms of authority and organization, this distinction makes a fundamental difference.

[49] Zook 2006: 67.

in events such as the uprisings of the 2011 "Arab Spring" was novel, this was more in the activists' methods than in their goals (which remained focused on regime change within particular states).[50] Similarly, diaspora communities often use new communication technologies for traditional goals: strengthening pre-existing national identities and ties to distant (territorial) homelands. Thus, these fundamentally non-political forms of organization are unlikely to threaten a resilient political form like the territorial state. Nonetheless, the possibility of a "no-place" where economic transactions, political activism, and social interactions "take place" does present the possibility for the emergence of something new.

The modern state was founded on a collection of narratives about and representations of the world, a major component of which was supplied (and continues to be supplied) by maps. The question remains, then, as to whether new technologies and practices will strengthen, transform, or replace those foundations. Focusing on the intersection between technological changes, ideas of legitimate authority, and political practices offers the best means of approaching this fundamental issue. The time may come when governments look at new representations and, like Louis XIV in the face of Cassini's more accurate measurement of France, lament the "loss" of authority that was never really theirs in the first place.

---

[50] For a discussion of the ambiguous effects of "liberation technologies" in the Arab Spring and other regime transformations, see Diamond and Plattner 2012.

References

Adler, Emanuel. 2005. *Communitarian International Relations: The Epistemic Foundations of International Relations*. New York: Routledge.

Adler, Emanuel, and Vincent Pouliot, eds. 2011. *International Practices*. Cambridge University Press.

Agnew, John. 1994. "The Territorial Trap: The Geographical Assumptions of International Relations Theory." *Review of International Political Economy* 1(1): 53–80.

2009. *Globalization and Sovereignty*. Lanham, MD: Rowman & Littlefield.

Akerman, James R. 1984. "Cartography and the Emergence of Territorial States in Western Europe." In John F. Sweets, ed. *Proceedings of the Tenth Annual Meeting of the Western Society for French History*. Lawrence: University of Kansas Press.

1995. "The Structuring of Political Territory in Early Printed Atlases." *Imago Mundi* 47: 138–54.

2002. "American Promotional Road Mapping in the Twentieth Century." *Cartography and Geographic Information Science* 29(3): 175–91.

Allmand, Christopher. 1988. *The Hundred Years War: England and France at War, c. 1300–c. 1450*. Cambridge University Press.

Anderson, Benedict. 1991. *Imagined Communities*, rev. edn. London: Verso.

Anderson, Perry. 1974. *Lineages of the Absolutist State*. London: Verso.

Anghie, Antony. 2004. *Imperialism, Sovereignty and the Making of International Law*. Cambridge University Press.

The Anglo-Saxon Chronicle. 1912. Trans. James Ingram. London: Everyman Press.

Archer, Margaret. 1995. *Realist Social Theory: The Morphogenetic Approach*. Cambridge University Press.

Arendt, Hannah. 1966. *The Origins of Totalitarianism*. New York: Harcourt.

Astengo, Corradino. 2007. "The Renaissance Chart Tradition in the Mediterranean." In David Woodward, ed. *The History of Cartography*, vol. III, *Cartography in the European Renaissance*. University of Chicago Press.

Badie, Bertrand. 2000. *The Imported State: The Westernization of the Political Order*, trans. Claudia Royal. Stanford University Press.

Baldwin, Robert C. D. 2007. "Colonial Cartography under the Tudor and Early Stuart Monarchies, ca. 1480–ca. 1640." In David Woodward, ed. *The History of Cartography*, vol. III, *Cartography in the European Renaissance*. University of Chicago Press.

Barber, Peter. 1992. "England I: Pageantry, Defense, and Government: Maps at Court to 1550." In David Buisseret, ed. *Monarchs, Ministers, and Maps: The Emergence of Cartography as a Tool of Government in Early Modern Europe*. University of Chicago Press.

——— 1997. "Maps and Monarchs in Europe, 1550–1800." In Robert Oresko, G. C. Gibbs, and H. M. Scott, eds. *Royal and Republican Sovereignty in Early Modern Europe*. Cambridge University Press.

——— 2007. "Mapmaking in England, ca. 1470–1650." In David Woodward, ed. *The History of Cartography*, vol. III, *Cartography in the European Renaissance*. University of Chicago Press.

Barkawi, Tarak. 2010. "On the Limits of New Foundations: A Commentary on R. Harrison Wagner, *War and the State*." *International Theory* 2(2): 317–32.

Bartelson, Jens. 2009. *Visions of World Community*. Cambridge University Press.

Bartlett, Robert. 1993. *The Making of Europe: Conquest, Colonization and Cultural Change, 950–1350*. Princeton University Press.

Bassett, Thomas J. 1994. "Cartography and Empire Building in Nineteenth-Century West Africa." *Geographical Review* 84(3): 316–35.

Baudrillard, Jean. 1988. *Jean Baudrillard, Selected Writings*, ed. Mark Poster. Stanford University Press.

Bauman, Zygmunt. 1998. *Globalization: The Human Consequences*. New York: Columbia University Press.

Beaulac, Stéphane. 2004. *The Power of Language in the Making of International Law. The Word Sovereignty in Bodin and Vattel and the Myth of Westphalia*. Leiden and Boston: Martinus Nijhoff Publishers.

Bergin, Joseph, ed. 2001. *The Seventeenth Century: Europe 1598–1715*. Oxford University Press.

Berry, Mary Elizabeth. 2006. *Japan in Print: Information and Nation in the Early Modern Period*. Berkeley: University of California Press.

Bhambra, Gurminder K. 2007. *Rethinking Modernity: Postcolonialism and the Sociological Imagination*. New York: Palgrave MacMillan.

Biggs, Michael. 1999. "Putting the State on the Map: Cartography, Territory, and European State Formation." *Comparative Studies in Society and History* 41(2): 374–405.

Bijker, Wiebe E., Thomas P. Hughes, and Trevor J. Pinch, eds. 1989. *The Social Construction of Technological Systems: New Directions in the Sociology and History of Technology.* Cambridge, MA: MIT Press.

Bishai, Linda S. 2004. *Forgetting Ourselves: Secession and the (Im)possibility of Territorial Identity.* Lanham, MD: Lexington Books.

Black, Antony. 1992. *Political Thought in Europe, 1250–1450.* Cambridge University Press.

Black, Jeremy, ed. 1987. *The Origins of War in Early Modern Europe.* Edinburgh: John Donald.

1997a. *Maps and History: Constructing Images of the Past.* New Haven, CT: Yale University Press.

1997b. *Maps and Politics.* University of Chicago Press.

1999. "Warfare, Crisis, and Absolutism." In Euan Cameron, ed. *Early Modern Europe: An Oxford History.* Oxford University Press.

2002. *Europe and the World, 1650–1830.* London: Routledge.

Bloch, Marc. 1961. *Feudal Society,* 2 vols., trans. L. A. Manyon. University of Chicago Press.

Bonney, Richard. 1988. *Society and Government in France under Richelieu and Mazarin, 1624–1661.* London: Macmillan.

Borges, Jorge Luis. 1990. *Dreamtigers,* trans. Mildred Boyer and Harold Morland. Austin: University of Texas Press.

Bourdieu, Pierre. 1990 [1980]. *The Logic of Practice,* trans. Richard Nice. Stanford University Press.

Brenner, Neil. 1999. "Beyond State-Centrism? Space, Territoriality, and Geographic Scale in Globalization Studies." *Theory and Society* 28(1): 39–78.

Brenner, Neil, and Stuart Elden. 2009. "Henri Lefebvre on State, Space, Territory." *International Political Sociology* 3(4): 353–77.

Brotton, Jerry. 1997. *Trading Territories: Mapping the Early Modern World.* Ithaca, NY: Cornell University Press.

Buisseret, David. 1984a. "The Cartographic Definition of France's Eastern Boundary in the Early Seventeenth Century." *Imago Mundi* 36: 72–80.

1984b. "Comment on Session: Cartography and Power in the Seventeenth Century." in John F. Sweets, ed. *Proceedings of the Tenth Annual Meeting of the Western Society for French History.* Lawrence: University of Kansas Press.

1992a. "Introduction." In David Buisseret, ed. *Monarchs, Ministers, and Maps: The Emergence of Cartography as a Tool of Government in Early Modern Europe.* University of Chicago Press.

1992b. "Monarchs, Ministers, and Maps in France before the Accession of Louis XIV." In David Buisseret, ed. *Monarchs, Ministers, and Maps:*

The Emergence of Cartography as a Tool of Government in Early Modern Europe. University of Chicago Press.

2003. *The Mapmakers' Quest: Depicting New Worlds in Renaissance Europe.* Oxford University Press.

2007a. "French Cartography: The *ingénieurs du roi*, 1500–1650." In David Woodward, ed. *The History of Cartography*, vol. III, *Cartography in the European Renaissance.* University of Chicago Press.

2007b. "Spanish Peninsular Cartography, 1500–1700." In David Woodward, ed. *The History of Cartography*, vol. III, *Cartography in the European Renaissance.* University of Chicago Press.

Bukovansky, Mlada. 2002. *Legitimacy and Power Politics: The American and French Revolutions in International Political Culture.* Princeton University Press.

Bull, Hedley. 1977. *The Anarchical Society.* New York: Columbia University Press.

Bull, Hedley, and Adam Watson, eds. 1984. *The Expansion of International Society.* Oxford University Press.

Bunce, Valerie. 1999. *Subversive Institutions: The Design and Destruction of Socialism and the State.* New York: Cambridge University Press.

Burch, Kurt. 2000. "Changing the Rules: Reconceiving Change in the Westphalian System." *International Studies Review* 2(2): 181–210.

Buzan, Barry. 2004. *From International to World Society? English School Theory and the Social Structure of Globalization.* Cambridge University Press.

Buzan, Barry, and Richard Little. 2000. *International Systems in World History.* Oxford University Press.

Campbell, Tony. 1987. "Portolan Charts from the Late Thirteenth Century to 1500." In J. B. Harley and David Woodward, eds. *The History of Cartography*, vol. I, *Cartography in Prehistoric, Ancient, and Medieval Europe and the Mediterranean.* University of Chicago Press.

Carlsnaes, Walter. 1992. "The Agency–Structure Problem in Foreign Policy Analysis." *International Studies Quarterly* 36(3): 245–70.

Castells, Manuel. 1996. *The Information Age: Economy, Society, and Culture*, vol. I, *The Rise of the Network Society.* Oxford: Blackwell.

Casti, Emanuela. 2007. "State, Cartography, and Territory in Renaissance Veneto and Lombardy." In David Woodward, ed. *The History of Cartography*, vol. III, *Cartography in the European Renaissance.* University of Chicago Press.

Chrisman, Nicholas. 2005. "Full Circle: More than Just Social Implications of GIS." *Cartographica* 40(4): 23–35.

Cline, Howard F. 1964. "The *Relaciones Geográficas* of the Spanish Indies, 1577–1586." *Hispanic American Historical Review* 44(3): 341–74.

Collins, James B. 1995. *The State in Early Modern France*. Cambridge University Press.

Cooley, Alexander. 2005. *Logics of Hierarchy: The Organization of Empires, States, and Military Occupations*. Ithaca, NY: Cornell University Press.

"A Corpus of Maps of 'Germania' (before *c.* 1700)." 1993. *Imago Mundi* 45: 19.

Cosgrove, Denis. 1992. "Mapping New Worlds: Culture and Cartography in Sixteenth-Century Venice." *Imago Mundi* 44: 65–89.

    2001. *Apollo's Eye: A Cartographic Genealogy of the Earth in the Western Imagination*. Baltimore, MD: Johns Hopkins University Press.

Covini, Maria Nadia. 2000. "Political and Military Bonds in the Italian State System, Thirteenth to Sixteenth Centuries." In Philippe Contamine, ed. *War and Competition between States: The Origins of the Modern State in Europe, 13th–18th Centuries*. New York: Clarendon Press.

Crampton, Jeremy W. 2001. "Maps as Social Constructions: Power, Communication, and Visualization." *Progress in Human Geography* 25(2): 235–52.

    2003. *The Political Mapping of Cyberspace*. Edinburgh University Press.

    2004. "GIS and Geographic Governance: Reconstructing the Choropleth Map." *Cartographica* 39(1): 41–53.

    2006. "The Cartographic Calculation of Space: Race Mapping and the Balkans at the Paris Peace Conference of 1919." *Social and Cultural Geography* 7(5): 731–52.

    2009. "Cartography: Maps 2.0." *Progress in Human Geography* 33(1): 91–100.

    2010. *Mapping: A Critical Introduction to Cartography and GIS*. Malden, MA: Wiley-Blackwell.

    2011. "Cartographic Calculations of Territory." *Progress in Human Geography* 35(1): 92–103.

Crampton, Jeremy W., and John Krygier. 2006. "An Introduction to Critical Cartography." *ACME: An International E-Journal for Critical Geographies* 4(1): 11–33.

Croxton, Derek. 1999. "The Peace of Westphalia of 1648 and the Origins of Sovereignty." *International History Review* 21(3): 569–91.

Curry, Anne. 1993. *The Hundred Years War*. New York: St. Martin's Press.

Curry, Michael R. 2005. "Toward a Geography of a World without Maps: Lessons from Ptolemy and Postal Codes." *Annals of the Association of American Geographers* 95(3): 680–91.

Dalché, Patrick Gautier. 2007. "The Reception of Ptolemy's *Geography* (End of the Fourteenth to Beginning of the Sixteenth Century)." In David Woodward, ed. *The History of Cartography*, vol. III, *Cartography in the European Renaissance*. University of Chicago Press.

Day, John D. 1995. "The Search for the Origins of the Chinese Manuscript of Matteo Ricci's Maps." *Imago Mundi* 47(1): 94–117.

De Dainville, F. 1970. "How Did Oronce Fine Draw His Large Map of France?" *Imago Mundi* 24: 49–55.

Deibert, Ronald J. 1997. *Parchment, Printing, and Hypermedia: Communication in World Order Transformation.* New York: Columbia University Press.

Delano-Smith, Catherine. 2000. "Maps and Religion in Medieval and Early Modern Europe." In David Woodward, Catherine Delano-Smith and Cordell Yee, eds. *Plantejaments i objectius d'una història universal de la cartografia / Approaches and Challenges in a Worldwide History of Cartography.* Barcelona: Institut Cartogràfic de Catalunya.

Dessau, Adalbert. 1968. "The Idea of Treason in the Middle Ages." In Frederic L. Cheyette, ed. *Lordship and Community in Medieval Europe. Selected Readings.* New York: Holt, Rinehard, and Winston.

Dessler, David. 1989. "What's at Stake in the Agent–Structure Debate?" *International Organization* 43(3): 441–73.

Diamond, Larry, and Marc F. Plattner, eds. 2012. *Liberation Technology: Social Media and the Struggle for Democracy.* Baltimore: Johns Hopkins University Press.

Dickinson, Joycelyne G. 1955. *The Congress of Arras, 1435: A Study in Medieval Diplomacy.* Oxford: Clarendon Press.

Dilke, O. A. W. 1987. "Cartography in the Ancient World: A Conclusion." In J. B. Harley and David Woodward, eds. *The History of Cartography,* vol. I, *Cartography in Prehistoric, Ancient, and Medieval Europe and the Mediterranean.* University of Chicago Press.

Dodge, Martin, and Rob Kitchin. 2001. *Atlas of Cyberspace.* London: Pearson Education.

Doty, Roxanne Lynn. 1997. "Aporia: A Critical Exploration of the Agent–Structure Problematique in International Relations Theory." *European Journal of International Relations* 3(3): 365–92.

Downing, Brian M. 1992. *The Military Revolution and Political Change: Origins of Democracy and Autocracy in Early Modern Europe.* Princeton University Press.

Duby, Georges. 1968. "The Nobility in Eleventh- and Twelfth-Century Mâconnais." In Frederic L. Cheyette, ed. *Lordship and Community in Medieval Europe. Selected Readings.* New York: Holt, Rinehard, and Winston.

Dunbabin, Jean. 1988. "Government." In J. H. Burns, ed. *The Cambridge History of Medieval Political Thought, c. 350–c. 1450.* Cambridge University Press.

Dunn, Christine E. 2007. "Participatory GIS: A People's GIS?" *Progress in Human Geography* 31(5): 616–37.

Duvall, Raymond, and Jonathan Havercroft. 2008. "Taking Sovereignty Out of This World: Space Weapons and the Empire of the Future." *Review of International Studies* 34(4): 755–75.

Eco, Umberto. 1994. *How to Travel with a Salmon and Other Essays*, trans. William Weaver. New York: Harcourt, Brace.

Edgerton, Samuel Y., Jr. 1975. *The Renaissance Rediscovery of Linear Perspective*. New York: Basic Books.

1987. "From Mental Matrix to *Mappamundi* to Christian Empire: The Heritage of Ptolemaic Cartography in the Renaissance." In David Woodward, ed. *Art and Cartography: Six Historical Essays*. University of Chicago Press.

Edney, Matthew H. 1993. "Cartography without 'Progress': Reinterpreting the Nature and Historical Development of Mapmaking." *Cartographica* 30(2/3): 54–68.

1997. *Mapping an Empire: The Geographical Construction of British India, 1765–1843*. University of Chicago Press.

2009. "The Irony of Imperial Mapping." In James R. Akerman, ed. *The Imperial Map: Cartography and the Mastery of Empire*. University of Chicago Press.

Edson, Evelyn. 1997. *Mapping Time and Space: How Medieval Mapmakers Viewed Their World*. London: The British Library.

Edwards, Clinton R. 1969. "Mapping by Questionnaire: An Early Spanish Attempt to Determine New World Geographical Positions." *Imago Mundi* 23: 17–28.

Ehrensvärd, Ulla. 1987. "Color in Cartography: A Historical Survey." In David Woodward, ed. *Art and Cartography: Six Historical Essays*. University of Chicago Press.

Eisenstein, Elizabeth L. 1979. *The Printing Press as an Agent of Change*. Cambridge University Press.

2005. *The Printing Revolution in Early Modern Europe*, 2nd edn. Cambridge University Press.

Elden, Stuart. 2010. "Land, Terrain, Territory." *Progress in Human Geography* 34(6): 799–817.

Ellison, Nicole B., Charles Steinfield, and Cliff Lampe. 2007. "The Benefits of Facebook 'Friends:' Social Capital and College Students' Use of Online Social Network Sites." *Journal of Computer-Mediated Communication* 12(4): 1143–168.

Elman, Benjamin A. 2006. *A Cultural History of Modern Science in China*. Cambridge, MA: Harvard University Press.

Elrod, Richard B. 1976. "The Concert of Europe: A Fresh Look at an International System." *World Politics* 28(2): 159–74.

Ertman, Thomas. 1997. *The Birth of the Leviathan: Building States and Regimes in Medieval and Early Modern Europe.* Cambridge University Press.

Evans, R. J. W. 1992. "Essay and Reflection: Frontiers and National Identities in Central Europe." *International History Review* 14(3): 480–502.

Febvre, Lucien. 1973. "*Frontière*: The Word and the Concept." In Peter Burke, ed. *A New Kind of History: From the Writings of Febvre.* London: Routledge & Kegan Paul.

Ferguson, Yale H., and Richard W. Mansbach. 1996. *Polities: Authority, Identities, and Change.* Columbia: University of South Carolina Press.

Fernández-Santamaria, J. A. 1977. *The State, War, and Peace: Spanish Political Thought in the Renaissance, 1516–1559.* London: Cambridge University Press.

Finer, Samuel E. 1997. *The History of Government from the Earliest Times,* 3 vols. Oxford University Press.

Fischer, Markus. 1992. "Feudal Europe, 800–1300: Communal Discourse and Conflictual Practices." *International Organization* 46(2): 427–66.

Fletcher, Owen. 2011. "Google Applies for Online Map License in China." *Wall Street Journal Online,* June 14.

Foucault, Michel. 1970. *The Order of Things: An Archeology of the Human Sciences.* New York: Vintage Books.

Fowler, Kenneth. 1971. "Truces." In Kenneth Fowler, ed. *The Hundred Years War.* London: Macmillan.

Frängsmyr, Tore, J. L. Heilbron, and Robin E. Rider, eds. 1990. *The Quantifying Spirit in the 18th Century.* Berkeley: University of California Press.

Fritsch, Stefan. 2011. "Technology and Global Affairs." *International Studies Perspectives* 12(1): 27–45.

Ganshof, François L. 1970. *The Middle Ages: A History of International Relations,* trans. Rémy Inglis Hall. New York: Harper & Row.

George, Alexander L., and Andrew Bennett. 2005. *Case Studies and Theory Development in the Social Sciences.* Cambridge, MA: MIT Press.

Gerhardt, Hannes, Philip E. Steinberg, Jeremy Tasch, Sandra J. Fabiano, and Rob Shields. 2010. "Contested Sovereignty in a Changing Arctic." *Annals of the Association of American Geographers* 100(4): 992–1002.

Giddens, Anthony. 1984. *The Constitution of Society: Outline of the Theory of Structuration.* Oxford: Polity Press.

1985. *The Nation-State and Violence. Volume Two of A Contemporary Critique of Historical Materialism.* Berkeley: University of California Press.

Gilman, Nils. 2009. "Hacking Goes Pro." *Engineering and Technology Magazine* 4(3), February 16.

Gilpin, Robert. 1981. *War and Change in World Politics.* Cambridge University Press.

Goodchild, Michael F. 2006. "GIScience Ten Years after *Ground Truth.*" *Transactions in GIS* 10(5): 687–92.

2007. "Citizens as Sensors: The World of Volunteered Geography." *GeoJournal* 69(4): 211–21.

Gorski, Philip S. 2003. *The Disciplinary Revolution: Calvinism and the Rise of the State in Early Modern Europe.* University of Chicago Press.

Gottman, Jean. 1973. *The Significance of Territory.* Charlottesville: University Press of Virginia.

Grafton, Anthony. 1992. *New Worlds, Ancient Texts: The Power of Tradition and the Shock of Discovery.* Cambridge, MA: Harvard University Press.

Greenblatt, Stephen. 1991. *Marvelous Possessions: The Wonder of the New World.* University of Chicago Press.

Gross, Leo. 1948. "The Peace of Westphalia, 1648–1948." *American Journal of International Law* 42(1): 21–41.

Guarini, Elena Fasano. 2003. "Geographies of Power: The Territorial State in Early Modern Italy." In John Jeffries Martin, ed. *The Renaissance: Italy and Abroad.* London: Routledge.

Gustafsson, Harald. 1998. "The Conglomerate State: A Perspective on State Formation in Early Modern Europe." *Scandinavian Journal of History* 23(3): 189–213.

Hacking, Ian. 1975 [2006]. *The Emergence of Probability,* 2nd edn. Cambridge University Press.

1990. *The Taming of Chance.* Cambridge University Press.

1995. *Rewriting the Soul: Multiple Personality and the Sciences of Memory.* Princeton University Press.

2002. *Historical Ontology.* Cambridge, MA: Harvard University Press.

Häkli, Jouni. 2001. "In the Territory of Knowledge: State-Centred Discourses and the Construction of Society." *Progress in Human Geography* 25(3): 403–22.

Hale, John. 1971. *Renaissance Europe: Individual and Society, 1480–1520.* Berkeley: University of California Press.

2007. "Warfare and Cartography, ca. 1450 to ca. 1640." In David Woodward, ed. *The History of Cartography,* vol. III, *Cartography in the European Renaissance.* University of Chicago Press.

Hall, Rodney Bruce. 1999. *National Collective Identity: Social Constructs and International Systems.* New York: Columbia University Press.

Hall, Rodney Bruce, and Friedrich V. Kratochwil. 1993. "Medieval Tales: Neorealist 'Science' and the Abuse of History." *International Organization* 47(3): 479–91.

Harley, J. B. 1987. "The Map and the Development of the History of Cartography." In J. B. Harley and David Woodward, eds. *The History of Cartography*, vol. I, *Cartography in Prehistoric, Ancient, and Medieval Europe and the Mediterranean*. University of Chicago Press.

——— 1989. "Historical Geography and the Cartographic Illusion." *Journal of Historical Geography* 15(1): 80–91.

——— 2001. *The New Nature of Maps: Essays in the History of Cartography*. Paul Laxton, ed. Baltimore, MD: Johns Hopkins University Press.

Harley, J. B., and David Woodward, eds. 1987a. *The History of Cartography*, vol. I, *Cartography in Prehistoric, Ancient, and Medieval Europe and the Mediterranean*. University of Chicago Press.

——— 1987b. "Concluding Remarks." In Harley and Woodward, eds. *The History of Cartography*, vol. I, *Cartography in Prehistoric, Ancient, and Medieval Europe and the Mediterranean*. University of Chicago Press.

——— 1992. *The History of Cartography*, vol. II, book i, *Cartography in the Traditional Islamic and South Asian Societies*. University of Chicago Press.

——— 1994. *The History of Cartography*, vol. II, book ii, *Cartography in the Traditional East and Southeast Asian Societies*. University of Chicago Press.

Harvey, P. D. A. 1987a. "Local and Regional Cartography in Medieval Europe." In J. B. Harley and David Woodward, eds. *The History of Cartography*, vol. I, *Cartography in Prehistoric, Ancient, and Medieval Europe and the Mediterranean*. University of Chicago Press.

——— 1987b. "Medieval Maps: An Introduction." In J. B. Harley and David Woodward, eds. *The History of Cartography*, vol. I, *Cartography in Prehistoric, Ancient, and Medieval Europe and the Mediterranean*. University of Chicago Press.

Headrick, Daniel R. 2000. *When Information Came of Age: Technologies of Knowledge in the Age of Reason and Revolution 1700–1850*. Oxford University Press.

Hebbert, F. J., and G. A. Rothrock. 1990. *Soldier of France: Sébastien Le Prestre de Vauban, 1633–1707*. New York: Peter Lang.

Heffernan, Michael. 2002. "The Politics of the Map in the Early Twentieth Century." *Cartography and Geographic Information Science* 29(3): 207–26.

Heilbron, J. L. 1990. "Introductory Essay." In Tore Frängsmyr, J. L. Heilbron, and Robin E. Rider, eds. *The Quantifying Spirit in the 18th Century*. Berkeley: University of California Press.

Henrikson, Alan, K. 1975. "The Map as an 'Idea': The Role of Cartographic Imagery during the Second World War." *American Geographer* 2(1): 19–53.

Herbst, Jeffrey. 2000. *States and Power in Africa: Comparative Lessons in Authority and Control*. Princeton University Press.

Herrera, Geoffrey L. 2006. *Technology and International Transformation: The Railroad, the Atom Bomb, and the Politics of Technological Change*. Albany, NY: SUNY Press.

Hill, Henry Bertram, ed. and trans. 1961. *The Political Testament of Cardinal Richelieu*. Madison: University of Wisconsin Press.

Hobson, John M. 2004. *The Eastern Origins of Western Civilization*. Cambridge University Press.

2009. "Provincializing Westphalia: The Eastern Origins of Sovereignty." *International Politics* 46(6): 671–90.

Holsti, K. J. 2004. *Taming the Sovereigns: Institutional Change in International Politics*. Cambridge University Press.

Holzgrefe, J. L. 1989. "The Origins of Modern International Relations Theory." *Review of International Studies* 15(1): 11–26.

Hopf, Ted. 2010. "The Logic of Habit in International Relations." *European Journal of International Relations* 16(4): 539–61.

Hostetler, Laura. 2001. *Qing Colonial Enterprise: Ethnography and Cartography in Early Modern China*. University of Chicago Press.

Israel, Fred L., ed. 1967. *Major Peace Treaties of Modern History, 1648–1967*, vol. I. Philadelphia: Chelsea House Publishers.

Jackson, Peter. 2008. "Pierre Bourdieu, the 'Cultural Turn' and the Practice of International History." *Review of International Studies* 34(1): 155–81.

Jackson, Robert H. 1990. *Quasi-states: Sovereignty, International Relations and the Third World*. Cambridge University Press.

Jackson, Robert H., and Carl G. Rosberg. 1982. "Why Africa's Weak States Persist: The Empirical and the Juridical in Statehood." *World Politics* 35(1): 1–24.

Jacob, Christian. 1996. "Toward a Cultural History of Cartography." *Imago Mundi* 48: 191–98.

Jahn, Beate. 1999. "IR and the State of Nature: The Cultural Origins of a Ruling Ideology." *Review of International Studies* 25(3): 411–34.

2000. *The Cultural Construction of International Relations: The Invention of the State of Nature*. New York: Palgrave.

Johnson, Richard G. 1999. "Negotiating the Dayton Peace Accords through Digital Maps." United States Institute of Peace, Virtual Diplomacy Report 8, February 25, 1999.

Kagan, Richard L., and Benjamin Schmidt. 2007. "Maps and the Early Modern State: Official Cartography." In David Woodward, ed. *The History of Cartography*, vol. III, *Cartography in the European Renaissance*. University of Chicago Press.

Kain, Roger J. P., and Elizabeth Baigent. 1992. *The Cadastral Map in the Service of the State: A History of Property Mapping*. University of Chicago Press.

Kantorowicz, Ernst H. 1957. *The King's Two Bodies: A Study in Mediaeval Political Theology*. Princeton University Press.

Karamustafa, Ahmet T. 1992a. "Introduction to Islamic Maps." In J. B. Harley and David Woodward, eds. *The History of Cartography*, vol. II, book i, *Cartography in the Traditional Islamic and South Asian Societies*. University of Chicago Press.

——— 1992b. "Military, Administrative, and Scholarly Maps and Plans." In J. B. Harley and David Woodward, eds. *The History of Cartography*, vol. II, book i, *Cartography in the Traditional Islamic and South Asian Societies*. University of Chicago Press.

Karrow, Robert. 2007. "Centers of Map Publishing in Europe, 1472–1600." In David Woodward, ed. *The History of Cartography*, vol. III, *Cartography in the European Renaissance*. University of Chicago Press.

Kayaoglu, Turan. 2007. "The Extension of Westphalian Sovereignty: State Building and the Abolition of Extraterritoriality." *International Studies Quarterly* 51(3): 649–75.

Keen, M. H. 1968. "The Laws of War in the Late Middle Ages." In Frederic L. Cheyette, ed. *Lordship and Community in Medieval Europe. Selected Readings*. New York: Holt, Rinehard, and Winston.

Keene, Edward. 2002. *Beyond the Anarchical Society: Grotius, Colonialism and Order in World Politics*. Cambridge University Press.

King, Geoff. 1996. *Mapping Reality: An Exploration of Cultural Cartographies*. London: Macmillan.

King, P. D. 1988. "The Barbarian Kingdoms." In J. H. Burns, ed. *The Cambridge History of Medieval Political Thought, c. 350–c. 1450*. Cambridge University Press.

Kivelson, Valeri A. 1999. "Cartography, Autocracy, and State Powerlessness: The Uses of Maps in Early Modern Russia." *Imago Mundi* 51(1): 83–105.

Klinghoffer, Arthur Jay. 2006. *The Power of Projections: How Maps Reflect Global Politics and History*. Westport, CT: Praeger.

Kobrin, Stephen J. 2001. "Sovereignty @ Bay: Globalization, Multinational Enterprise, and the International Political System." In Alan Rugman and Thomas Brewer, eds. *The Oxford Handbook of International Business*. New York: Oxford University Press.

Koeman, Cornelis. 1970. *Joan Blaeu and his Grand Atlas*. Amsterdam: Theatrum Orbis Terrarum.

Koeman, Cornelis, Günter Schilder, Marco van Egmond, and Peter van der Krogt. 2007. "Commercial Cartography and Map Production in the Low Countries, 1500–ca. 1670." In David Woodward, ed. *The History of Cartography*, vol. III, *Cartography in the European Renaissance.* University of Chicago Press.

Kokkonen, Pellervo. 1998. "State, Territorial Expansion, and the Meaning of Maps: Some Perspectives on the Eighteenth-Century Mapping of the Baltic Sea." *Cartographica* 35(3/4): 55–66.

Konvitz, Josef W. 1987. *Cartography in France, 1660–1848: Science, Engineering, and Statecraft.* University of Chicago Press.

    1990. "The Nation-State, Paris and Cartography in Eighteenth- and Nineteenth-Century France." *Journal of Historical Geography* 16(1): 3–16.

Krasner, Stephen D. 1993. "Westphalia and All That," in Judith Goldstein and Robert Keohane, eds. *Ideas and Foreign Policy.* Ithaca, NY: Cornell University Press.

    1999. *Sovereignty: Organized Hypocrisy.* Princeton University Press.

    2001. "Rethinking the Sovereign State Model." *Review of International Studies* 27(5): 17–42.

Kratochwil, Friedrich. 1986. "Of Systems, Boundaries, and Territoriality: An Inquiry into the Formation of the State System." *World Politics* 39(1): 27–52.

    1989. *Rules, Norms, and Decisions. On the Conditions of Practical and Legal Reasoning in International Relations and Domestic Affairs.* Cambridge University Press.

Krishna, Sankaran. 1996. "Cartographic Anxiety: Mapping the Body Politic in India." In Michael J. Shapiro and Hayward R. Alker, eds. *Challenging Boundaries: Global Flows, Territorial Identities.* Minneapolis: University of Minnesota Press.

Kula, Witold. 1986. *Measures and Men,* trans. R. Szreter. Princeton University Press.

Lake, David A. 2003. "The New Sovereignty in International Relations." *International Studies Review* 5(3): 303–23.

    2009. *Hierarchy in International Relations.* Ithaca, NY: Cornell University Press.

Latour, Bruno. 1987. *Science in Action: How to Follow Scientists and Engineers through Society.* Cambridge, MA: Harvard University Press.

Lefebvre, Henri. 1991 [1974]. *The Production of Space,* trans. Donald Nicholson-Smith. Cambridge, MA: Blackwell.

Lesaffer, Randall, ed. 2004. *Peace Treaties and International Law in European History: From the Late Middle Ages to World War One.* Cambridge University Press.

Leyser, K. 1975. "Frederick Barbarossa, Henry II, and the Hand of St James." *English Historical Review* 90(356): 356.

Linklater, Andro. 2002. *Measuring America: How the United States Was Shaped by the Greatest Land Sale in History*. New York: Penguin.

Lukowski, Jerzy. 1999. *The Partitions of Poland: 1772, 1793, 1795*. New York: Longman.

Lynn, John A. 1999. *The Wars of Louis XIV, 1667–1714*. London: Longman.

2003. *Battle: A History of Combat and Culture*. Boulder, CO: Westview Press.

Lyons, Martyn. 2006. *Post-Revolutionary Europe, 1815–1856*. New York: Palgrave.

Mahoney, James. 1999. "Nominal, Ordinal and Narrative Appraisal in Macrocausal Analysis." *American Journal of Sociology* 104(4): 1154–1196.

Marino, John. 1992. "Administrative Mapping in the Italian States." In David Buisseret, ed. 1992. *Monarchs, Ministers, and Maps: The Emergence of Cartography as a Tool of Government in Early Modern Europe*. University of Chicago Press.

Martines, Lauro. 1979. *Power and Imagination: City-States in Renaissance Italy*. Baltimore, MD: Johns Hopkins University Press.

Mattingly, Garrett. 1955. *Renaissance Diplomacy*. Cambridge: Riverside Press.

McLuhan, Marshall. 1962. *The Gutenberg Galaxy: The Making of Typographic Man*. University of Toronto Press.

McNeill, William H. 1982. *The Pursuit of Power: Technology, Armed Force, and Society since A.D. 1000*. University of Chicago Press.

Mead, William R. 2007. "Scandinavian Renaissance Cartography." In David Woodward, ed. *The History of Cartography*, vol. III, *Cartography in the European Renaissance*. University of Chicago Press.

Meurer, Peter H. 2007. "Cartography in the German Lands, 1450–1650." In David Woodward, ed. *The History of Cartography*, vol. III, *Cartography in the European Renaissance*. University of Chicago Press.

Meyer, John W., John Boli, George M. Thomas, Francisco O. Ramirez. 1997. "World Society and the Nation-State." *American Journal of Sociology* 103(1): 144–81.

Michael, Bernardo A. 2007. "Making Territory Visible: The Revenue Surveys of Colonial South Asia." *Imago Mundi* 59(1): 78–95.

Migdal, Joel S. 2004. "Mental Maps and Virtual Checkpoints: Struggles to Construct and Maintain State and Social Boundaries." In Joel S. Migdal, ed. *Boundaries and Belonging: States and Societies in the Struggle to Shape Identities and Local Practices*. Cambridge University Press.

Mignolo, Walter D. 1995. *The Darker Side of the Renaissance: Literacy, Territoriality, and Colonization*. Ann Arbor: University of Michigan Press.

Miller, Christopher C. 2006. "A Beast in the Field: The Google Maps Mashups as GIS/2." *Cartographica* 41(3): 187–99.

Milner, Helen. 1991. "The Assumption of Anarchy in International Relations Theory: A Critique." *Review of International Studies* 17(1): 67–85.

Miquelon, Dale. 2001. "Envisioning the French Empire: Utrecht, 1711–1713." *French Historical Studies* 24(4): 653–77.

Mitteis, Heinrich. 1975. *The State in the Middle Ages: A Comparative Constitutional History of Feudal Europe*. Amsterdam: North-Holland Pub. Co.

Monmonier, Mark. 1995. *Drawing the Line: Tales of Maps and Cartocontroversy*. New York: Henry Holt.

Mukerji, Chandra. 1997. *Territorial Ambitions and the Gardens of Versailles*. Cambridge University Press.

2006. "Printing, Cartography, and Conceptions of Place in Renaissance Europe." *Media, Culture and Society* 28(5): 651–69.

Muldoon, James. 1999. *Empire and Order: The Concept of Empire, 800–1800*. New York: St. Martin's Press.

Munck, Thomas. 1990. *Seventeenth Century Europe: State, Conflict and the Social Order in Europe, 1598–1700*. New York: St. Martin's Press.

Mundy, Barbara E. 1996. *The Mapping of New Spain: Indigenous Cartography and the Maps of the Relaciones Geográficas*. University of Chicago Press.

Murphy, Alexander B. 2012. "Territory's Continuing Allure." *Annals of the Association of American Geographers*, DOI: 10.1080/00045608.2012.696232, published online July 2012.

Neocleous, Mark. 2003. "Off the Map: On Violence and Cartography." *European Journal of Social Theory* 6(4): 409–25.

Newman, David, and Anssi Paasi. 1998. "Fences and Neighbors in the Postmodern World: Boundary Narratives in Political Geography." *Progress in Human Geography* 22(2): 186–207.

Nexon, Daniel H. 2009. *The Struggle for Power in Early Modern Europe: Religious Conflict, Dynastic Empires, and International Change*. Princeton University Press.

O'Gorman, Edmundo. 1961. *The Invention of America*. Westport, CT: Greenwood Press.

Onuf, Nicholas. 1989. *World of Our Making: Rules and Rule in Social Theory and International Relations*. Columbia: University of South Carolina Press.

Onuf, Peter, and Nicholas Onuf. 1993. *Federal Union, Modern World: The Law of Nations in an Age of Revolutions, 1776–1814*. Madison, WI: Madison House.

Organization of African Unity (OAU). 1964. "Border Disputes among African States." Resolutions Adopted by the First Ordinary Session of the Assembly of Heads of State and Government Held in Cairo, UAR, from 17 to 21 July, AHG/Res.16(I).

Osiander, Andreas. 1994. *The States System of Europe, 1640–1990: Peacemaking and the Conditions of International Stability*. Oxford: Clarendon Press.

2001a. "Before Sovereignty: Society and Politics in *Ancient Régime* Europe." *Review of International Studies* 27(5): 119–45.

2001b. "Sovereignty, International Relations, and the Westphalian Myth." *International Organization* 55(2): 251–87.

2007. *Before the State: Systemic Political Change in the West from the Greeks to the French Revolution*. Oxford University Press.

Padrón, Ricardo. 2002. "Mapping Plus Ultra: Cartography, Space, and Hispanic Modernity." *Representations* 79(1): 28–60.

2004. *The Spacious Word: Cartography, Literature, and Empire in Early Modern Spain*. University of Chicago Press.

Pagden, Anthony. 1995. *Lords of All the World: Ideologies of Empire in Spain, Britain, and France, c. 1500–c. 1800*. New Haven, CT: Yale University Press.

Parker, Geoffrey. 2001. *Europe in Crisis: 1598–1648*, 2nd edn. Oxford: Blackwell.

Parsons, Craig. 2007. *How to Map Arguments in Political Science*. Oxford University Press.

Pedley, Mary Sponberg. 1984. "New Light on an Old Atlas: Documents concerning the Publication of the *Atlas Universel* (1757)." *Imago Mundi* 36: 48–63.

Pelletier, Monique. 1998. "Cartography and Power in France during the Seventeenth and Eighteenth Centuries." *Cartographica* 35(3/4): 41–53.

2007. "National and Regional Mapping in France to about 1650." In David Woodward, ed. *The History of Cartography*, vol. III, *Cartography in the European Renaissance*. University of Chicago Press.

Petrella, Marco. 2009. "Guillaume Delisle's *Carte du Duché de Bourgogne*: The Role of Central and Peripheral Authorities in the Construction of a Provincial Territory in France in the Early 18th Century." *Journal of Map and Geography Libraries* 5(1): 17–39.

Petto, Christine Marie. 2007. *When France Was King of Cartography: The Patronage and Production of Maps in Early Modern France*. Lanham, MD: Lexington Books.

Philpott, Daniel. 2001. *Revolutions in Sovereignty: How Ideas Shaped Modern International Relations*. Princeton University Press.

Pickles, John, ed. 1995. *Ground Truth: The Social Implications of Geographic Information Systems*. New York: The Guilford Press.

——— 2004. *A History of Spaces: Cartographic Reason, Mapping, and the Geocoded World*. New York: Routledge.

Poggi, Gianfranco. 1978. *The Development of the Modern State: A Sociological Introduction*. Stanford University Press.

Prescott, J. R. V. 1987. *Political Frontiers and Boundaries*. London: Allen and Unwin.

Procopé, John. 1988. "Greek and Roman Political Theory." In J. H. Burns, ed. *The Cambridge History of Medieval Political Thought, c. 350–c. 1450*. Cambridge University Press.

Quaini, Massimo. 2007. "Cartographic Activities in the Republic of Genoa, Corsica, and Sardinia in the Renaissance." In David Woodward, ed. *The History of Cartography*, vol. III, *Cartography in the European Renaissance*. University of Chicago Press.

Raj, Kapil. 2000. "Colonial Encounters and the Forging of New Knowledge and National Identities: Great Britain and India, 1760–1850." *Osiris* 2nd ser., 15: 119–34.

Randles, W. G. L. 2000a, [1988]. "The Emergence of Nautical Astronomy in Portugal in the XVth Century." In *Geography, Cartography, and Nautical Science in the Renaissance: The Impact of the Great Discoveries*. Aldershot: Ashgate.

——— 2000b [1994]. "Classical Models of World Geography and Their Transformation Following the Discovery of America." In *Geography, Cartography, and Nautical Science in the Renaissance: The Impact of the Great Discoveries*. Aldershot: Ashgate.

Reinhartz, Dennis. 1997. *The Cartographer and the Literati: Herman Moll and His Intellectual Circle*. Lewiston, NY: Edwin Mellen Press.

Reisser, Wesley J. 2012. *The Black Book: Woodrow Wilson's Secret Plan for Peace*. Lanham, MD: Lexington Books.

Rekacewicz, Philippe. 2000. "Mapping Concepts (*cartographier la pensée*)." *Public Culture* 12(3): 703–6.

Reus-Smit, Christian. 1999. *The Moral Purpose of the State*. Princeton University Press.

Revel, Jacques. 1991. "Knowledge of the Territory." *Science in Context* 4(1): 133–61.

Reyes, Alvaro, and Mara Kaufman. 2011. "Sovereignty, Indigeneity, Territory: Zapatista Autonomy and the New Practices of Decolonization." *South Atlantic Quarterly* 110(2): 505–25.

Reynolds, Susan. 1997. *Kingdoms and Communities in Western Europe, 900–1300*, 2nd edn. Oxford: Clarendon Press.

Rombai, Leonardo. 2007. "Cartography in the Central Italian States from 1480–1680." In David Woodward, ed. *The History of Cartography*, vol. III, *Cartography in the European Renaissance*. University of Chicago Press.

Rosenberg, Justin. 1994. *The Empire of Civil Society*. London: Verso.

Rose-Redwood, Reuben S. 2006. "Governmentality, Geography, and the Geo-coded World." *Progress in Human Geography* 30(4): 469–86.

Roth, Robin. 2009. "The Challenges of Mapping Complex Indigenous Spatiality: From Abstract Space to Dwelling Space." *Cultural Geographies* 16(2): 207–27.

Ruggie, John G. 1983. "Continuity and Transformation in the World Polity: Toward a Neorealist Synthesis." *World Politics* 35(2): 261–85.

1993. "Territoriality and Beyond: Problematizing Modernity in International Relations." *International Organization* 47(1): 139–74.

Russell, Joycelyne G. 1986. *Peacemaking in the Renaissance*. Philadelphia: University of Pennsylvania Press.

Sack, Robert David. 1986. *Human Territoriality: Its Theory and History*. Cambridge University Press.

Sahlins, Peter. 1989. *Boundaries: The Making of France and Spain in the Pyrenees*. Berkeley: University of California Press.

1990. "Natural Frontiers Revisited: France's Boundaries since the Seventeenth Century." *American Historical Review* 95(5): 1423–451.

Sandman, Allison. 2007. "Spanish Nautical Cartography in the Renaissance." In David Woodward, ed. *The History of Cartography*, vol. III, *Cartography in the European Renaissance*. University of Chicago Press.

Sassen, Saskia. 2002. "Towards a Sociology of Information Technology." *Current Sociology* 50(3): 365–88.

2006. *Territory, Authority, Rights: From Medieval to Global Assemblages*. Princeton University Press.

Scharfe, Wolfgang. 1998. "President, King's Jester, and Cartographer: Jakob Paul von Gundling and the First Domestic Map of Brandenburg, 1724." *Cartographica* 35(3/4): 11–24.

Schilder, Günter. 1979. "Willem Jansz. Blaeu's Wall Map of the World, on Mercator's Projection, 1606–07 and Its Influence." *Imago Mundi* 31: 36–54.

Schmitt, Carl. 2003 [1974]. *The Nomos of the Earth*, trans. G. L. Ulmen. New York: Telos Press.

Schroeder, Paul W. 1986. "The 19th-Century International System: Changes in the Structure." *World Politics* 39(1): 1–26.

1994. *The Transformation of European Politics: 1763–1848*. Oxford: Clarendon Press.

2000. "International Politics, Peace, and War, 1815–1914." In T. C. W. Blanning, ed. *The Nineteenth Century: Europe 1789–1914*. Oxford University Press.

Schulz, Juergen. 1987. "Maps as Metaphors: Mural Map Cycles of the Italian Renaissance." In David Woodward, ed. *Art and Cartography: Six Historical Essays*. University of Chicago Press.

Scott, James C. 1998. *Seeing Like a State: How Certain Schemes to Improve the Human Condition Have Failed*. New Haven, CT: Yale University Press.

Seligman, Matthew S. 1995. "Maps as Progenitors of Territorial Disputes: Two Examples from Nineteenth-Century Southern Africa." *Imago Mundi* 47: 173–83.

Serchuk, Camille. 2006. "Picturing France in the Fifteenth Century: The Map in BNF MS Fr. 4991." *Imago Mundi* 58(2): 133–49.

Sewell, William H., Jr. 1992. "A Theory of Structure: Duality, Agency, and Transformation." *American Journal of Sociology* 98(1): 1–29.

Sivin, Nathan, and Gari Ledyard. 1994. "Introduction to East Asian Cartography." In J. B. Harley and David Woodward, eds. *The History of Cartography*, vol. II, book ii, *Cartography in the Traditional East and Southeast Asian Societies*. University of Chicago Press.

Skinner, Quentin. 1978. *The Foundations of Modern Political Thought*, 2 vols. Cambridge University Press.

Smith, Thomas W. 1999. *History and International Relations*. London: Routledge.

Soll, Jacob. 2009. *The Information Master: Jean-Baptiste Colbert's Secret State Intelligence System*. Ann Arbor: University of Michigan Press.

Solon, Paul. 1984. "Frontiers and Boundaries: French Cartography and the Limitation of Bourbon Ambition in Seventeenth-Century France." In John F. Sweets, ed. *Proceedings of the Tenth Annual Meeting of the Western Society for French History*. Lawrence: University of Kansas Press.

Spruyt, Hendrik. 1994. *The Sovereign State and Its Competitors*. Princeton University Press.

1998. "Historical Sociology and Systems Theory in International Relations." *Review of International Political Economy* 5(2): 340–53.

2000. "The End of Empire and the Extension of the Westphalian System: The Normative Basis of the Modern State Order." *International Studies Review* 2(2): 65–92.

2002. "The Origins, Development, and Possible Decline of the Modern State." *Annual Review of Political Science* 5: 127–49.

2005. *Ending Empire: Contested Sovereignty and Territorial Partition.* Ithaca, NY: Cornell University Press.

Steinberg, Philip E. 2005. "Insularity, Sovereignty, and Statehood: The Representation of Islands on Portolan Charts and the Construction of the Territorial State." *Geografiska Annaler* 87(4): 253–65.

2009. "Sovereignty, Territory, and the Mapping of Mobility: A View from the Outside." *Annals of the Association of American Geographers* 99(3): 467–95.

Strandsbjerg, Jeppe. 2008. "The Cartographic Production of Territorial Space: Mapping and State Formation in Early Modern Denmark." *Geopolitics* 13(2): 335–58.

Strange, Jeffrey J., and Cynthia C. Leung. 1999. "How Anecdotal Accounts in News and in Fiction Can Influence Judgments of a Social Problem's Urgency, Causes, and Cures." *Personality and Social Psychology Bulletin* 25(4): 436–49.

Strayer, Joseph R. 1970. *On the Medieval Origins of the Modern State.* Princeton University Press.

Sturdy, David J. 2002. *Fractured Europe: 1600–1721.* Malden, MA: Blackwell.

Talbert, Richard J. A., and Richard W. Unger, eds. 2008. *Cartography in Antiquity and the Middle Ages: Fresh Perspectives, New Methods.* Boston: Brill.

Taschen, Benedikt, and Peter van der Krogt. 2006. *Atlas Maior of 1665,* by Joan Blaeu. Hong Kong: Taschen.

Taussig, Michael. 1984. "Culture of Terror – Space of Death. Roger Casement's Putumayo Report and the Explanation of Torture." *Comparative Studies in Society and History* 26(3): 467–97.

Te Brake, Wayne. 1998. *Shaping History: Ordinary People in European Politics, 1500–1700.* Berkeley: University of California Press.

Teschke, Benno. 2003. *The Myth of 1648.* London: Verso.

Thelen, Kathleen. 2003. "How Institutionalism Evolves: Insights from Comparative Historical Analysis." In James Mahoney and James Rueschemeyer, eds. *Comparative Historical Analysis in the Social Sciences.* New York: Cambridge University Press.

Thomson, Janice E. 1994. *Mercenaries, Pirates, and Sovereigns.* Princeton University Press.

Thongchai Winichakul. 1994. *Siam Mapped: A History of the Geo-body of a Nation.* Honolulu: University of Hawai'i Press.

Thrower, Norman J. 1999. *Maps and Civilization: Cartography in Culture and Society,* 2nd edn. University of Chicago Press.

Tibbets, Gerald R. 1992. "The Beginnings of a Cartographic Tradition." In J. B. Harley and David Woodward, eds. *The History of Cartography,* vol. II, book i, *Cartography in the Traditional Islamic and South Asian Societies*. University of Chicago Press.

Tilly, Charles. 1992. *Coercion, Capital, and European States, AD 990–1992*. London: Blackwell.

Tombs, Robert. 2000. "Politics." In T. C. W. Blanning, ed. *The Nineteenth Century: Europe 1789–1914*. Oxford University Press.

Trachtenberg, Marc. 2006. *The Craft of International History: A Guide to Method*. Princeton University Press.

Turnbull, David. 1996. "Cartography and Science in Early Modern Europe: Mapping the Construction of Knowledge Spaces." *Imago Mundi* 48: 5–24.

Ullman, Walter. 1949. "The Development of the Medieval Idea of Sovereignty." *English Historical Review* 64(250): 1–33.

Valerio, Vladimiro. 2007. "Cartography in the Kingdom of Naples during the Early Modern Period." In David Woodward, ed. *The History of Cartography*, vol. III, *Cartography in the European Renaissance*. University of Chicago Press.

Vann, James. 1992. "Mapping under the Austrian Habsburgs." In David Buisseret, ed. *Monarchs, Ministers, and Maps: The Emergence of Cartography as a Tool of Government in Early Modern Europe*. University of Chicago Press.

Vigneras, L. A. 1962. "The Cartographer Diogo Ribeiro." *Imago Mundi* 16: 76–83.

Vu, Tuong. 2010. "Studying the State through State Formation." *World Politics* 62(1): 148–75.

Wagner, R. Harrison. 2007. *War and the State: The Theory of International Politics*. Ann Arbor: University of Michigan Press.

Wainwright, Joel, and Joe Bryan. 2009. "Cartography, Territory, Property: Postcolonial Reflections on Indigenous Counter-Mapping in Nicaragua and Belize." *Cultural Geographies* 16(2): 153–78.

Walker, R. B. J. 1993. *Inside/Outside: International Relations as Political Theory*. Cambridge University Press.

Wallerstein, Immanuel. 1974. *The Modern World System*, vol. I. Orlando, FL: Academic Press.

Waltz, Kenneth N. 1979. *Theory of International Politics*. Reading, MA: Addison-Wesley.

Watson, Adam. 1992. *The Evolution of International Society: A Comparative Historical Analysis*. London: Routledge.

Wendt, Alexander. 1987. "The Agent-Structure Problem in International Relations Theory." *International Organization* 41(3): 335–70.

1999. *Social Theory of International Politics*. Cambridge University Press.

Wendt, Alexander, and Daniel Friedheim. 1995. "Hierarchy under Anarchy: Informal Empire and the East German State." *International Organization* 49(4): 689–721.

Whittaker, C. R. 2004. *Rome and Its Frontiers: The Dynamics of Empire.* London: Routledge.

Wight, Colin. 1999. "They Shoot Dead Horses Don't They? Locating Agency in the Agent-Structure Problematique." *European Journal of International Relations* 5(1): 109–42.

Wight, Martin. 1977. *Systems of States.* Leicester University Press.

Wimmer, Andreas, and Brian Min. 2006. "From Empire to Nation-State: Explaining Wars in the Modern World, 1816–2001." *American Sociological Review* 71(6): 867–97.

Wolfart, Philip D. 2008. "Mapping the Early Modern State: The Work of Ignaz Ambros Amman, 1782–1812." *Journal of Historical Geography* 34(1): 1–23.

Wood, Denis. 1992. *The Power of Maps.* New York: The Guilford Press.

2010. *Rethinking the Power of Maps.* New York: The Guilford Press.

Woodward, David. 1985. "Reality, Symbolism, Time and Space in Medieval World Maps." *Annals of the Association of American Geographers* 75(4): 510–21.

1987. "Medieval *Mappaemundi.*" In J. B. Harley and David Woodward, eds. *The History of Cartography,* vol. I, *Cartography in Prehistoric, Ancient, and Medieval Europe and the Mediterranean.* University of Chicago Press.

1996. *Maps as Prints in the Italian Renaissance: Makers, Distributors, and Consumers.* London: The British Library.

2000. "'Theory' and *The History of Cartography.*" In David Woodward, Catherine Delano-Smith, and Cordell Yee, eds. *Plantejaments i objectius d'una història universal de la cartografia / Approaches and Challenges in a Worldwide History of Cartography.* Barcelona: Institut Cartogràfic de Catalunya.

2007a. "Cartography in the Renaissance: Continuity and Change." In David Woodward, ed. *The History of Cartography,* vol. III, *Cartography in the European Renaissance.* University of Chicago Press.

2007b. *The History of Cartography,* vol. III, *Cartography in the European Renaissance.* University of Chicago Press.

Woodward, David, and G. Malcolm Lewis, eds. 1998. *The History of Cartography,* vol. II, book iii, *Cartography in the Traditional African, American, Arctic, Australian, and Pacific Societies.* University of Chicago Press.

Yee, Cordell D. K. 1994a. "Chinese Maps in Political Culture." In J. B. Harley and David Woodward, eds. *The History of Cartography,* vol. II, book ii, *Cartography in the Traditional East and Southeast Asian Societies.* University of Chicago Press.

1994b. "Taking the World's Measure: Chinese Maps between Observation and Text." In J. B. Harley and David Woodward, eds. *The History of Cartography*, vol. II, book ii, *Cartography in the Traditional East and Southeast Asian Societies.* University of Chicago Press.

Yonemoto, Marcia. 2003. *Mapping Early Modern Japan: Space, Place, and Culture in the Tokugawa Period (1603–1868).* Berkeley: University of California Press.

Young, Oran R. 2009. "Whither the Arctic? Conflict or Cooperation in the Circumpolar North." *Polar Record* 45(232): 73–82.

Zandvliet, Kees. 2007. "Mapping the Dutch World Overseas in the Seventeenth Century." In David Woodward, ed. *The History of Cartography*, vol. III, *Cartography in the European Renaissance.* University of Chicago Press.

Ziman, John. 2000. *Real Science: What It Is, and What It Means.* Cambridge University Press.

Zook, Matthew. 2006. "The Geographies of the Internet." *Annual Review of Information Science and Technology*: 53–78.

Zook, Matthew, and Martin Dodge. 2009. "Mapping Cyberspace." In Rob Kitchin and Nigel Thrift, eds. *The International Encyclopedia of Human Geography.* Oxford: Elsevier.

Index

Cambridge Studies in International Relations

CPSIA information can be obtained at www.ICGtesting.com
Printed in the USA
LVOW07s0230010116

468754LV00017B/266/P